The Russ Howard Story

RUSS HOWARD   •   BOB WEEKS

BICENTENNIAL

1807

WILEY

2007

BICENTENNIAL

John Wiley & Sons Canada, Ltd.

Library and Archives Canada Cataloguing in Publication

Howard, Russ
    Hurry hard: the Russ Howard story / Russ Howard, Bob Weeks.

Includes index.
ISBN 978-0-470-83955-3

    1. Howard, Russ.   2. Curlers (Athletes)—Canada—Biography.
I. Weeks, Bob II. Title.

GV845.62.H68A3 2007   796.964092   C2007-900519-5

Production Credits:
Cover design: Ian Koo
Jacket photos (front and spine)
Top: Adrian Wyld/CP Images
Bottom left and spine: Adrian Wyld/CP Images
Bottom right: Michael Burns Photography
Interior text design: Adrian So
Wiley Bicentennial Logo: Richard J. Pacifico
Printer: Tri-Graphic

John Wiley & Sons Canada, Ltd.
6045 Freemont Blvd.
Mississauga, Ontario
L5R 4J3

Printed in Canada
1 2 3 4 5 TRI 11 10 09 08 07

To all the members of Team Howard—
Bill, Barb, Glenn, Wendy, Steven and Ashley.

Contents

Acknowledgements

WHEN I WAS FIRST asked to write a book, I have to admit that I had no idea what it would entail. At times I felt a bit like I was standing on the ice wearing sliders on both feet. For that reason, I'm extremely thankful to a number of people who have guided me through the process to produce what you have in your hands.

Bob Weeks, my co-author, who put my memories into words, was the perfect partner for this book. Bob has followed my career for a long time, from the early days in Ontario through to Briers and World Championships and Olympics. His research skills were vital in helping jog my memory and his patience was limitless as we worked on this project. We had a great time sitting in my kitchen, reliving curling memories.

Wendy, my wife, has always encouraged me to follow my dreams, even when it meant sacrifices on her part. She's been there every step of the way, always lending support, always giving me the confidence I needed to get over the next hurdle, whether that was on the ice or off. After raising our two wonderful children, Ashley and Steven, and managing our successful real estate careers with Re/Max, she still managed to spend hours with me working on this book. I love you honey. Thanks for everything. Now you can sign us up for those dance lessons!

I feel I am the luckiest man in the world to have Ashley and Steven as my children. I will never forget standing on the podium, the most wonderful moment in my sporting career, and looking down and seeing the smiles, the tears of joy, and the pride on their faces. What a thrill, at my age, to have such a memory.

My parents, Barb and Bill Howard, as you will read in the book, were strong supporters of Glenn and I throughout our entire lives. They were always there for us, and their work ethic and dedication are values I hope we have been able to pass along to our children.

My brother, Glenn, who is one of the most talented players I have ever curled with, has shared so many memories with me. The years we curled together, in the 1980s and '90s were wonderful and I feel Glenn was the best vice in the world. These days, I am so proud to watch him as a successful skip of his own team.

Wendy's parents, Doreen and Ross Thompson, were also very supportive throughout the years, and without all the babysitting they did for us, I don't know if I would have been able to enjoy my curling as much. Their help allowed Wendy to be with me at every major curling event.

Curling is a team sport and I have been fortunate in my 40 years of playing this grand old game to have some incredible memories, with an amazing amount of world class teammates. Every one has been talented and our friendships will last a lifetime. A note to you all—when you get to seniors, keep your heads up, I'll be waiting for you!

I am fortunate enough to have had sponsorship support for our many teams throughout the years and each and everyone is appreciated. Without the assistance of sponsors, curlers like myself do not have the opportunity to compete in bonspiels across the country in preparation for national and international titles. A special thanks to AMJ Campbell VAN LINES and CEO Bruce Bowser who became a wonderful friend over the past 15 years of our association. Bruce was very instrumental in my relocation to the Maritimes and AMJ Campbell is a class organization, and I have worn their crest proudly.

To everyone who has supported me throughout my career and to the many who have watched me grow up, I say thank you. I was very fortunate to spend much of my life in the Midland/Penetanguishene area in Ontario, where the residents have been involved in various fundraising activities and celebrations over the years. I'll treasure those memories forever. It was difficult to relocate our family to Moncton in 1998, but the support we have received here has been tremendous. How fortunate we are to have a second hometown. And to Newfoundland and Labrador, thank you for adopting me! In fact, thank you Canada, I have never felt so proud to be Canadian.

Russ Howard
January 2007

The Pinnacle 1

IT WAS ALMOST SURREAL. The moment that every athlete dreams of was upon me and I was really almost having a hard time believing it. Here I was, in a faraway land, in a place that I never even knew existed a year or so earlier, ready to step up to the top level of the Olympic podium. It was a breathtaking scene. Out in front of me as far as my eyes could see were people, cheering and waving Canadian flags. Flanking me on both sides were the teammates with whom I'd shared this remarkable journey, a collection of youngsters less than half my age. Despite this seeming incongruity in years, we were definitely together at this moment as we mounted the platform, our hands joined and then raised overhead to meet the cheers from the throng out in front of us.

It was hard to hear the announcements, which came in three different languages—English, French and Italian—but our names were clear, and one sentence still rings in my ears: "gold medal winners and Olympic champions." We had made it.

To the left of us were the Americans, led by skip Pete Fenson, who had almost derailed our dream a few days earlier in the Palaghiaccio ice rink at Pinerolo, the town fifty kilometres from Torino where the curling had been staged. Fenson and his team had proven to be worthy opponents, fuelled by the support of the massive U.S. Olympic program. Their prize would be the bronze medal and as they received their awards, it was clear from the looks on their faces that they weren't disappointed with the finish. It was the best Olympic performance by an American men's team.

On our right were the Finns, a remarkable rink that had defied the odds to earn the silver medal. Their skip, the towering Markku Uusilpaavalniemmi, had gone to extraordinary lengths to reach the medal podium. With limited availability to curling rinks in Finland, Uusilpaavalniemmi had physically built his own four-sheeter on which he practised his craft. He and his team had scared us in our gold medal game. While the foursome was solid all week, he had almost single-handedly dragged them to the Olympic title. They seemed to accept their silver medals begrudgingly, receiving them as a prize that might have been better.

A moment later, it was our turn. I was handed a bouquet of flowers that never really registered although I held them as tightly as I would a newborn baby. But it was the next reward for which I'd been waiting. I bowed over and a single ribbon holding a medal that looked like a golden compact disc was placed over my head. As I stood up, I felt the weight of the one-pound medallion drop to my chest, and my eyes fixed on it. It twinkled in the lights and again, I felt as if this must be some sort of dream.

I was standing on the stage at the Olympics with a gold medal around my neck. A few minutes earlier, before heading out onto the stage to the medal plaza, I'd been speaking with Prime Minster Stephen Harper, who phoned to congratulate us on our Olympic victory. Now I was hearing my name being called out as Olympic champion.

I was still stunned, but it had to be true, had to be really happening.

I looked out into the crowd and among the thousands of spectators, I could spot three beaming faces, those belonging to my wife,

Wendy, and two kids, Steven and Ashley. At that moment, I thought I would lose it. I could feel their eyes meet mine and in an instant, tears began to well up inside of me. It was all I could do to keep the dam from bursting.

Wendy, my wife and best friend, had sacrificed so much over my curling career. She'd stayed at home on countless weekends while I barnstormed around the world, throwing rock after rock. She'd never had those romantic vacations to the south or the fancy birthday dinners like most wives. When she did follow me, it was to places like Saskatoon or Hamilton—in March—where we holed up in a hotel room, preparing for the next game and sharing my fears about some future opponent or situation.

Steven and Ashley had become solid curlers in their own right—both having played in national championships—and were here to see their dad achieve the ultimate in sporting success. They, too, had been on the short end of the stick when it came to growing up with me as a father. My curling travels meant I had missed too many special events and important moments in their lives as I chased my dream. But that didn't matter to them right now. They were the proudest three people in that crowd of ten thousand. Their faces beamed, they waved at me, and it seemed perfect to be there together.

It had cost us a small fortune to be here as a family, and the treatment the three of them and the families of my teammates had received during their stay in Italy had been less than ideal. They had faced long delays, cancelled reservations, transportation nightmares and price gouging on tickets. Just to be here at this special moment, to watch me receive my medal, had meant a six-hour journey with multiple connections, made part of the way on foot, the rest on buses. At this point, they weren't even sure how they were going to get back to their hotel, which was in San Secondo, an hour's drive—if they'd had a car. The buses had stopped running long ago.

But they didn't seem to care or have an ounce of concern for themselves. They were there cheering me on, celebrating my achievement.

And again, I had to pinch myself. Could this all really be happening? Was it possible that I was now a gold medal winner at age fifty?

I had won many championships, world and Canadian championships, Ontario and New Brunswick championships. I had won hundreds of bonspiels and cashed scores of first-place cheques. I have a basement full of trophies and medals, but nothing could compare to the moment I was experiencing now; nothing could ever match the newest reward that was hanging from my neck.

What made this so hard to comprehend was that just six months prior, I had no inkling that I was even going to the Olympics. As far as I was concerned, my Olympic dream was over. The team I had played with had lost out on all the possible qualifying routes to get to the Canadian Curling Trials in Halifax, the competition that determined Canada's representatives to the 2006 Games in Torino, Italy. I was fully expecting to watch that event—easily the best competition in curling—on television at home.

I had been a part of every prior Canadian Olympic qualifying that had ranged from a training camp style process in 1987 to the previous two qualifying events, where teams played a Brier-like competition to determine Canada's entry to the games. Each time I had come up short, failing to win what was increasingly becoming the pinnacle for every curler.

I had watched Ed Lukowich capture the bronze in 1988, when curling was a demonstration sport in Calgary. I'd seen Mike Harris, a friend and rival in Ontario during the early 1990s, take silver in 1998. And in 2002, I'd watched Edmonton's Kevin Martin, one of the toughest competitors I'd ever played, win silver after an agonizing loss in the final in 2002.

I'd always thought that 2006 was my last shot at becoming an Olympian, which meant reaching the Trials the previous year. There were a number of ways to get into that ten-team field including winning a Brier or earning enough points in the Canadian Team Ranking System, a complicated process set up by the Canadian Curling Association to track team performance. Despite my best efforts, we'd failed to make it, and at my advanced age (I would be fifty during the Torino Games), and with the talented youth coming up through the ranks across Canada, I had resigned myself to the fact that the Olympics had passed me by.

But one summer afternoon in 2005, my phone rang. At the other end of the line was Toby McDonald, a lawyer from St. John's, but best known among curlers as the third on Newfoundland's only Brier-winning rink. He was calling to see if I'd be interested in serving as the fifth man or reserve player for Brad Gushue's rink, a team of young but exceptionally talented Newfoundlanders who had earned one of the spots in the Trials.

Although the Gushue rink had won the world junior championship and had played in the Brier, the Canadian men's curling championships, it was still quite green when it came to competition at the elite level. To make it to the Olympics meant winning the Trials, which was arguably tougher than the Games themselves. The Brier has one team representing each province. The Trials had no geographical restrictions—it was simply the ten best teams in all of Canada. It meant taking on and beating the likes of Randy Ferbey and Kevin Martin, both from Alberta and ranked as the two best teams in curling. That wouldn't happen at the Brier where only one of those two rinks could make it into the field. And it meant surviving in a pressure-packed environment filled with media scrutiny and doing it on live television.

Gushue and his team of Mark Nichol, Jamie Korab and Mike Adam didn't have that experience, and they knew it. McDonald had signed on as coach and along with the team had drawn up a list of people they wanted to ask to be fifth player. McDonald told me I was at the top of the list. Normally, the position of fifth player is one of the more unenviable in curling. It meant you were part of the team, but barring some sort of injury or illness, the role ranged from scouting future opponents to carrying the brooms on and off the ice. The fifth man rarely gets to play and even when he does, it might only be for a game or two. He's there just in case one of the regulars can't compete.

He's equal parts coach, cheerleader and travel co-ordinator. About the only positive benefit was that you got a seat at ice level for all the games. For a person as competitive as me, it would have been a tough assignment, like keeping a racehorse locked up in the barn.

But at the Trials, the fifth man role had taken on a different meaning. Because there were no geographical restrictions on who you could assign to the role—as there are at a Brier, where teams must choose a player from the province they are representing—teams were taking the best players they could find to fit the roles they needed.

The Martin rink, for example, had signed up Scott Bailey, the superb lead for Wayne Middaugh's rink. At first glance, that might have seemed unusual. Bailey was a talented player but certainly higher-profile curlers were available, most of them skips. But Martin knew that his lead, Don Bartlett, had a wonky back that could give out at any time. The need for this team was someone who could step in and replace Bartlett, and they had found that in Bailey.

Gushue's requirement was different. He had the shots but he needed guidance from someone who knew when to play them. They needed help from someone who had been there before, someone who had dealt with all that goes on at championships. And more important, someone who had won those same championships.

In short, they were looking to me.

After carefully considering the commitment, I accepted but even then I had no idea that I'd be going to Italy, let alone playing in the Olympics and winning a gold medal. We had only a few months to prepare for the Trials and I was hoping to be able to give the team a crash course in everything I knew. But not long into our training, I was asked to bring my knowledge to the ice as a player, suiting up for some big events on the competitive circuit for curlers, the World Curling Tour. At first, I thought it would be a temporary role, but the more I played, the better were the results. We did well in these events. And then, remarkably, I was asked to consider being a full-time player.

By the time we arrived at the Trials, I was throwing second stones and calling the game. The wild ride continued when we won the Trials and then did the same thing in Italy, capturing gold. And now I was standing on the podium, dressed in my Canadian uniform, experiencing something that had seemed almost impossible a few months earlier.

I turned to the right and there in front of me the Maple Leaf had started its ascent to the highest flagpole. The first few notes of the national anthem started to ring in my ears, and I joined my teammates in boldly—and perhaps badly—singing "O Canada." I don't think I've ever felt more Canadian than I did at that moment.

As the last few notes died out, a wave of cheers grew from the crowd, gaining in intensity. The flags began to wave again, and it was finally sinking in.

After thousands of games, countless rocks thrown and trips to the far reaches of the world, I had put a cap on my career by achieving the ultimate.

I could believe it now. I was an Olympic champion.

The Start

FOR SOMEONE WHO HAS LOVED the sport of curling for forty years, I'm almost embarrassed to say that I don't remember the first time I stepped onto the curling ice (maybe because it was forty years ago!). I do know that it happened at the Midland Curling Club in my hometown of Midland, Ontario, and I'm certain it was under the watchful eye of my father, Bill, when I was about ten or eleven. My father and mother were avid curlers, and in the winter months, the curling club was the hub of their social world.

Ever since I can remember, curling was around our house and always around our lives. On most nights of the week my parents would be off to the curling club. Sometimes it was my father, sometimes my mother and sometimes it was both of them together for mixed curling or some club function. Around the dinner table, my brother Glenn (who was six years younger) and I would also hear about their games, about who they were up against that night or whether they won or lost the night before.

In that way, I don't think we were any different than any other family in a small town in Canada. That's just what happens all across the country in small towns like Midland. In winter, you're either a hockey family or a curling family, but ours was actually both.

My mom and dad introduced me to hockey when I was five. You had to know my dad, if you were going to play hockey, you were going to do it right. As soon as I showed interest in the sport, my father built a state-of-the-art backyard rink that was just slightly smaller than NHL size—and that was only because the neighbours wouldn't allow him to flood their backyard. The rink had boards of official size—sixteen inches long, sixteen inches high and six inches thick. Two sets of lights were hung that were so bright you could read a newspaper at midnight at the other end of the yard!

Maintaining a rink is hard work and my dad was out there night after night, shovelling and flooding, flooding and shovelling. Finally, one day he came up with another brainstorm—he invented what was to my knowledge the world's first human-powered Zamboni. He took a five-foot piece of lumber, covered it in burlap, secured a half-inch copper pipe along the middle, closed off the ends of the pipe and drilled small holes in it so the water would seep out, soak the burlap and provide a nice, even flood. He attached the handle of an old lawn mower to the piece of wood and ran the hose to it so it attached to the pipe, providing the water.

We pulled this baby Zamboni around on cold nights and it would melt the slush left from the day of skating, replacing it with a fine layer of water that immediately froze into a perfect sheet of ice.

With such a great rink, every kid in the neighbourhood descended on our place after school, night after night, for pickup games. The only thing that stopped the games was snow, of which Midland got a lot. But my dad was undeterred by Mother Nature's white stuff. He bought the Rolls Royce of snowblowers. Even though the rink was roughly a hundred feet behind our home, if the wind was right, this monster of a snowblower would blow the snow off the rink, over our house and onto the street where it fell on the unsuspecting traffic going past our door.

I played competitive hockey up until I was seventeen. One year our rep team finished second in Ontario. I was a skilled forward and

I loved the game, but once the defencemen got to be as big as trees, I knew hockey wasn't a long-term choice for me. My mother also helped my decision making by giving me an ultimatum. "Looking at your report card, you are going to have to make a decision between hockey, curling and school. You're too busy and something has to go." I told her I was going to miss school, she laughed but at that point, my hockey career was over.

Although I loved hockey, curling had been growing on me for a long time. When we were quite young, we'd accompany our parents to the club, spending a couple of hours in the upstairs lounge with other area kids whose folks were throwing rocks. (I guess it was cheaper than a babysitter!) We were left to run wild—something not that uncommon in those days—and on one occasion, I managed to lock another boy into the bathroom and jam the lock so tight, the fire department had to be called to get him out.

I can remember being up there watching the games and hearing the sounds of the rocks colliding and the corn brooms pounding on the ice. There was also a lot of yelling for teams to sweep, I remember. Those were intriguing sounds for a seven- or eight-year-old. They would draw me into the games even though at that point, I had little idea of what was going on. But the sweeping, the sliding, the noise of the stones hitting each other was captivating.

My mother was a social curler and she enjoyed the camaraderie of the game. I don't think she ever had the desire to play in the Canadian championship. She was more intent on the pure enjoyment of the sport and being with her friends. That doesn't mean she didn't have a competitive streak in her. Or so one would think! I can remember being at the provincial track and field meet in Grade 8, which was held at our local high school, located basically just on the other side of my backyard. I was taking part as a member of a relay team, running the third leg of the race. As the gun went off our team settled into second place but by the time the baton was handed to me, we were fifth out of five teams. Just as I started to run, out of the corner of my eye I saw someone running along the inside of the track at the same speed as me—it was my mother. She had walked through two and a half acres of brush, scaled the eight-foot fence and was racing beside me, yelling encouragement.

People have asked me why I yell so much on the curling ice and I always answer, "Because it works." My mother proved that to me because with her at my side and in my ear, I passed all four other runners as if they were standing still, handing the baton to our fastest runner. I still remember slowing down and veering off to the left after making the pass and watching in pride as my teammate hit the final straightaway on his way to certain victory. The only person he didn't beat was my mother!

Mom's life revolved around her family and various jobs she held such as working for a lawyer or as secretary at the local church. She always seemed busy no matter what she was doing and always seemed to be smiling when she was doing it.

My father's approach to the game was quite different. He was more competitive than my mother. He had a good reputation within the curling club, usually winning more than losing, and although he didn't often venture too far beyond the club for bonspiels, he did have a competitive streak. Even so, he was always good-natured. He loved to compete and loved to play the game. I guess I got those competitive fires from him.

A long-time employee of Loblaws, he managed the grocery stores in Midland and Collingwood for thirty years. In anything he did—the skating rink is a good example—he poured himself into it completely, studying everything he could get his hands on, talking to anyone who had any sort of expertise. If you wanted to buy a new car, he'd produce the *Consumer Reports* issue on new cars. If you wanted to buy new golf clubs, he'd have information on the best brands and the recommendations of the experts. If you were looking for a new fridge, he'd be able to give you the literature that rated the top brands. He always did his homework and was thorough about everything.

He was that way with curling, too. He'd study the games of the best players in the club and see what strategies they were using and

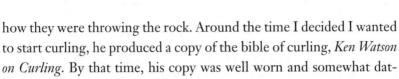

how they were throwing the rock. Around the time I decided I wanted to start curling, he produced a copy of the bible of curling, *Ken Watson on Curling*. By that time, his copy was well worn and somewhat dated—it was published in 1950, but it covered the basics, and I pored over that book for hours on end.

My father was always big on getting me to learn the fundamentals of the curling delivery. He would stress things like balance and foot position and how to hold the broom. Time after time when all I wanted to do was fire the rock down the ice so it would hit some of the other rocks and make loud crashing noises, he'd be prodding me to keep my back straight and keep a proper grip on the rock. At the time, these lessons weren't a lot of fun, but I think they are a large part of why my delivery is so solid to this day—it was built on a solid foundation of fundamentals, taught to me by my father.

My dad was also quite innovative, especially when it came to sports. In golf he was a ten handicap, which was remarkable considering his work didn't allow him much time to play. I can remember that he took a label maker and wrote out the words "Slow Backswing Stupid" and taped it on to the top of his driver as a reminder of how to swing the club (this was long before the Nike Swoosh!)

In curling in the 1940s and '50s, before sliding to the hog line was possible, my father sourced out Teflon from Dupont of Canada. He found that Teflon was the perfect material to let you slide effortlessly without dragging, and that meant a better curling delivery. He'd buy sheets of the stuff in three-foot lengths and three-quarters of an inch thickness, then trace out the bottom of a curling shoe on it. The shoe-shaped piece of Teflon would be cut out and then stitched onto the bottom of the shoe, with the stitching countersunk so it wouldn't drag on the ice. This material, that only my father had, was sought after in the '70s. He received phone calls asking for it from Al Hackner and other greats. From the first time I threw rocks, I've always had three-quarter-inch Teflon on the bottom of my shoe.

When my father retired, he became an icemaker at the Midland Curling Club. Like everything else, it didn't take him long to get proficient at making a great curling surface. He took courses, he read books and he would learn from the best, going to the provincial championships to get instruction from Shorty Jenkins, who was tops in the business. Dad also wasn't afraid to experiment, trying new ways to make the ice better. He made pretty good ice but he was still using tap water, and the chemicals in the water made the ice slower as the game went on. It also became very swingy.

To combat that, my dad and I got the bright idea of polishing the sliding surface of a rock to see if it would improve things. He went out and bought the world's most powerful car polisher and some polishing compound, flipped over one of the white lead rocks on an outside, lesser used sheet of ice and buffed away. When we were finished, we put the rock on the ice for an hour or so to let it cool down and then I gave it a test run. We were used to seeing the rocks curl about four feet or more from the centre line out to the wings, but when I threw the polished stone, it went down the centre of the sheet as if it was on a conveyer belt, never bending an inch, slamming into the back boards, with more than hack weight. We decided the other seventy-nine rocks should be left alone. I won a lot of games that winter choosing the red rocks instead of the white on that sheet.

The Midland Curling Club was located on the town's fairgrounds, next to the hockey rink and baseball diamond. It was an old building, having been constructed in 1919, but had lots of character. There were five sheets of curling ice, a bar and lounge on the main floor, locker rooms in the basement and a banquet room upstairs. There was an old billiards table in the basement that was so large some people believe the club was built around it. It seems almost impossible that it could have been carried into the club. It had seen better days by the time I began to play on it, but I spent many hours using it nonetheless. The roof of the club was of a Quonset hut style and in the winter, no one dared park their car near the club building because the ice and snow would come sliding down, landing with a tremendous crash in the parking lot. On other occasions, when the snow stayed up there, members were called out to shovel it off so it didn't cause the roof to cave in.

The club was run entirely by the members who took turns volunteering to be the bartender, the cook, the dishwasher or the custodian. Members pitched in and did their part, and in some ways, that was a key to the success of the place. There was a genuine commitment to the facility, and we all felt pride in how it operated.

Of course, the curling club was just one sports centre in Midland, a town located on the shores of Georgian Bay about an hour and a half north of Toronto. There was a wide array of places to get your sports fix. There were football fields and arenas, baseball diamonds and tennis courts. And being on the water also provided plenty of opportunity for recreation. It also meant Midland was a popular destination in the summer months. With all the cottagers and tourists, Midland's population tripled to about forty-five thousand in July and August.

The boating and water sports drew people as did Midland's other attraction, the Martyrs' Shrine, an historic church that honours early Jesuit missionaries such as Jean de Brébeuf, who were responsible for bringing Christianity to Canada almost four hundred years ago. It's accompanied by Sainte-Marie Among the Hurons, a recreated seventeenth-century village that shows how these early missionaries lived.

Despite this famous attraction, Midland was still a small centre, with a population of about fifteen thousand. While there might be some disadvantages to growing up in a small town, they were outweighed by opportunities to play just about every sport, and growing up, I took full advantage of that. If there was a game being played, I'd sign up and give it a try. If there was an opportunity to ride a bike or play a game of baseball or throw a football around, I was there. I loved sports and played constantly. My parents encouraged that and gave us the chance to play as much as we could.

One sport I don't think they were too happy about was wagon racing. That's not really an official sport, but it was one that Glenn and I tried out one afternoon, much to my parents' mortification. One of the first times they left Glenn and I alone, with me in charge (I was 10, Glenn was 4), I decided it would be interesting to see how fast our wagon could go. In Midland, one of the main streets, Hugel Avenue, has a steep descent that ends at Georgian Bay. If there was snow on it, it would make a pretty good ski run.

On this particular day, I took Glenn and the wagon to the top of the hill, and sat him in the front. I pushed off and then jumped into the back. Down the hill the two of us went, picking up speed with every foot. By the time we got halfway down the hill, we were going fast...very fast. Only then did it dawn on me that there were no brakes on our little red wagon and so I began weaving from side to side, to slow us down somewhat. We passed cross street after cross street and just about the time we reached our peak speed, we crossed a street where a car was waiting at the stop sign, certainly never expecting the vehicle to which it was yielding to would be a wagon. As we sped past, I looked over and there were my parents looking out through the windshield, absolutely astonished. Somehow we managed to stop the wagon before it ended up in the bay. Neither of us was hurt but we heard about that little incident from my parents for some time.

With the big difference in age, Glenn and I didn't hang around together a lot, but we did the normal things that brothers do. We'd wrestle and chase each other around—I remember once chasing him and he wound up running right through the screen door, ripping the screen right off. As he got a little older, we'd play in the same pickup games of whatever happened to be the sport du jour. As the older brother, I did try to look out for Glenn whenever possible.

When he started curling, I tried to help him, sometimes too much. One year when he was in the high school playdowns, I remember watching one of his games and from the crowd, frantically trying to get his attention to tell him he was calling the wrong strategy.

On another occasion, we were playing in a junior-senior golf tournament at CFB Borden near Barrie. Both of us were good golfers and there was really only one other team in the region that could challenge us for the title. That team had won the tournament for the previous two years and I was determined to win it this year. The format was such that both players drove, then switched and hit each other's ball for the second shot. From that point, we chose the best of the two balls and alternated shots into the hole.

We were tied with the other duo on the seventeenth hole, a par five. We chose Glenn's drive, and I managed to get the second one onto the green about thirty feet from the pin. The other team did the same, but ended up about fifteen feet away. Glenn was putting for eagle, and I could tell he was extremely nervous, knowing just what was on the line. He prepared himself and then got set near the ball and tried to take a practice stroke. As he did, however, the heel of his putter nicked the toe of his golf shoe, deflecting the putter head onto the golf ball, sending it sideways. Now we were laying three and still thirty feet from the cup.

Glenn, who was fifteen, was so upset, he walked off the green and slammed his putter into a patch of rough, burying it halfway up the shaft. He was on the verge of tears. I was doing all I could not to laugh at the predicament and Glenn's reaction. Remarkably, I sank the next putt for a birdie, and our opponents three-putted for a par, putting us one up going to eighteen, and we hung on to win.

While it wasn't the most memorable of moments for Glenn, it did show just how intense he was at sports, how spirited he was when it came to competing. We both shared those traits, which helped us later in life when we took to the curling rink for more serious contests.

Early in my teenage years I wouldn't say I was absorbed by curling. I certainly enjoyed it and it was a big part of my winters. It wasn't until high school that I played on an organized school team. And organized is a loose term. I played a four-end game every Tuesday and Thursday after school. During the year, I played in two or three bonspiels. In one of those events, a school bonspiel, my boys' team made it to the final where we were up against a mixed team skipped by a cute girl named Wendy Thompson. Six ends later, the woman who would become my wife was celebrating her championship victory by an 8–3 margin. It's something I've never been allowed to forget. In fact these days, whenever I teach a junior clinic, my daughter, Ashley, prompts a junior in the crowd to ask the loaded question: "Have you ever been beaten by a girl?" I have to answer, "Yes, and that would be Ashley's mother." Wendy and I went on to curl together in a lot of mixed bonspiels after that—that was one way to keep her from beating me again.

My father owned a driving range in town so we were around golf a lot. Just as with curling, my dad taught me the fundamentals of the sport—grip, posture, stance, alignment—and allowed me to experiment with the game at a young age. I was six when he bought me a membership at the local club. At that age, I didn't do much except whack the ball around and maybe play one or two of the par threes, but I loved being outdoors and hitting that little white ball around on the grassy field.

Every son has the memory of the first time he was able to beat his dad at a game of golf. Mine is permanently etched in my memory. When I was about twelve we were playing the last hole, with me trailing by two strokes. The eighteenth was a par three and it didn't seem likely that I'd be able to close the gap on my father. My tee shot came to rest on the front edge of the green, while my father knocked his right over the flagstick onto the back edge of the green, where it then rolled over a slope and down into a creek.

Because of where his ball entered the creek, Dad's next shot—after fishing the ball out of the water—was impeded by a large bridge with wooden support poles set in a criss-cross pattern. He tried to hit his wedge through an opening in the wooden supports but the ball hit the bridge and fell into the creek. The next attempt produced the same result. So did the third and the fourth and the fifth. Finally, on the eighth try my persistant father got the ball onto the green. I whipped him that day, and the news spread throughout the club. That fall, at our closing banquet, my father was presented with a wooden replica of the bridge, a reminder of that fateful day.

As I grew older I would spend more and more of the winter months at the curling club, throwing rocks. I loved practising and I would do it for hours. (I still do today.) I continued to watch my parents' games, too, and began to get a better understanding of the strategy, at first just getting a handle on scoring and then learning the basics of the game.

Gradually, I turned into a rink rat, spending hours at the club, practising and playing. I started to become a decent player, certainly one of the better ones in my area. I made the high school team in Grade 10 and soon after, I was skipping it. I would play in junior bonspiels around the region and did quite well against older kids.

When I was about twelve, my father introduced me to a fellow named John Scott, who was probably the best player in our area. He had won the Territories (the combined area of Yukon and Northwest Territories) championship three or four times before that region had a spot in the Brier. My father asked him if he would watch me throw a few rocks and maybe offer me some tips. I can remember trundling out to the ice and Scott asking me what I was struggling with.

"My draws," I answered.

I went down to the other end of the ice to show him my stuff, threw four rocks and put all four in the four foot.

"Ernie Richardson wishes he had as many problems as you do, kid," commented an impressed Scott, comparing me to the four-time Canadian champion. That was the end of the lesson.

As I grew older, I began to really enjoy playing skip and the challenge that brought. Skips are responsible for deciding what shot should be played and how it should be played. Some curlers don't like that responsibility—I lived for it. There were two main reasons I loved top spot. One was the strategy. I was always intrigued by how an end could change after every shot. The rocks would be sitting in one position and after another player's turn, an entirely new set of possibilities existed. I'd have to react to those possibilities thinking not only about the ice conditions, but the strengths and weaknesses of the opposition and my own team.

The other reason I liked skipping was that I enjoyed throwing the last shot, which can make or break the game. It wasn't ego; it was just that the shots were usually tougher and meant more. I loved having that responsibility and opportunity. It never occurred to me that some people might fear that; for me it was thrilling. I never really thought about missing, but concentrated on how I was going to make the shot. Of course, I didn't always make that last brick, but to have the chance excited me.

Because the junior team I skipped was so avid, we were allowed to compete in the men's ranks in Midland. That was a wonderful opportunity to learn the game. I've always believed that the only way to improve is to play against teams that are better than I am. Although the teams we were playing against were only club teams who rarely played in any serious competition, many of them had been around a while and seen a lot more than I had.

Even though the strategy of the game in those days was pretty basic, I ate it up, trying to learn as much as I could and oftentimes getting taught a good lesson that came along with a loss. Still, we managed to hold our own against the men and it helped us immensely.

I went to a few bonspiels in Penetanguishene and Elmvale, and continued the school curling, which was almost always played in Orillia. When I was seventeen, the team I skipped managed to reach the final of the Ontario Junior Tankard, a provincewide competition. The true Ontario championship, the one that sent the winner on to play in the Canadian Junior, was still the Schoolboy championship. Teams in that event were made up of players from the same school. In later years the Tankard usually provided stronger teams and better competition, and became the official Ontario championship, with the winner going on to the national final

The competition was being held at the Toronto Cricket, Skating and Curling Club, on Wilson Street in Toronto, a posh establishment in the big city. When we arrived at the club parking lot, I knew we weren't in Midland anymore. I'd never seen a club like this. It had a figure skating pad separated by a wall from a six-sheet curling rink. There were upstairs and downstairs viewing lounges that were as formal as I'd ever seen at any curling facility. Everyone seemed to be wearing a jacket and tie. I had no idea curling clubs could be as stylish as this. As the country bumpkins, we definitely felt out of place.

That we weren't from the big city was made even more apparent by our uniforms. After qualifying for the provincial final, we didn't go out and get matching jackets, as most of the other teams did. Instead, our mothers knitted us big shawl-collared fisherman's sweaters, and to make matters worse, they didn't even knit four the same colour or style. We looked like four Charlie Farquharsons with brooms.

Despite appearances, we managed to finish runner-up to Dave Merklinger of Ottawa, whom I would face many times again during the course of my career. It was a big step to make it that far, and I was gaining confidence with every rock of every game. More to the point, I was really in love with the game. I simply couldn't get enough of it, and every chance I could get, I was throwing rocks. I was ready to take my game to the next level.

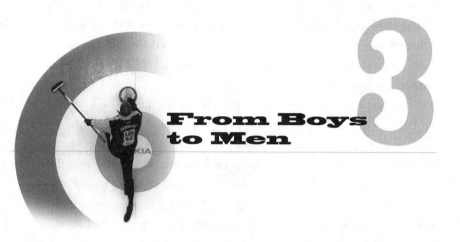

From Boys to Men

3

GRADUATING TO MEN'S CURLING didn't seem like a big thing. I had been playing against the men as a junior but when I turned twenty, I was able to enter men's competitions, including the playdowns that led to the Brier.

The first year I played in men's competitions, 1976, I played with Paul Macdonald, who was, in my estimation, the best curler in Midland—and I was not alone in that opinion. It was quite an honour to throw third rocks for this guy, and he became my curling mentor. But I was naive. For me, the curling world started and ended in the Midland area. There was our club, the nearby Penetang club and then, if you wanted a real road trip, you could drive the fifteen minutes over to Elmvale. Although I had curled in different clubs in various junior competitions, I never even thought about looking for teammates anywhere else but my club. It was simple—I lived in Midland, I curled in Midland, so I should find the other three best curlers in the club and put a team together.

That theory started with Paul, who was fifteen years older than me. He was a good player who had won a fair bit around our little area. Our team that year was rounded out by Len Patterson and a first-year curler named Kent Carstairs. Kent had recently been transferred to Midland from Toronto by his company. He had grown up in a fairly toney section of Toronto; his parents lived around The Bridle Path—known as Millionaire's Row—so it was a bit of an adjustment coming to Midland.

But Kent jumped right in, especially at the curling club where he became a fixture, playing three or four times a week, which is a lot for anyone, let alone a new curler. He always seemed to be on the ice that first year, and I was enthusiastic about the possibility of making him a teammate when I saw him sweep. Even though he'd only been playing for a couple of months, he was an awesome sweeper, slinging the straw fast and hard, rock after rock. Later, at the 1980 Brier, he was voted the best sweeper, and that field included the Wilson brothers from Saskatchewan, two legendary pounders of the corn. In those pre-push broom days, Kent used a big Cat brand broom and he could sweep at an incredible speed. It was really something to see.

Teams didn't assemble the way they do now. While most competitive rinks these days are formed mere moments after the end of the previous season, back then, we put teams together late in the fall, just in time to enter the playdowns and maybe warm up with a couple of spiels.

With one notable exception, that team with Paul as skip really only played in events close to home—the regular men's night and perhaps one bonspiel. That was our preparation for my first official run at the Brier.

It did include a couple of games against a notable international team. In the fall of 1977, the reigning world champion, Ragnar Kamp and his team from Sweden, played in the biggest cashspiel in Toronto, the Molson Classic at the Royal Canadian Curling Club. Kamp was scheduled to compete in another event two weeks later and Paul Macdonald got the idea to invite them to Midland on their week off. After a few phone calls, the invitation was accepted and the club organized an exhibition game between our rink and the Swedes. The night of the contest, the club was jammed with spectators crammed into every square inch of viewing space. It was a good close game and Ragnar drew for one in the tenth end to tie the game. Being an exhibition, Paul decided it would end in a tie, which didn't sit well with me. Being the competitor that I was, I wanted to play the extra end because I knew we had a good chance to beat the world champs, which would have been a thrill.

As luck would have it, we faced them again the next week at the bonspiel in Penetanguishene with both of us making it to the final undefeated. In front of another full house, we had a scoreless game after five ends. Behind the glass, Kamp's father, who served as the team coach, leaned over to my father and said: "Your son will win." My father asked why he would make that prediction and Kamp explained that he was taking shooting percentages, tracking the proficiency of each curler. None of us had ever heard of this system, which became standard at all national and international championships a few years later. At that point in the game, we outcurled the Swedes 83 per cent to 72. The elder Kamp explained that gap would eventually show on the scoreboard and he was correct. We won the game 6-3 and collected $2,000 for the victory. More important in my mind was the fact we defeated the world champions. This was the defining moment for me—from that point on, I wanted to be a competitive curler.

Our playdown run started with a win at the zone level, the first stage in the Ontario playdown process. The zone level involved all the clubs in our area—there were about twenty. Our zone was one of sixteen in the province. Two teams moved to the next stage, the regional playdown, which pitted all the zone winners against each other (there were four regions in the province; each region included four zones). Two teams from each region went on to the provincial final.

We did well enough in our region to get to the final, where we played a team from our area, skipped by Gary Turner. Turner was from Elmvale, which had a small but active two-sheet curling club. In our little part of the province, Turner was The Guy. He'd been to the provincial finals before, and he won most of the area bonspiels. Even though I was new to curling in the men's division, I knew Turner's was the team to beat.

It was the best two out of three to move on to the provincials. We went the full three games—Turner won the first, we won the second— and I can still feel the blisters on my hands from the corn brooms. I was playing third and had to sweep, in games that lasted twelve ends. We ended up playing thirty-seven ends in one day (that may be another reason I wanted to skip, so I could avoid all that sweeping!).

Although we put up a brave effort, Turner wound up beating us in the third game and went on to the provincials. Turner finished with a 2 and 7 record, but was very competitive in the 7 losses. It was just remarkable that a team from a two-sheet club in rural Ontario even made it to the provincial final.

Although we didn't make it any further, the team stayed together. We had one last adventure, and it was my first trip to the United States. Somehow, Paul had heard about this bonspiel in Chicago and we decided the squad was in need of a road trip. So off we went, heading for the Windy City. Our trip was what you might expect from four guys on a twelve-hour drive. Three of us kept a steady intake of rum and Coke going—we wouldn't let Paul, the driver, touch anything, which didn't make him too happy—as we motored towards the United States. By the time we reached the border, we were feeling no pain, and it wasn't until Paul pulled the car up to the customs booth that I started to get nervous. I'd never made the crossing before and, a little juiced, I was starting to shake. Would we get in trouble for being drunk? I envisioned us getting thrown in some jail and left to rot.

"What's your purpose in the United States?" asked the guard in a serious tone. "We're curling," Paul said. As the only sober one in the car, we had decided he would be the only one to speak, perhaps hiding the state of the rest of us, although I'm sure the smell of booze was wafting out the car window.

The response from the big burly man leaning in our door floored us all. "What do they call a curling event?" he questioned. All four of us quickly answered in unison: "Bonspiel!" The guard laughed and waved us through. Obviously we'd lucked out and found a fellow curler.

When we reached Chicago, we decided that after the lengthy journey during which we'd been imbibing pretty much the whole way, the proper thing would be to go out to a bar for a few more. I vaguely remember heading out with the boys, and I have a few recollections of the bar we went to. But the next morning, I remember waking up with the other three guys looking at me.

"How do you feel?" asked Paul.

"I'm exhausted and my shoulder hurts," I answered. "Why are you asking?"

"You had a seizure last night," Kent stated.

"Like a Bloody Caesar?"

"No, like a real seizure."

They filled me in on the few hours that had apparently not been recorded in my memory banks. After trying to go drink for drink with these older guys, I had gone to sleep feeling no pain. In the middle of the night, I apparently fell out of the bed, landing hard on my shoulder—it was so bad that to this day I can't throw a football. I then had some sort of attack where my body convulsed and shook. When that subsided, the guys put me back in bed.

In the morning, they took me to the hospital as a precaution and after a brief examination, I was pumped full of liquids—the first diagnosis was dehydration.

When the doctor came in he asked one simple question: "What were you drinking last night?

"Rum," I replied.

"Don't ever drink rum again."

With that he left, and I went to the bonspiel.

I took his advice and to this day, I've never had another drink of rum, and I rarely drink since that night, other than the odd beer here and there. I think my aversion to alcohol stems from that incident, which scared the heck out of me.

The results of that bonspiel aren't in my memory banks either, which likely means we didn't win. What I do remember is that most of the American teams used push brooms to sweep. We were all using Rink Rats (a big foam-style broom) and corn brooms; we thought it was quite humourous to see these Yanks, who had picked up the push brooms from their many games against Scottish teams, scrubbing away with these little brooms. It seemed so backward.

Of course, the Americans had the last laugh. Within a couple of years push brooms were the standard. The first appearance of a push broom in Canada was in the 1980 Brier, my first. The guy who led the push broom invasion to Canada was Paul Gowsell. He skipped the first big-name team to use push brooms. They were much more effective on the rocks because they never left the ice surface, and continuous pressure could be put directly on the rock's path. They were also less taxing on the body, so you could sweep a lot more effectively, especially on multiple-game days. It didn't take long for the conversion to be made.

While our Midland rink didn't qualify for the provincials and we didn't have any success in Chicago, I did manage one big victory that year. Ontario had a competition, called the Colts, for new curlers. It was for players who had less than seven years' experience at the men's level. It was intended to be a championship for the up-and-coming players as well as those who weren't quite good enough to make it to the Ontario men's final.

I took a team of Kent, Jim Clarke and Lindy Hurlbut—all local players who were about my own age—to the provincial title. For me, this was a huge achievement, especially because I was skipping. I had played third all year, but I knew that skip was my natural position. I'd skipped all through junior and had only dropped down to third for Paul, the best skip in the men's section at Midland. Winning the Colts was a huge boost of confidence and it showed me that despite being pretty green in terms of strategy, I was ready to reassume the position.

There's really no set way to determine who plays what position, but it used to be that the best player was skip and so on down through the positions. That made sense because the skip's rocks are, generally speaking, the most important of the end. Even in the early days of my competitive career, I would play teams where the leads were quite green. But skips had to do more than just throw good shots. They also had to be good with game strategy and at reading the ice, picking up on the nuances of how a particular sheet of ice was running. I was getting better and better at all that and so the next year, 1977, Paul and I switched places. He played third and I threw last rocks and skipped the game.

We picked up Len Patterson at lead and had a good year, winning a lot of games in our club play and the bonspiels we entered. When the playdowns came, we hit our stride, and I was really starting to feel good again, throwing the last rock. After a lot of tough games, some good shots and a little luck, we made it to the provincials.

In those days, the Midland–Penetanguishene area was pretty much a dead zone for competitive curling. In the Toronto area, there were lots of great teams such as those skipped by Paul Savage, Joe Gurowka, Earle Hushagen and Jim Sharples. London was another hotbed, with Ken Buchan, Jim Waite and Bruce Munro. Gary Turner's trip to the provincial finals the year before was the first for a rink from our zone and it was big news. When I qualified, the local paper asked me what my goal was. "I just want to do better than 2–7," was my reply, indicating I was hoping to improve on Turner's mark.

The prognosticators weren't so sure. In the *Ontario Curling Report*, the bible for the game in the province, Alf Phillips Jr., the Brier-winning skip from 1967, handicapped the field and had us at 0–9 with the comment: "Nice guys finish last."

Ouch.

That provincial final was my baptism into arena curling. It was the second year that the Ontario final had been held in an arena instead of a curling club, and Shorty Jenkins was providing the ice. Shorty, in my opinion the best icemaker who's ever walked the planet, became the master at providing stellar conditions in arenas, and this year was no different. The ice was keen and had movement to it, making it ideal for a big championship.

The favourite that year was a team from St. Thomas, skipped by Jim Waite. He was the hot skip in the province that year. (Coincidentally, when I went to the Olympics in 2006, he served as the team leader, the sort of guide and liaison for everything that was going on at the Games.) Savage was also in the field. At that time in Ontario, he was The Man. He'd been to the Brier three times and was winning just about everything on the cash circuit in our area. He was also the antithesis of the curlers I knew. At twenty-nine, he was young, brash, cool and fearless on the ice. He was also from the big city, Toronto, while I was this country bumpkin.

I remember hearing about Savage when I was starting out and watching him and his team on the old CBC Curling Classic, a made-for-television curling competition that would show one game a week between two of the top teams in Canada. He was pretty much my idol. He came to a junior curling camp in Midland in the early 1970s and he asked all the kids to name their favourite curler. I emphatically said, "Paul Savage."

So when we stepped on to the ice at the provincial final, I was somewhat in awe. What's funny about that game is that I have absolutely no recollection of his third that year, a competitor who would play a large role in my curling career—Ed Werenich.

Werenich and Savage were my chief opponents for the next two decades. We'd have plenty of battles and also join forces for a number of confrontations with curling's governing bodies. It was a great rivalry that not only made both our teams better, but I'd say served to fuel a growth of the sport in Southern Ontario.

For that '77 championship, Paul also had a front end of Ron Green and Reid Ferguson, two huge guys who swept so hard with Rink Rats that you almost felt as if the ice was going to shatter beneath them. It was scary to see them sweep. They were a very impressive team, to be sure. During our game, I remember Paul asking Ron to throw up a corner guard (a stone off to the side, in front of the rings) in one of the early ends. What was going on here, I thought? I was so green I started to chuckle to myself. I thought he'd missed. No one intentionally played a shot to that part of the ice. How could this guy be so good if he was calling shots like that? When he scored three points on us by using that corner guard, I wasn't laughing any more.

Paul went on to win that Ontario championship and took his team to second place at the Brier in the days before there was a playoff. He missed out by one game to Jim Ursel's Quebec rink.

By my thinking, of course, Savage had just lost out to Ursel. I had just been nipped by Savage at the provincials so that meant that I was close to being able to win a Brier. That was my curling version of six degrees of separation. Yup, I was still a little naive when it came to understanding the big picture of curling. There were so many games between where I was and where teams led by skips such as Savage and Ursel were; there was so much to learn. Coming close to beating Savage was like standing in the foothills of Mount Everest and saying I was close to reaching the summit.

I knew what I wanted to do when I was curling, but the rest of my life wasn't so clear. After I finished high school, where I was a mediocre student at best, I went to Georgian College in Barrie, Ontario, to study journalism. The program had us doing a little bit of everything. One of the highlights was acting as disc jockey on the campus radio station. I'd go in and spin records—yes, actual vinyl LPs—by artists like Elton John, KC and the Sunshine Band and ABBA. That part, I liked.

But there were also courses that drove me nuts. I had to take things such as sociology and psychology, and they just didn't fit with me. I never understood how they applied to the real world. That left me without a lot of enthusiasm. With every passing month, it was becoming clear to me that school wasn't my forte. I've never been one to read a lot, and I think that was one reason I didn't enjoy my time at Georgian—at least in terms of the school work—all that much.

But when it came to sports, it was, "Where do I sign up?" I played on the golf team; I played touch football, volleyball, badminton and whatever else was available. There was no curling at the college, which was too bad because I had two curlers plus myself sitting in my homeroom.

I went to the assistant athletic director, Jim Martin, who became a good friend (probably because I spent almost as much time in the gym as the classroom), and inquired if there was any way we could form a college team. Martin approached the school but was turned down. By the start of October, there was some hope on the horizon; the hockey team had decided after its 0–13 start the previous year to disband the program, and there was now money in the coffers to start a curling program. We began playing Tuesday nights at the Stroud Curling Club, about a half-hour from the college.

We ended up with about forty students religiously making the trip to Stroud that first year. From that group we formed competitive mixed, men's, and women's teams to compete in the Ontario college championships. Our men's team, although not the most talented squad ever assembled, taught me about team belief and camaraderie. These guys were great friends and believed that I could do no wrong. They really helped me be confident.

Glen Robinson, my lead, was a wonderful guy who only curled socially once a week. We put him at lead because he tended to fall over—unintentionally, of course—on takeouts. Danny Asselin and I had curled together in high school. He also had not played competitively and ended up being our second, even though he couldn't throw hard enough to crack an egg. That left a good friend, Dave Godward from Orillia, as my third. He had done some curling and, more important, didn't mind my yelling for sweeping, because he was deaf in one ear.

To top it all off, Martin had volunteered to be our coach, even though he'd never seen a curling rock in his life and knew absolutely nothing about the game. He provided the moral support, even though he wasn't always sure if we were winning or losing.

Despite the drawbacks, we managed to win our zone and our region, and make it to the provincial championship in Kirkland Lake—Martin got to drive the van on that trip, another of his coaching duties. This was quite an accomplishment, to make it out of the Southern Zones to the Provincials with such a green team.

It was one of those magical weeks that only happens a couple of times in a life. My team struggled so badly that they had to believe completely in their skipper, and that gave me a tremendous amount of confidence. Game after game after game, the opposition would have five stones in the rings and I would manage to get my first one in behind the cover of guards. The other skip would try to follow that down and wreck on a guard, and I would throw another perfect draw, and we would get our two. I was having one of those weeks where everything worked.

We won our first five games, all on the last shot, and most of them by stealing points—scoring when we didn't have last shot in an end. It was a seven-game round robin with no playoffs. The top record would win. At 5–0 we just had to win our sixth game. By this time, our lead had three tensor bandages on his sliding leg, our second was nauseated and couldn't stand the pressure, and our third was deaf in both ears. Martin was eating Maalox like Smarties. Once we taught Jim the game, he became increasingly nervous as the bad ends piled up and anxiously watched as we managed by smoke and mirrors to work through the event. To add more excitement, the roof at the Kirkland Lake arena was full of holes. Unfortunately the weather had turned warm, and most of the snow turned to water and ended up coming through the roof and onto the ice surface. There were pools of water all over the curling sheet, and for the first and only time in my life, my curling game was rained out.

The Cinderella story continued, however. I managed to make a double takeout with my last shot to win our sixth game, and the seventh game became meaningless because no one could catch us in the standings. We still had to play to complete the round robin, and just to keep the coach on edge, we scored two in the tenth and final end to win our seventh consecutive game on the last shot.

This was the first provincial championship title for Georgian College. With the curling win and points for being the top golfer, I was chosen Athlete of the Year. I returned to the college for its twenty-fifth anniversary and was named Athlete of the Quarter Century.

After a year in journalism, I quit, having squeaked a passing grade. I switched to Hotel and Resort Management, where I passed about ninety per cent of my courses, but I hated it. A lot of the classes didn't make any sense, but I slogged through them. I didn't see why I needed to understand how to interpret a poem or why it was important to know when John Cabot landed in Canada. Courses like sociology, history and psychology didn't have a lot of relevance for me. Math, however, made sense, because I could see its purpose.

Outside the classroom, my real passion was golf rather than curling. I held four course records and had posted a sixty-one at my home course, which was one shot off the lowest score ever recorded, although our course was slightly shorter than six thousand yards, which was the criterion for a regulation-length golf course.

I'd been a decent enough player to get some inquiries about attending school in the U.S. on a golf scholarship, but I never pursued that. I look back and think that if I'd made any effort, I could have gone to the States. Still, I would have had to deal with the whole schoolwork issue south of the border and that may be one reason I never pursued this option.

But there were other factors that played into that decision, too. I was a small town kid and I wasn't really interested in leaving home. Midland was the right place for me. That's why Georgian College, despite the frustrations that came along with the work, was a perfect fit.

To continue my passion for golf, I had been working part time at the Brooklea Golf Club, moving up the ranks from back shop club cleaner to front shop attendant. I became a course rat, playing pretty much every day and working whenever I wasn't playing. I got to be a good player, probably one of the best in the region, and could shoot under par at the course. Brooklea wasn't about to host the Canadian Open, but it was a decent enough track that had a steady clientele. Most were locals, but in the height of the summer season, it was also an attraction for cottagers and tourists. I enjoyed working with people, greeting them and trying to help them get more out of their day. And that realization led me to finally pursue a career.

When I finished my last class at Georgian College, I left the campus and drove straight to Brooklea. The course was my new home and where I wanted to be. For the next six or seven years, I learned the business of golf under a British professional named John Caygill. He taught me all sorts of things about the job of being a professional, but one thing he never did was enroll me in the Canadian Professional Golfers Association program for assistants, the certification system that provides the CPGA designation. All the while I was working as a golf pro, I hadn't joined the CPGA, something that would hurt me dearly later on.

My golf career was blossoming even without the CPGA, and my curling also continued to improve. In the 1978–79 season, I was still playing with Paul and Kent, and we added Carl McAllen, who replaced Len Patterson, whose job had been transferred. It was a good team as far as being competitive in the region, but having had a taste of a higher level at the 1977 provincials, I knew that if I wanted to achieve more, I'd have to get a stronger team.

The first step in that equation—breaking up the old team—wasn't hard. Carl wasn't interested in playing competitively. He had a family and responsibilities that took precedence over curling. He wasn't interested in going to the big cashspiels at the Royals in Toronto or Whitby and playing for money, which was what I wanted to do.

Paul was getting older and I think in some ways he probably still wanted to curl, but he moved aside when it was clear Kent and I were going in another direction. It was sad to part with Paul but I wanted a more competitive team. We needed two new curlers, and we were getting smart. Rather than look only at the Midland Curling Club, we expanded our search all the way to Penetanguishene and found the two best curlers at that club, Larry Merkley and Bob Ruston.

Merkley was a wonderful guy and the best curler at Penetang. We had butted heads a number of times in area spiels and playdowns. He was a bit older than I was and a tremendous athlete—a good hockey player, a great tennis player, a decent golfer. His daughter later played on the Canadian national tennis team. Larry, who played third, always had a great work ethic, which I really liked. He may not have known the game as well as someone like Paul Savage, but what he lacked in knowledge, he more than made up for with enthusiasm. Larry was an unbelieveable team player, and like the college team had a strong belief in my abilities.

Bob, the second, was a real fun-loving guy who was also a good athlete. He could play just about any sport, and he was a good curler. But as the year went on, I learned that he probably wasn't cut out for competitive curling. It wasn't that he couldn't play, he just didn't have the fire in the belly you need to succeed in competition. There was nothing wrong with that, but the rest of us were there to go as far as we could.

But that year we started out full of optimism. I was enjoying skipping and was starting to get a bit of an understanding of strategy at the top levels. We didn't start playing until about mid-fall of 1979. That was the way it worked for teams in our area. The ice never went into the clubs until much later than the rinks in Toronto, where teams had been playing for a month or six weeks before we took our first slides. Part of that was probably the cost of keeping the ice, something that was easier financially on the big curling clubs in Toronto.

Our year consisted of playing those big cash events at the Royals and Whitby again, filled in with a few local spiels. I think we won about $2,000, which probably didn't even cover our expenses for hotels, meals and gas. That was how we prepared for the playdowns. Somehow we made it through the zone and regional qualifying and ended up at the Ontario championships in Brampton. It was exciting to be skipping at that event, and to see my name up there on the draw board and in the media.

Alfie Phillips, in his annual ranking of contenders in the *Ontario Curling Report*, picked us to go 4–5. Bob Fedosa was the defending champion and the favourite, with Savage right behind.

The ice at Brampton was great, thanks to Shorty Jenkins and his magic touch. It was exceedingly quick (twenty-seven seconds from hog line to tee line), and I loved that because it allowed for a lot of finesse shots such as draws, freezes and taps, my strengths; a lot of the other guys, however, didn't love the ice. We jumped out to win our first seven games and, I think, stunned just about everybody. Fedosa, meanwhile, lost his first seven.

Throughout my curling career, if there was an easy way or a hard way to win a championship or get to the next level, my team always seemed to take the hard way. Both times we won the Brier and the Worlds, we had to go through the Challenge Round, which was a last-chance playdown for teams that had lost out along the traditional route. It was similar to the repechage in rowing and was a real crapshoot and a tough way to make it to the provincial final.

In 1980, we didn't have to go through that, but we did make it tough on ourselves. Heading into the eighth draw, we were two games up on Bob Charlebois, a savvy curler who'd been to the Brier. Mathematically, he was the only team that could catch us. He was playing Savage in the eighth round, and if he lost that game or his next one, or if we won one of the final two games, we were off to the Brier.

Of course, as soon as you start thinking like that, the inevitable happens. Welcome to curling…here we were with seven wins, no losses, playing the defending champion, on his home turf, who had been devastated all week and had lost all seven of his games, and of course, you know the rest of the story. Fedosa arose from the dead to hand us our first loss. Meanwhile, Savage looked like he mailed in his game against Charlebois, which was upsetting. Our loss and Charlebois' victory made the final round-robin game the deciding contest of the Ontario finals.

We went into the final round against an old friend of mine, Max MacIntyre. We had played MacIntyre in our regions many a time and had a wonderful record against his team. MacIntyre had long been eliminated from winning the provincials and, with nothing to lose, was dangerous. He came out and made everything...hit and rolls, freezes, taps. It was unreal. Every time he'd come down the ice after some sensational shot, he would look at me and say: "Sorry, Russ."

We lost to him, and Charlebois won his last one, which meant a playoff the next morning. The press was really behind Charlebois and down on us, writing things like "The Kid's Bubble Has Burst" or "The Dream Is Over." We were starting to wonder if we were indeed in over our heads.

We knew we had to prepare for a big battle with Charlebois, a notoriously slow player, who liked to drag things out. Games in those days didn't have any time clocks, as they do now, and the round-robin contest we played against him took four hours and twenty-five minutes. It was a marathon. We called him the Human Rain Delay. I remember that as we were finishing up the round-robin match, the other teams were coming into the rink to start the next draw. For that round-robin game, we played Charlebois and then went right out for our next game.

With that in mind, I elected to go to the hotel to get as much rest as possible, knowing the playoff could be a marathon. But unbeknownst to me, Bob and Kent decided the best way to handle everything was to go back to their roots. All week, they'd been good boys. They'd curled and gone to the hotel and rested. Bob loved curling, but he also loved having a beer after the game, and he hadn't done that all week. Kent was never one to shy away from a beer either so the two of them decided that nothing would put the charge back in their game better than a few cold ones.

So they went out and had fun, and the next morning, they never curled better. Of course, they did not tell me they went out until we won. I was the young guy, and they were always protecting me from stuff I didn't really need to know. I probably would have blown a gasket thinking about them out on the town right before a big game, but it worked.

The ice in that final was really quick. I remember in the first end, however, coming up a foot short with my first rock. Charlebois hit and rolleded out, and I threw a split for two, pushing both a rock that was just off the rings and my shooter into the house. We ended up winning 6–2.

When the last rock came to rest we just exploded—we were going to the Brier. Larry threw his broom up, and it hit the roof. He went nuts. I think he may have had a better idea of what we'd just accomplished.

Wendy, who was just about to become my wife, had no idea what we'd done, but she was no less excited. She phoned her mother with the good news: "Mom, you won't believe it. Russ was curling and he won a trip to Calgary." She didn't understand it was to represent Ontario in the Canadian championship.

One of the reasons I think we won that game and the title was that the ice was so perfect. Savage had told the press that the ice really favoured me because I had the best delivery. He was the best reader of the ice at that time, but reading the ice didn't matter because every sheet was consistent, and the speed never changed. His advantage was negated, while mine was enhanced. Over the years, Shorty Jenkins made phenomenal curling ice for the Provincial playdowns, which gave me great confidence. Just knowing he was in the building always helped us raise our level of play.

The hours I'd spent working on my delivery had paid off. My father had always drilled a lesson into me—on good ice, if there's a guy with a good technique and a guy with a bad technique, at the end of the day, you know who's going to win. I always felt that when I was playing Savage I had an advantage. He had a good delivery, but it was awkward-looking to me. His left arm, which he used to throw the stone, was bent, and his body was twisted. Certainly it was still effective—he'd won a lot using it—but there was a greater chance of something going wrong. It was the same thing in later years against Eddie Werenich. One reporter said of Eddie's delivery: "Eddie's delivery is like watching a drunk trying to stand up in a canoe." Style or not, Eddie went on to be one of the best skips who every lived.

We went back to Midland after our win, and while the town celebrated, we found ourselves in the middle of a political issue. Two of us—Kent and I—were from the Midland Curling Club. But Bob and Larry were Penetanguishene members. There was a lot of pulling and pushing to figure out where the team was from. Both clubs wanted to say they were the home of the Ontario champions and call us their own.

My father had become the manager at the Penetanguishene Curling Club after retiring from Loblaws, so we elected to play from there. That went over like a lead balloon with the folks at the Midland club. But there was no way we were going to win that one. Thankfully, any animosity was put on the back burner, and there were a number of fundraising parties at both clubs where they'd hold fifty-fifty draws and raffles, which helped us defray the costs of missing work for a week and taking our wives to the Brier, as well.

Three of us were pretty pumped to be heading to the Brier, but Bob was an exception. On the plane to Calgary, Bob leaned over and told me something that left me stunned. "I'm never doing this again," he said. "I don't enjoy it. I'm not having any fun." I'd had him out practising every day because, in my mind, there was only one game plan to take to Calgary—to win. In those days, we never did any physical workouts in a gym, but we threw a lot of rocks. Bob didn't want to do that. He wanted to play his game and have a few beers.

That year at the Brier, there were officials stationed on the ice to chart violations. There was a long list of infractions that ranged from moving while an opposition member was throwing; sweeping a bit too early; and not standing in the right spot. The infractions were a precursor to what was to come a few years later when the Canadian Curling Association added officials to judge whether players had released the stone before crossing the hog line. They had the authority to remove a rock from play, but at the 1980 Brier, there were no penalties. Players were handed a sheet with all their violations on it.

One game, Bob got his sheet and he had 143 violations. I might have two or three in a game. "So what?" he said, after looking at his tally, "Where's the beer?" He definitely had a fun-loving attitude, and I loved him for that, but it probably wasn't the best way to come into a Brier.

One of Bob's most memorable incidents came in our game against BC. They had a player named Kelly Horrigan, who was known as Horrible Horrigan. (His brother, Tim, skipped the team.) He was a brash, loud fellow, and I think because I was new to this level of curling, he was trying to intimidate us. Bob saw that, and after a while, Bob got in Kelly's face and told him to cut it out. The two of them really got into a shouting match, and the officials had to step in and break it up.

One thing about Bob is that he'll never die of stress. I don't think he liked the pressure of the Provincials or the Brier.

The 1980 Brier was also the first one sponsored by Labatt. Macdonald Tobacco sponsored the event for fifty years. Then the brewery stepped in and made a lot of changes. Labatt put up the money to host the event, and they helped create the party atmosphere that's part of the Brier today, by adding things like the Brier Patch, a huge bar that is the watering hole for five or six thousand curling fans. They were a great sponsor, but at the start, they really didn't understand the traditions of the event.

They didn't make too many mistakes, but one big one was in the crest they gave every participant. For almost every past Brier, if a team won its province, the players received a crest, known as the Purple

Heart, which became the symbol of participation in the national championship. It was the crest every curler wanted on his uniform.

But Labatt decided to create its own crest and brought out this round white one that quickly became known as the Doily.

When we were handed the white crest, we were crushed. I'd only been involved in curling for a short period, but I knew the Purple Heart was it. It was like the Green Jacket in golf's Masters Tournament. It was curling's Holy Grail.

The Quebec team got two Doilies. They first received one in French and complained, and got a second one in English.

At the Brier, there was a big movement to get the Purple Heart back, and in the end, Labatt issued all the teams a new Labatt Purple Heart. I still have that Doily, though—it's definitely a collector's item.

While there were a few bumps as they learned the ropes, Labatt really did treat us like kings. We stayed in the best hotels and had a huge per diem and free everything at the rink. Every team had a driver on call who would take us anywhere and everywhere. We really weren't used to this kind of treatment. Usually, we got into our own car and drove to the next spiel. It was the big time, or it sure felt like it. In later years, this type of treatment from Labatt, coupled with the huge crowds in excess of a hundred thousand for the week, became an incredible motivator to get back to the Brier.

On the ice was an amazing collection of teams. There was Rick Folk from Saskatchewan; there was Jim Ursel from Quebec, who'd won it all in 1977. There were two unknowns from Northern Ontario named Al Hackner and Rick Lang; and there was Earl Morris, who was skipping Manitoba and would eventually skip in three Briers from three different provinces. Earl happens to be the father of John Morris, a talented curler who would go on to win a world junior champion-ship and finish second in the Brier. There was also the flamboyant Paul Gowsell from Calgary, who'd won two world junior titles and was making his first appearance at the Brier.

Our first Brier game was against Ursel, and I was shaking in my boots. Here I was, a rookie, and I had to shake hands with Ursel, whose sweater was covered in Purple Hearts. We used to call them scare badges, and Ursel was pretty scary. To make matters worse, just the day before, we'd run into Warren Wallace, who lived in Barrie. We'd curled against him from time to time in our area playdowns, and when he was living in Quebec he had played one year for Ursel. He'd come to watch the Brier, and we ran into him in the lobby of our hotel. He went on and on about how good Ursel was and that we shouldn't worry if he cleaned our clocks. Talk about positive thoughts to take into a game!

As it turned out, we were three down playing the eighth end, and I had a fairly simple double takeout for two points, but ended up just chipping one rock and scoring only one. I was devastated. I was two down to Ursel in my first Brier game. Somehow we managed to steal one in the ninth and then did the same thing in ten and then, in the extra end, we got two to win 9–7. That was such a shock, especially in the days before the Free Guard Zone, the offense-stimulating rule brought into the game in 1994. That type of comeback almost never happened.

So I had my first Brier win, and what a memory it was. We high-fived, rushed back to the change room, had some laughs and headed back to the parking lot to the team van, where low and behold, in the back of our van was Warren Wallace. Obviously, a converted fan. Warren was a great guy who continued to follow our career, even though he lived in British Columbia and we lived in Ontario. Ironically, seven years later in 1987 when we managed to win the Brier and represent Canada at the World Championships in Vancouver, we were thrilled to have a friend such as Warren Wallace, who volunteered to be our driver for the week. It was a thrill I'll never forget.

After that first Brier game against Ursel, I learned another aspect of the championship for which I wasn't really ready: the media. At the Ontario final, there was a handful of reporters, but at the Brier it grew almost tenfold. It also didn't take long to realize that I had to be careful about what I said. I didn't want to say something that could be interpreted as being negative towards another team. That could easily add fuel to the opponents' tanks or cause the fans to get on me and throw me off my game. There were occasions in my career when what I said was interpreted differently than I meant, causing some problems. But at that Brier, I didn't mind talking to the media. I'd like to think that I've always had a pretty good relationship with the press, and if they're talking to a player, it usually means that player is winning.

We started off 4–1 that week; the loss was to Hackner, who stole the last end to beat us. After the first five games, things started to unravel. We were pretty naïve about how things operated. We started to go to the Brier Patch at night, and the late nights started to catch up with us. As well, there were parties that we thought were command performances. There was a joint Ontario party, called the North–South, where curlers and officials from Southern Ontario and Northern Ontario got together. We went to that. We were invited to Atlantic night, and we went to that. If there was a banquet that started at 7:30, we'd show up at 6:30. It took me a while to learn that if the banquet started at 8:00, we didn't leave the hotel until 8:30, and then we'd have one Coke at the banquet and leave. But in 1980, we were almost the last to leave every one of these bashes.

All of a sudden it was Tuesday and we were exhausted. It wasn't really all the drinking—I still wasn't drinking much, if anything—but just going out and doing everything, the festivities, the banquets, the media requirements and all the rest. We lost two or three games at the end of the week to teams we probably should have beaten, in large part because we were running on empty.

One of the big attractions at the 1980 Brier was Paul Gowsell. He was a wild guy who looked more like a ZZ Top exile than any Brier competitor I'd ever seen. He had long red hair and a scraggily beard. He was really a curling rebel, and his was the first team to use push brooms at the Brier. They'd won almost everything that year on the cashspiel circuit, earning something like $75,000, which was huge back then.

His carefree attitude allowed him to party all week. He even ordered a pizza in the middle of a round-robin Brier game when his opponent was taking too long to play. He was quoted as saying that I would never be a good curler because I yelled too loud, which I found ironic because he could belt out the notes too.

That year, Gowsell had a record of 17–1 against Folk, but he never got the chance to play Folk in the final. After finishing with an 8–3 mark in the round robin, he ran into Hackner in the semi and missed a fairly routine double to lose. I think if he'd won that game he would have won the Brier. It's always seemed strange to me that Gowsell only ever made it to one Brier, but 1980 was his one and only appearance.

Hackner went on to lose to Folk in the final, which was an event. That was the first Brier to have playoffs, something Labatt brought in for television. Prior to that, the Brier was a straight round robin, and the team with the best record won. The old format allowed for an anti-climactic finish when a team had an unmatchable record going into the last draw. The playoffs saw the team with the best round-robin record advance directly to the final, while the second- and third-place teams met in the semifinal. It worked well, and curling was never the same.

On the plane ride back from Calgary, I was upset that I'd finished with a losing record of 5–6. Ontario should do better than that, I thought. Savage wouldn't have had a losing record. I thought like that for a long time, but when the next curling season rolled around, I was playing in the little cashspiel in Elmvale and people came up and asked about the Brier, about Gowsell, about the atmosphere and playing in an arena. It suddenly dawned on me that it was a real thrill to have played in the Brier. It didn't matter how I'd finished, I'd played in the Brier. And after one taste, I knew I wanted more.

Back to the Brier

4

THE START OF THE 1980–81 season was totally different than any before. I was the reigning Ontario champion, and that meant all sorts of extra attention, invitations to big cashspiels, and every time our team stepped on the ice, our opponents were out to get us. I was also getting better at understanding the landscape in terms of what it took to get to the Brier and to compete on the cash circuit in Ontario. I knew I needed to practise a lot more, play in bigger events and play more often. I was also starting off with a change in the lineup. At the end of the 1980 season, Bob Ruston surprised none of us by saying he'd had enough. He had his Purple Heart and was happy to go back to playing once or twice a week in the club and having a few beers with the boys after the game. I don't know if Bob ever understood how good a curler he was, but he was clear about what he enjoyed, and competitive curling wasn't it.

I wasn't quite sure what I was going to do about replacing Bob, but I'd already done my usual scouting around Midland and Penetang and come up with a couple of possibilities. It never occurred to me that someone from Barrie or Toronto would be interested in playing for me. But one summer afternoon at the golf club the phone rang and at the other end was Bob Charlebois. This was the same Bob Charlebois who had skipped the team I had defeated in the playoff to win Ontario.

In 1979–80, he'd probably been the best player in the province. His team had won the most money, and he had been to two Briers, in 1971 and 1976. He was a big, tall, lanky fellow who had a graceful delivery that sort of unfolded from the hack. It almost seemed as if he was already at the hog line before his foot left the hack. His call surprised me. I was twenty-three, coming off a losing record at the Brier, and the guy I had beaten in the final, who was probably the best skip in the province, was calling.

"Russ," he said. "I know you're down a player for next year. I'd like to come and play third for you."

I was stunned. I couldn't figure out why he'd want to play for me, but it certainly seemed to solve all my problems. We needed a curler and we were going to replace Bob Ruston with Bob Charlebois, who was a veteran from Toronto who wanted to play hard and get to the Brier. Larry agreed to move down to second, and Kent was, in my mind, one of the best leads in the country. He'd gone from never throwing a rock in 1976 to the Brier in 1980. He was working hard at it, too, throwing rocks and training.

I have to admit that with Charlebois on the team and having just come off a Brier year, I had high expectations for the team. We did the full circuit that year, hitting most of the major bonspiels on the Ontario tour, and we expected big things. But it couldn't have been worse. We were just plain awful, and most of it—it not all of it—was due to the relationship I had with Charlebois. Throughout the first few bonspiels, he was constantly telling me what shots to play and how to skip. He was incessant about keeping control of the team, and I became intimidated. I started to fall into a shell, getting more and more frustrated with him and playing worse and worse. I didn't enjoy going to the games because I knew I'd get beaten up every time I stepped on the ice. I expect that from my opposition, but never from my teammates.

In some ways, it was like school. If I wasn't enjoying myself, I wasn't motivated, and I definitely wasn't enjoying myself. I didn't feel like the skip—I was just a rock thrower and broom holder for Charlebois.

Over the months we played, I also came to realize what a lot of other curlers in Ontario already knew: Charlebois was an unusual guy. He was a talented curler, yes, but he marched to a different drum than the rest of the world. He had different ideas on just about everything.

As the season went on, it became Larry, Kent and I on one side and Bob on the other. There was a lot of tension between us all as we entered the playdowns. We somehow managed to win our zone level but, somewhat mercifully, we lost at the regions, and that was it. Normally, we'd enter the Challenge Round, the second-chance bonspiel and the last way to get a spot in the Ontario final. It's an extremely tough way to make it, but almost every competitive team that loses out early goes. But so strong were the tensions on this team that Bob told us he wasn't interested in playing. Just like that, he quit the team. I don't think any of us were really surprised at his move. After a year of playing with Bob, nothing really surprised us. We picked up another player to replace him for the Challenge Round, lost, and our season was done. The defending champions didn't make it back to the provincial final.

Towards the end of that year, curling really hadn't been on the front burner for me. That may be why we did so poorly. But I was more interested in pursuing Wendy. Wendy was a curler and a golfer, which made us a perfect fit. We'd curled together (this was after she'd beaten me in our famous high school bonspiel) and we'd golfed together. There weren't many girls in Midland who curled and golfed, so our paths crossed a great deal. For a few summers, we'd golf with another couple, Dale Faint and Rob Roberts. They were dating, but Wendy and I were just friends. But that friendship grew stronger. We'd follow up our golf games with trips to Dairy Queen and pretty soon Wendy and

I were an item. Although she was a year ahead of me, we dated through high school until graduation took us to different places. Wendy went to Toronto, to St. Michael's College to study health record administration. I had another year of high school and then headed to Georgian College. We managed a long-distance relationship for two years, driving between Midland and Toronto, but when Wendy graduated, her only job option was in Sioux Lookout, a small community in Northwestern Ontario. Long-distance relationship took on a new meaning, and we decided it was time to part. Deep inside, I'm not sure either of us really wanted to end things, but common sense told us it would be pretty tough to continue seeing each other.

Two years later, Wendy got a new job in Huntsville, about forty-five minutes from Midland. I'd heard she moved back to the region and ran into her once in a while when she came to town. In the spring of 1980, I asked her out one weekend when she was home visiting her folks. She suggested we go golfing and invited her parents so it would be a very casual afternoon. I didn't want to go to Brooklea because I had been dating the owner's daughter, so I suggested Orr Lake, a course about fifteen minutes from Midland. After three holes, Mr. and Mrs. Thompson found some reason to disappear, and Wendy and I played on together. That afternoon was memorable for two reasons. I shot twenty-nine on the nine-hole course, which was the course record. And more important, Wendy and I got back together. We were engaged in November 1980, and that made the year curling with Bob somewhat more bearable. I'd see Wendy and the troubles on the ice would disappear. She was a great listener and was my sounding board when I became frustrated. That is something that has carried through to today. I know that I would not be the curler I am today without her beside me.

In 1981, I took a winter job making the ice at the Huntsville Curling Club, in part to supplement my income and also to be close to Wendy, who was working in that town.

One day, Doug Flowers, the owner of Goldine Curling Supplies, dropped in for a routine visit and brought with him a gentleman named Hiroshi Kobayashi from Japan. He met Doug through some contacts and expressed an interest in starting curling in Japan.

I took Hiroshi on to the ice and gave him a crash course in curling. I showed him a little bit about the game, worked on his delivery and explained the scoring system. He was definitely enthused.

Over the next few decades, Hiroshi popped up when I least expected it. I met him at the 1983 Ontario championships, and he told me he was impressed with the curling and the enthusiasm of the crowd. I ran into him at the 1987 World Curling Championships, where he was an observer for the fledgling Japanese Curling Association. Hiroshi had formed that group a few years earlier. After we won the world championship that year, he invited me to Japan to promote the sport. Warren Hansen, the CCA's director of events and a world-class teacher, Wendy and I accepted the invitation and in the fall of 1987, we went to Karuizawa. This was a wonderful resort area with state-of-the-art sport facilities: an indoor rink for curling or hockey, a half-mile outdoor speed skating oval, a training facility, all at the foot of the mountains. The facilities were great, but the conditions for curling were not. The first rocks I threw on the ice only made it half-way down the sheet. I knew something was wrong so I started asking questions: what kind of water were they using, what kind of pebble head, what was the ice temperature? Everything they told me was perfect. I was mystified. I asked if they recently scraped the ice because of the frost level. They told me they finished scraping just before I arrived using a brand new Ice King scraper. When I checked that out, I found the problem. No one had taught them to unwind the scraper blade from its shipping position, which was dead flat. I gave the blade 10 or 12 cranks to give it some angle and ran it up and down the sheet twice. We re-pebbled the ice and I threw one. To the amazement of the ice making crew, the rock sailed smoothly the length of the sheet. The Japanese onlookers were overjoyed. They were cheering, they were jumping up and down, and all the top Japanese curlers wanted to throw on that sheet immediately.

Once the ice was in top shape, I was out throwing rocks by myself and Hiroshi asked if some of the top curlers in the country could come out and challenge me in a draw to the button contest. Each curler would throw a draw to the button and I would attempt to beat it. For some reason that day, I was unbeatable. If my opponent put it on the side of the button, I was on the pin. If I was only in the eight foot, they would be in the twelve foot. Each time I won, I glanced at Hiroshi and he said "Lucky." That became his nickname for me.

Hiroshi concluded the visit with a bonspiel, complete with a piper, signage, sheet dividers and carpeted walkways. I won the men's division with three relatively new curlers and Wendy won the women's, playing with three women who had come up from the Canadian embassy.

We went back a year later, this time with my team of Kent Carstairs, Tim Belcourt and Larry Merkley, sparing for Glenn who had work commitments. On this trip, Larry and I spent a great deal of time teaching the Japanese about icemaking. One example came when we reflooded the outside sheet which, through hockey use, was eight inches lower on one side of the sheet than the other.

We had a third visit in 1989, this time with Pete Corner, Wayne Middaugh, Glenn and myself. I was becoming a veteran of this trip but it was a new experience for the other three. We had a great time, except for Pete who is allergic to seafood, which is prevalent in much of the Japanese food. Many of the meals, which were very delicious, came in the form of a stew, with all kinds of weird and wonderful things. Peter didn't want to risk eating something that wouldn't agree with him so he ate boiled white rice for breakfast, lunch and dinner. Wayne was another story. He didn't have a fish allergy; he was just allergic to anything that didn't look right. Glenn and I can eat everything, but as our trip went along our front end was wasting away. At one point during the trip, we were driving from Tokyo to

Karuizawa and in the back of our van was a bag of about 30 small mandarin oranges. We weren't out of Tokyo and the bag was empty, devoured by Pete and Wayne.

"These are the best oranges I've ever eaten," Pete yelled up to the driver, who we nicknamed Hurray because we couldn't pronounce his name. Hurray looked back in the rear view and told us they should be, they were $9 a piece!

It was a different world over there to be sure. We were asked to play golf at a course where the green fee was $350 American. A steak dinner, at that time, was roughly $100. By the time we got back to Tokyo at the end of our trip, Wayne and Pete found salvation. Right outside of our hotel were the famous Golden Arches, a sight for sore eyes, or in this case, stomachs.

There was also a political reason for this third trip to Japan. Hiroshi had done a wonderful job of growing the game of curling in the three short years that I had been over. The sport went from a couple of hundred curlers on my first visit to 9,000 by year three, all wearing the same grey Goldline curling shoes that I was wearing! Hiroshi asked us to accompany him, wearing our World Championship jackets, to meet the president of the Japanese Olympic Committee. Japan was awarded the 1998 Winter Olympics and Hiroshi had been asked to explain curling to the Japanese committee. We spent the afternoon, explaining our sport and answering questions to the very interested dignitaries. We heard a couple of years later that Japan had asked the International Olympic Committee to add curling as an official Olympic sport when they hosted the 1998 Olympics. When it came to a vote on whether curling should join the Olympic family Japan was onside.

Ironically, one of the dissenting votes cam from Canadian Ken Reid, the former downhill skier. If it wasn't for the strength of the Japanese commitment—spearheaded by Hiroshi—curling may not have become an Olympic sport.

It was somewhat fitting, then, that I next saw Hiroshi in Torino, a few moments after winning the gold medal. As I was talking to the press I heard a voice up in the stands: "Lucky!" There was Hiroshi, applauding the win. Lucky indeed.

In 1981, while we stayed close to home when choosing a teammate, we made the same mistake: we didn't get a player who would fit with the rest of us. We picked a player named Steve Strong, who had just finished his junior career curling with my brother, Glenn. My thinking was all local. Steve was from Midland and was probably the best player coming out of junior. He curled for Glenn, so he must be good, and there was nobody else in Midland who could fit the bill. So we signed him up.

But, just as with Charlebois, it was a bad mix. He was on a different wavelength than the rest of us. For instance, that year we had to go to the Challenge Round, and when we went out on the ice for our first game, he was nowhere to be found. There we were into our last chance to get to the Brier and we started with a three-man team. He finally showed up in the fifth end, no reason given for being late.

That year was another waste, as the experiment with Strong didn't work. He was at least a lot easier to be around than Charlebois, but the bottom line was the same.

While we might not have won anything on the ice, I did learn one valuable lesson from Strong and Charlebois: chemistry is a vital part of any team. If the team doesn't get along, it doesn't matter how good the players are; the team will be hard pressed to perform on the ice. To this day, I've always made chemistry one of the first components in selecting teammates.

The next year, chemistry wasn't a problem. Glenn finally turned nineteen and was ready to join the men's ranks. He was a great young curler, having been schooled, as I had, by my father. Dad instilled the same basic fundamentals in Glenn as he did in me, and it showed. Glenn's delivery was pure, and like me, he loved to practise. We'd have long sessions of throwing rocks, critiquing each other's deliveries and trying to beat each other.

In his first year in the men's ranks, Glenn played second. Larry moved back to third. Kent was continuing to improve as a lead.

We had a solid season on the cashspiel circuit and eased through our playdowns to make it to the Ontario final. We thought we had a pretty good chance, but that year belonged to the Dream Team.

Ed (Eddie) Werenich, Paul Savage, John Kawaja and Neil Harrison were the toast of Ontario curling that year. Heck, they were the toast of Canada. The rink included four of the best players in the Toronto area who weren't shy about anything. Before they stepped on the ice, the predictions ran from they'd self-destruct by Thanksgiving to they'd win everything.

Being from Toronto, they'd cornered the publicity market, and when they started to win and kept winning, they were everywhere. I couldn't open up a curling publication and not read about their exploits, winning cars at this spiel, winning cash at that one. Even the mainstream media in Toronto were following their exploits. Eddie was very vocal and received a lot of great press, not only for his team, but for the game. As much as it was hard to admit they were the best team in the world at the time, any press was good press for our sport and it really motivated our team. We knew they were the team to beat.

I thought Kawaja was probably the best curler in the world. It seemed as if he never missed—didn't matter if it was a hit, draw, tap or freeze. Kawaja was always the driving force behind Eddie's teams, that year included. We had so many mental battles with those guys over the years, and Kawaja would just stare us right in the eye with a look that said: "Why are you even out here?" I don't know if there's been a stronger curler mentally than he was. He was intimidating in a sort of fearless way.

As it turns out, Werenich—the Wrench—was probably the best curler on that team; he just didn't look the part. Here was this short, pudgy little guy who looked like he was going to fall over when he delivered it, but the rock ended up perfectly every time. Or so it seemed. And I don't know if there's been anyone better as a strategist. Certainly he was far ahead of everyone else. He was always thinking two, three or four shots ahead. And he was fearless in calling his team to play very difficult shots. He knew they would make them ninety-nine times out of a hundred, and having that confidence allowed him to put a lot of pressure on his opponents.

We were still learning the game, but I felt for the first time I had a team that was capable of competing. From 1976 to 1982, we hadn't improved our rink. We were just trotting out the same guys, most of whom were good curlers, but not at the level where they could win a Brier.

In some ways, we were the opposite of the Dream Team. They were four guys from across this big region of Toronto who had all been stars in their own right. We were four guys from the neighbour-hood. But we could compete.

As well, I was still grasping the strategy at the highest level. It had taken a while to get comfortable with skipping against some of the best players in the world, but I was feeling more and more confident as we headed to the provincials in 1983.

When we played Werenich, I don't think any of us had any trouble getting up for the game. We'd all read the press clippings and seen what his team had done, and that gave us a lot more incentive to beat them. Glenn was easily the most pumped, and he played really well as we handed them one of the few losses they had on their Brier run.

To me, that game was really the start of our long rivalry. We would knock heads against those guys so many times over the years, and we would always seem to be in a battle for the Ontario title. We were real competitors. Eventually it got to the point where they were going to win or we were going to win. That made it really fierce, and the results had a double impact. If we won, we were ecstatic because we were going to the Brier, but also because Werenich wasn't. If we lost we were miserable because we were done for another year, and we'd have to watch the Wrench play at the Brier.

That type of feeling never really lasted long, though. I cheered for them when they won the Brier in 1983 in Sudbury. I can remember watching the final at the curling club and saying to the man sitting next to me: "We beat those guys."

It was thrilling to watch. I was cheering for them; I've always had the attitude if someone's good enough to beat me then I'm in his camp. And Werenich winning that Brier was that six degrees of separation thing again. Even though I'd finished 5–4 at the Ontario finals, and lost out in a tiebreaker, I'd beaten Werenich and he'd gone on to win it all. I was close, or so I believed.

I had, to that point, skipped longer than Werenich, something else from which I drew confidence. He'd skipped in 1981 for the first time. I'd been doing it since 1976, and even though I was younger and he was better, smarter, knew the angles and had a better team, I thought, "I can do what he's doing."

The rivalry was really only on the ice. I never held any animosity towards him on a personal level. After games, I'd sit down and have a drink with him as is the custom in the eastern part of the country. They were all golfers, too, so we'd often talk about that when we weren't discussing curling. But there's no doubt that as soon as we stepped onto the ice, it was war.

I learned another side of Werenich in 1984 as both of us returned to the provincial final held that year in Peterborough. Joe Gurowka was the president of the Ontario Curling Association. He'd been a good curler, played in a couple of Briers, including one in which he teamed with Bob Charlebois. But as an administrator, he left a lot to be desired.

Gurowka held a meeting at the start of the week in which he outlined the rules and proceedings for all the teams. He went over the playoff scenarios and at one point said there was no way there could be a five-way tie. Werenich stood up and told him he was wrong, that there was indeed a possibility of five teams tying for first. Gurowka told him it wasn't possible, and Werenich told him he was wrong.

I couldn't believe my ears. Here was a curler challenging an official. That was unheard of; curlers were supposed to sit there and listen, or so I thought at that time in my career. Werenich had become known as someone who challenged curling authority. He spoke out when he believed matters were wrong, most often when matters affected the curlers. He griped that it seemed as if the administrators were making decisions without talking to the curlers. He'd speak out on everything from bad ice conditions to poor draw scheduling to the need for on-ice officials to enforce rules that had been monitored by the players. He really felt the curlers got the short end of the stick when it came to events like the Brier. He was incensed when he learned that the Canadian Curling Association made a lot of money from these events and put their officials up in hotels with expense accounts, while the curlers received very little. The discussion about a five-way tie for first was an example. How could people running the most important event in Ontario curling fail to realize it was possible for five teams to tie for first? What made matters worse was the president of the association telling curlers that such an occurrence wasn't possible.

With one draw left in the round robin, the combinations were ripe for Werenich's predicted five-way tie. Of course, he would have to lose his last game for it to happen, and while I don't think he's ever publicly acknowledged throwing the game, it's pretty much common knowledge in the curling circles that he did just that, creating this huge log jam of five teams that actually benefited him because he received a bye while the other four teams had to play off.

That was really when I began to understand why Werenich and Savage had done so much griping over the years. They knew the guys running the sport were constantly messing up, that there was a lot of poor management and little thought for the players.

In our first trip to the Brier in 1980, we sat there and believed everything the officials told us. Werenich and Savage were different. They'd laugh at some of the stuff they were told. They'd challenge things and always stand up for the rights of the curlers.

As Werenich began to get more and more time in front of the microphone, he'd speak out and let these officials know what he was thinking and how they were ruining the game. The press loved him for that, and so did the fans.

Once I had been to three or four Briers, I began to understand a lot of the problems Eddie had confronted. Although we were fierce competitors, we stood as one on a lot of these issues.

I loved Werenich for that, for really trying to improve the game.

Werenich won Ontario again in 1984 and went to the Brier. We managed to beat his team in our round-robin match, finishing in the five-way tie. We lost out to Brian DeRooy of Chatham in our fourth game of the day, necessitated by the massive tie Gurowka never anticipated.

The next year saw another change in my team lineup, which was becoming a regular thing. Larry Merkley decided he didn't have the time to commit to the competitive curling life any more and stepped back. Glenn had moved up to third in 1984, and Kent was solid at lead. We needed to fill a hole at second, and my thinking was that we need to find someone who would allow us to compete with Werenich. If we were going to get to the Brier, the road we would take would go through the Wrench.

We decided to expand our area of search, which had been limited to Midland and Penetang in the past. We went seventeen miles down the road to Elmvale and found Tim Belcourt.

Tim wasn't the best curler in the area. There were three or four players I probably would have chosen ahead of him if I was looking at pure rock throwing. On a scale of one to ten, he was about a six. The others were sevens, and I didn't know enough to go to Toronto and find a nine. And I never thought any of those Toronto players would want to come to Midland to curl.

What sold me was Tim's work ethic. He absolutely loved to curl. He would play the 7:00 p.m. game in Elmvale, leave after throwing his first two rocks in the last end, fly over to Midland and join us for our 9:00 p.m. game halfway through the first end. I knew, with that drive, he would improve quickly.

Things with the new team didn't start off all that well. Although we did all right on the cashspiel circuit, our Brier bid was nipped short when we lost in the regions to a talented curler named Doug Palmer, who made a gem of a shot with his last one to beat us. We were surprised at losing to him; that happens in curling. There's no such thing as a sure thing, no matter how good you are. We didn't survive the Challenge Round and so we missed the provincial final. That was the only year between 1983 and 2006 that we didn't make it to the provincial final.

The next year started off slowy, but then, what year didn't?

After struggling through the early season, I thought we were starting to hit our stride heading into the playdowns. But we went to the zone competition and stunk the joint out. We played in Stayner, and took on the local icemaker in our first game and lost. In the second game we were playing a team from the local legion league, and they hammered us.

That was a long car ride home. We were really dejected because we'd been to four or five provincial finals, which was pretty good for a team from our area. Remember that up until we made it to the provincials in 1977, there had been one team—one—from the region that had been to the Ontario finals. We'd made it in 1977, 1980, 1983 and 1984.

I was so dejected I thought about packing it in. Kent was talking about going to the Challenge Round again, but having just come off two devastating defeats, I wasn't up for it. The Challenge Round was for the top sixteen teams in Southern Ontario that had failed to qualify at the regional level. It was only a double knockout—two losses and you were gone, and only one team would survive. But Kent's non-stop optimism won me over.

I think that car ride was the turning point for that team. If I'd stuck to my guns and refused to go to the Challenge Round, we would have been done, I'm sure of it. It would have been so easy not to go on. The day we left Midland for the Challenge Round there was a huge snowstorm (we lived in the storm belt area of southern Ontario), and Wendy was not happy about us heading out on a three-hour drive through the storm. Our son, Steven, had been born in 1984, and Wendy couldn't understand why we would risk our lives for such a small chance at winning. Wendy was always supportive of my curling, so I reassured her that we would check the road conditions and return home if we felt it was unsafe to travel. We survived the trip, we won the Challenge Round, and the rest was magical.

The Challenge Round advanced us to the provincial final. It restored my confidence. I looked at the opponents we were going to face and I felt that we were every bit as good. That year, Werenich, to almost everyone's surprise, missed the Ontario finals. His Dream Team was long gone. With him not there, it meant one less obstacle in the way of getting another Purple Heart.

That year's provincial championship was held in Richmond Hill, and in the first round, there was one of the strangest incidents I've ever seen. The night of the opening draw, there was a tremendous rainstorm and the arena roof leaked. There was one spot where a steady drip fell onto Sheet Two, a game between Ian Scott of Renfrew and Garry Lumbard from Kingsville.

Icemaker Shorty Jenkins brought out a large green garbage can and positioned it under the leak. He stayed with it all game and masterfully pulled and lifted it to keep the curlers and their rocks from colliding with his drip catcher.

It brought new meaning to the term "garbage game."

In every run to a Brier or World Championship or Olympic medal, there are always points where you can look back and say you dodged a bullet. A quarter inch more curl with this rock or a foot more in distance with that rock and a game could have had a different outcome.

We had one of those moments in a tiebreaker contest against Larry Snow, a competent Ontario curler who became president of the Ontario Curling Association and a real leader in the sport. Snow was as straight a shooter as there was out there, and it was proven in our important game against him.

After a four-way tie for second place—Ottawa's Wayne Tallon, with whom I would later curl when both of us moved to New Brunswick, won the round robin—we played Snow in a close contest. With my last rock, I was playing a quiet, come-around hit for two. Right out of my hand I was narrow, so I was screaming at the guys all the way down the sheet to sweep. It was really close to the guard, and just as it was about to go by, Tim's broom hit the guard, pushing it out of the way by about a quarter-inch. The shooter went on and made contact, and we scored two.

The other team's third, Robb English, immediately said to Tim: "You burned that rock." Tim admitted he did. Now the ball was in Snow's court. He could claim that the rock was going to wreck on the guard and, as a result, win the game. I went to him immediately. He was stationed right on the teeline at the time of the incident. I said to him: "I think it was going to get by, what did you see?"

Snow, being the honest guy he is, admitted that, yes, in his opinion, my shooter was going to slip past the guard. He held out his hand and said: "Good game."

I thought that was so big of him. Here was this competitor who'd never been to the Brier despite years and years of trying, and this was probably as good a chance as he was going to get, yet he did the right thing. If he'd said that the rock was going to wreck, he might be wearing a Purple Heart now, but he was honest and I remember commenting to the press on this and how it certainly reflected on Snow, but perhaps more on curlers in general. This is something I have loved about curling. As my dad always said, the game starts and ends with a handshake, and it really is a gentleman's game.

In the final, we went on to defeat Tallon, with three points in the sixth end proving to be the decisive moment. From the time we scored that three, all I could think about was getting back to the Brier.

Not long after our on-ice celebrations wrapped up, an official from the Ontario Curling Association (OCA) told us we had a number of tasks to do before we left. One was to name a fifth man. The Canadian Curling Association had recently added the position for all Brier teams, seeing it as an important position in case of injury or sickness.

We hadn't given it any thought, but it didn't take long for us to make our decision. Still wearing my curling gear, I changed shoes and raced into the parking lot, hoping I might catch our choice before he left to drive back to Penetanguishene. And there, just getting into his car, was Larry Merkley. I asked. He accepted, and for the next decade, he would always be our fifth, a role he filled superbly.

Inside the rink, Glenn, Tim and Kent were still celebrating, and with good reason. It had taken six years, but we were finally going back.

The 1986 Brier was held in Kitchener, and we were heading there as the home-province team. It was exciting because it was Glenn's first Brier. As well, he'd just finished university at Waterloo so he knew every second person there.

And I think just about everyone I knew from the Midland–Penetang–Elmvale triangle came at some point during the week, which added to the festivities.

Unlike our first trip, I felt we belonged this time. We had been pretty lucky to make it in 1980, but this time our team was strong. Some of the predictions had us as high as third; Ray Turnbull of TSN picked us as the dark horse.

One advantage to going back was that we knew what to expect, and we used that experience and paced ourselves for the long week ahead. We said no to a lot of stuff, despite the protests of Tim and Glenn, who were first-timers and wanted to experience everything.

But our slower pace paid off. We lost an early game to New Brunswick's Wade Blanchard 5–4 in an extra end. And late in the week, we lost to Alberta's Ed Lukowich 7–5. That left us at 9–2, which was good for a tie for first place, but because we were tied with Alberta, we fell into second place and the semi-final.

Before we played that game, I had a memorable encounter with a past Brier champ, Hec Gervais, who'd won the crown in 1974 and had been a dominant curler in the late 1960s and early 1970s. He was a mountain of a man, and I was in awe when I met him. He'd been one of the greats back in his day. I sat and listened as he talked about how much he loved the game and how he wished he was still playing. We talked about some of the players from his era, names I'd heard my father talk about, guys like Bob "Pee Wee" Pickering and the Richardsons.

I just loved hearing about the history of the game and the past greats; I think that's so important for our sport. I'm not sure if the Brier has done enough to honour the legends of the past, although I know that in recent years the Candian Curling Association has started to invite some of the past champions to the Briers. At the 2004 Brier the CCA honoured many of the game's greats, bringing together as many past Brier-winning skips as possible. I have a photo of all of them—including me—in my family room, and it's easily one of my favourites. It's important to recognize our past. Awareness of the game's history adds to the integrity of our game.

I was saddened at reading that Alf Phillips Jr. and John Ross, who won the 1967 Brier, had to pay to get into the Brier when it was in Ottawa in 1993. Can you imagine asking Gordie Howe to shell out to watch the Stanley Cup? I've always said that we should honour our champions, and a player who wins a Brier should have a lifetime pass to go to any Canadian men's championship.

After the Olympic victory, we were invited to the 2006 Brier in Regina, where we were brought out to be recognized. That night, I had the pleasure of going out to dinner with Sam Richardson of the famed Saskatchewan family that won four Briers. I couldn't get enough of Sam. We were fortunate at that dinner to be seated in a private room at the restaurant. I was at the opposite end of the table from Sam, but I listened to every word he said. He had some great stories, an amazing attitude and an incredible love of the game. Brad Gushue was sitting beside him, and I don't think he fully appreciated who Sam Richardson was or what he'd done. I felt a need for the young Newfoundland boys to sit and listen to the legendary stories, probably embellished, but nonetheless entertaining.

Back on the ice, Barry McPhee of BC was our opponent in the semi-final of that 1986 Brier, and we stole a single point in the extra end to beat him. We were one game away from winning it all, ten ends from being Canadian champions.

Before big games, my mind tends to race, and I babble on to Wendy about all sorts of things. What if we lose? What if we win? What if the ice is bad?

It's kind of crazy, but when I step on the ice, all that disappears, and I'm not worried about anything but the next shot. I guess it's a way for me to get rid of the nervous energy that builds up.

It was that way before our match with Lukowich. Once I put my foot on the ice, I was ready to try to win the Brier for me, for my team, for Ontario.

The game was fairly typical of contests in the days before the free guard zone rule. No one scored more than a single point in any end, although there were chances. In the fifth, Lukowich had to draw against five, and we managed to steal one. In the seventh, when my first rock picked and rubbed on a guard, he stole a point. We didn't play a very good seventh end, but we could have come out of it if I'd made that shot.

But the end everyone remembers is the ninth. We were one point down and had a nibbler off to the side. They had one in the back twelve. I threw an inturn hit at it, and if I'd made it, we would get two, and go one up coming home. Our plan was then to force Lukowich to one and win it in the extra end. That's how we mapped it out, anyway.

But as soon as I let it go, I panicked and yelled sweep—like I always seem to do—and the boys swept it. It looked great. We were worried about it bending too much because it was a swingy spot. Whether I threw it a hair harder than I should have or whether the ice got straighter—perhaps because of the TV lights that had been added for that game—I don't know. (That was my first time playing under TV lights.) Glenn says I split the broom, and he doesn't think we overswept it. But about halfway down the ice I said, "Uh-oh."

It hit and rolled out by about a half an inch.

We got one to tie it and he had the hammer coming home. Alberta scored one and won the Brier.

Losing in the Brier final, I thought, wouldn't be so bad. I would get over the initial disappointment—being so close and missing out—and then realize just how well I did. Second in Canada is no small achievement. But in a lot of ways, it's like being two steps from the top of Mount Everest and tumbling down all the way to the bottom. Everyone remembers the winner. And it seemed that year, everyone remembered who the winners beat.

After that game against Lukowich ended and we shook hands, I was reminded of losing every single day of that off season.

Not only that, but the reminders came in the form of: "You blew it," or "How did you manage to lose that?" or "What happened?"

I had a close friend in Midland who pulled me aside at the golf course one day and asked me if I had blacked out before throwing that rock in the ninth end.

The comments became relentless, and I had a lot of long nights of questioning myself and my abilities.

I replayed that shot in my head thousands of times. I knew I used to throw a lot of soft stuff for hits, but because it was a swingy spot, I decided, on that particular shot, to throw normal. If we didn't sweep the rock, we would have made it. I had just enough courage left in me to believe that I threw it the way I wanted. Otherwise I don't think I would have played another game.

All summer long it went on. No one congratulated us on making it to the final—they just asked why or how we blew it. It was hard at my job, too. I was greeting 200 people every day, and it seemed that 180 of them would shake my hand and say, "Too bad you missed that shot in the ninth."

I must have asked Glenn a hundred times that summer how I'd thrown that rock. Every time, he'd tell me I was right up the broom and the weight was perfect. The team certainly stuck together that summer. It was almost like we had to circle the wagons against the outside world.

It was bad enough that I had to listen to it all. What made it worse was that Wendy got it too. She was working at the golf course, and I can remember that after hearing, "Too bad your husband blew it," one too many times, she walked out the back door and broke down. She was sobbing uncontrollably.

That was about the last straw. I had to forget the shot. I had to believe we'd accomplished a lot in making it all the way to the final, that we were a great team. I had to convince myself I had thrown the shot I wanted to throw. The rock had missed, but it was no reason to jump off a tall building. Life would go on.

And at that point, I decided to make 1987 an absolute quest. I vowed to get back to the Brier and get the job done.

First Win

5

DESPITE ALL THE DETERMINATION, the focus and the hard work, our goal of making it back to the Brier in 1987 started with a thud. Although we enjoyed a good year in money events, we once again flopped in the playdowns. After making it all the way to the Brier final the year before, we lost out in our zone playdowns. That was almost an embarrassment, but it was becoming a habit. In fact, it got to be a joke with our team. We lost the zone? Hey, we must be headed to the Brier.

Once again, we set off for the Challenge Round and, if we hadn't won it the year before and gone as far as we did, I doubt we would have entered this time. The Challenge Round is such a crapshoot. If a team loses a game early in the event, it seems like it has to win about ten in a row to win it all. No matter how it does it, it has to be really lucky and really good to make it through, and 1987 was a perfect example of that.

We won our first three games, made it to the A final, and faced Gary Smokum from Barrie. Since Barrie was in our region, we'd played Smokum a number of times in various events. He definitely had one of the better teams in our area and he knocked us off in the A final, dropping us into the B side of the event. We managed to win the B side, which meant we had to beat Smokum twice to get to the provincial final.

Playing the ninth end, we were three down, and the ice conditions were horrible. Somehow we managed to steal one in the ninth and then steal two more in the tenth. In the extra end, Smokum needed to draw the four-foot to beat us, but came up light, so we still had life.

It came down to one game to determine which of the rinks would go to the provincial final. In that game, we were trailing by one point in the tenth end and scored one to tie it and force another extra end.

In the eleventh, with my last shot, I went around a centre guard to the top of the four-foot. Smokum could see about a third of my rock, and after missing his draw to the four to win the previous game, he elected to play a quiet hit and tap our rock out. It looked perfect all the way down the ice, and I resigned myself that this was as far as we were going to go, that our climb back had come up short. But then his rock straightened out and just clipped our rock. Both stones rolled and rolled and rolled, and when we looked down, ours was in by an inch. It was that close. With that inch, we were in, and Smokum was down the road.

I've always said that to win a Brier or even make it there, a team has to be good to be lucky or lucky to be good. There are just too many good teams in curling not to have some of the results come from luck. Let's face it: a team could be the best team in the world but they could always look back at a recent victory and realize just how close that came to being a loss. I think there is more opportunity for upsets in curling than in just about any other sport. I'm not going to beat Jack Nicklaus in a game of golf, but the best curling team in the world can make all eight shots in the first end while the opposition can miss their first seven but make the last one and be up 1–0.

Sometimes the luck doesn't come from the two competing teams, either. That was the case at the 1987 Ontario finals, held in Chatham. That year, curling officials across Canada had instituted judges at the hog line. There had been a feeling that many players were sliding across the line before letting go of the rock. To combat these rule breakers, two people would sit, one at each end of the hog line, and watch. Both judges had to agree that the player had gone too far before an infraction was registered. But what a penalty—the rock was removed from play.

At the 1986 Brier, the first to use the hog line officials, forty-seven rocks were pulled from play, and that sent the players into a tizzy. In most cases, the curlers were almost certain they hadn't crossed the line, that there had been human error. Television replays were not perfect, because of the camera angles, but they seemed to indicate that many times, the officials made errors.

In the last few years, since the Canadian Curling Association went to an electronic form of detection (sensors in the rock and at the hog line tell if the stone has been released in time), the number of infractions has plummeted. Did all these curlers suddenly become really proficient at releasing the stone before the hog line?

In the 1987 Ontario finals, one of the most glaring pulls of a rock occurred in our semifinal match with Paul Savage. We'd finished the round robin at 7–2, tied for top spot with Ed Werenich. We were relegated to second, however, thanks to the Wrench's eleventh-end draw to the button. He beat us in an extra end in our round-robin contest.

We were tied playing the eighth end with Savage holding last-rock advantage. He made a takeout for two and immediately the official came from the back of the sheet and told us there had been a hog line violation, that the rock had to be removed, and that the other stones had to be placed where they had been before the shot. This ruling allowed us to steal a point and take the lead.

I was stunned. Savage was livid.

In those days, Savage barely slid to the tee line. He said he'd never before been called for a hog line violation. I was at the far end of the sheet, not the best position to see if he was over, but for some reason, it registered in my mind that Paul was sliding out farther than usual on that particular shot. The ice was very quick, and we were all sliding to the hog line quicker than we were used to, but I never thought they would call it.

It certainly took guts for the official to make the call in the eighth end of the semifinal. But this gentleman took his role seriously and made the call to the best of his ability.

There was a lot of controversy surrounding the call. For some reason, there was only one official on the hog line, not the usual two. I heard later that the lone official quit the association because he took so much flak about his action.

The result of that rock pull meant that instead of being down two in the ninth end, we were one point up. Savage, an experienced veteran, regrouped and put a lot of pressure on us in the final two ends, but with some good shotmaking, we pulled it out.

That put us into the final against—guess who?—the Wrench. He no longer had the Dream Team, and we thought if we played aggressively we could put enough pressure on his new foursome in a big game that it might force some errors. It took six ends before we created the break we needed, sealing the victory with four points in the sixth. The mission was still alive; we were off to the Brier for the second consecutive year.

We knew we had received more than our fair share of breaks to win the 1987 Ontario title, but we'd qualified for the Brier, and we were going back determined to win. If there was any motivation needed at all, it was that we would not go through another summer like the last one.

I don't know if I've ever had a team that was as dialed in as that one was when we stepped onto the ice at the Agriplex in Edmonton. I was thirty-one, stubborn and driven, and I think Glenn and Kent were carrying some dogged determination too. They were almost mad on the ice, as if this was theirs and no one was going to take it from them. (Tim was different; he was the happy-go-lucky guy who kept us all loose. Sometimes I wondered if the guy had a pulse.)

The sports psychologists of today probably wouldn't have allowed us to play like that. The psychologists always tried to get Gushue's team to stay in their happy place all the time. But at the Brier that year, we went the other way. We went in thinking, "Who's our next opponent? I hope I hate him because if I hate him, I'll play better." (That attitude may have cost us a Brier in 1992 when we lost the final to Vic Peters. He was such a nice guy, and I couldn't be mad at him. I think if I had been able to get angry with him we might have won!)

The ice that week was atrocious, with inconsistent speed and curl due to bad frost. There were lots of crazy games with scores like 9–1 and 12–8 and 10–3. The frost was horrible, and we really had to be careful what part of the ice we were throwing on because it would only affect parts of the sheet. Conditions could vary drastically from the centre of the sheet to the side.

In the 1980s, the ice at the Brier was always unpredictable. The icemakers at Canadian championships were being challenged with big crowds and hot television lights, which affected the temperature in the building and created havoc with the surface. That was a big disadvantage for teams from Ontario. We'd play our provincials in arenas on perfect ice thanks to Shorty Jenkins and his magic. Shorty had worked hard to understand all the conditions that affected arena ice, such as humidity, ceiling height, airflow and temperature. Many other icemakers didn't have that experience. They were used to putting in ice in curling rinks, where conditions were more controlled. At the Brier, teams had to adjust strategy to combat the inconsistent conditions. And for some reason, the CCA wouldn't hire Shorty to do the Brier ice. It was almost as if they didn't want to admit that he knew more than their icemakers. Rather than swallowing their pride and getting great ice, they preferred to play their marquee event on the equivalent of a gravel road. I always believed if we were going to make our sport grow, we had to provide the best playing surfaces. If television audiences wanted to see great shotmaking, the icemakers could allow the players to do that. For a number of years, the largest television audiences were at the annual TSN Skins Game, a made-for-television event where some of the country's best players dazzled audiences with remarkable shotmaking. Many people attributed the great performances to the format. The organizers put different rules in play, and the rules forced teams to use aggressive strategy with lots of rocks in play. But the real reason the Skins Game was more exciting was due to the ice conditions Shorty Jenkins created. Without his playing surface, the event wouldn't have worked.

Despite the conditions at the 1987 Brier, we managed to win the round robin, losing two games, one to BC's Bernie Sparkes and the other to Gary Mitchell of New Brunswick. Sparkes ended up in the semifinal against Newfoundland's Mark Noseworthy. We decided to watch the game in the hotel on CBC, and we were hoping Noseworthy would win. Not that his team would be that much easier to beat, but we had lost to Sparkes in the round robin, and we knew he'd have a mental advantage.

Plus, there was the small fact that Sparkes had twelve Purple Hearts, more than any other curler. It wasn't likely that he'd be nervous playing in a Canadian final; Noseworthy might. The semi started off as a close game, and as we watched, I wasn't sure who we'd end up playing. Both teams were solid. But just as they reached the tenth end, the unbelievable happened—the CBC cut away from the game to go to local programming. I remember Dave Hodge making some negative comments about the decision, and that was it. We had to phone over to the rink to find out who won.

When we learned that Sparkes had won, I got a sick feeling. We knew he wasn't going to fold. We knew we were in for a tough game. I could feel the butterflies fluttering in my stomach. We'd climbed the mountain once again and made it to the Canadian final. I had spent the past twelve months thinking about the previous Brier final and all the what-ifs and if-onlys. Now the doubt was creeping into my mind. Did we have enough experience to beat the legendary Bernie Sparkes? Could we handle the Western crowds who would love to see Bernie win his first Brier as a skip? Would we be able to handle the field of straw their team created with their brooms, especially big Jim Armstrong?

If I'd known I would play in thirteen Briers, I might not have been so worried. But in Ontario, I had to beat Werenich and Savage, and I thought I might never have another chance. It was that tough. I also didn't want to be curling's version of the Buffalo Bills (the NFL team lost four consecutive Super Bowls), losing in consecutive finals.

I'd had twelve months of people telling me how useless I was, and I'd never before been scrutinized that closely. I had to learn to deal with it or it would shatter my confidence. The thought of going into another Brier final certainly caused me some trepidation, but more important, it was tough on Wendy. I could see the stress on her face. She's not only my Number One supporter, but my best friend. How could I explain to her that I wanted to be in this position, that competing at this level with these risks and rewards was what I loved? I wanted to win the national championship and I wanted to wear the Maple Leaf on my back and represent my country at the world championship.

Years later, Wendy said this was the defining moment of my career, the point where she knew how much I loved the sport and loved to compete at the highest level. In talking to Wendy, I gained the perspective I needed to compete in that final the next day. I realized the team had made it all the way through a long playdown road. We'd started in the club, then the zone, the Challenge Round, the Provincials, the Brier round robin and the Canadian final for the second straight year. This was quite a feat, and win or lose, we could be proud of our accomplishments. Being runner-up in the 1986 Brier had been the highlight of my career. One missed or made shot does not define a career. From that day forward I have always believed that pressure is self-inflicted. The farther the team goes, the less pressure there should be. If someone had said to me at the start of 1986 that I was going to come second in Canada, I would have been pretty happy. So why shouldn't I be happy being back in the final? I should be proud and realize that anything more was a bonus. To me, pressure is when I lose at the club level, not in the national final.

Call it experience, but this time, I went into the final with excitement. Sparkes' team was a good one. His front end, Jamie Sexton and Monte Ziola, was solid, and his third was big Jim Armstrong, a dentist who was the size of a Sherman tank and very intimidating. Before the Brier started, we were throwing practice rocks, and Armstrong came walking over to our sheet as we were finishing. I'd never seen the man before; he hadn't been at any of the spiels we'd played that year. He looked at me and without introducing himself said: "Bet you can't draw the rings."

I accepted the bet, and before I could throw, he took an inverted corn broom and swept the length of the ice. Those brooms had a centre of thick straw wrapped with regular straw and were really messy. They'd been banned in Ontario because of the debris they left on the ice (another step the Ontario Curling Association took to improve ice conditions before the rest of the country!) When Armstrong was done, it looked like a threshing machine had passed over the ice.

I stepped into the hack and, knowing I'd have to throw it a bit heavier, pushed off with about board weight—under normal conditions, just enough to make the rock go through the rings to the backboard. The rock didn't make the hog line, and it was going at right angles. Armstrong was standing there laughing.

That was my introduction to Big Jim, but it wasn't the last straw incident I had with him in that Brier.

The ice in the final had very little curl, which was predictable on arena ice in the pre-Shorty days. In the sixth end, with the score 3–2 for BC, we had a corner guard up on the right-hand side of the sheet. Sparkes was playing a hit on our stone, which was sitting in the twelve-foot circle on the left of the sheet. Before Sparkes threw, Armstrong went to the path that led behind the corner guard and swept all the debris away. That was because he knew the corn on the ice—in small amounts as opposed to what I had to face in our little pre-tournament bet—would help the rock curl in behind the guard. Technically it wasn't against the rules, but it wasn't exactly good sportsmanship. I got a little upset. He was clearing away the straw in an area he wasn't playing. He knew that if Sparkes hit and rolled out, we were going to have a good chance to bury one behind the guard.

And Sparkes did just that, leaving us that shot. As I walked down the sheet to throw my rock, I swept all the straw from the side boards, where Armstrong had put it, into the path of where my rock would go. I got about ten steps from the house when I ran right into Armstrong. I was staring at his chest. He smiled and said: "Don't ever do that again."

I'm sure he was hoping I would back down, but I didn't.

"Why?" I said. "Why can you move it away when you want to but I can't move it back when I want to?"

He didn't answer, just smiled, and I think that broke the ice. I'd stood up to him. And most of the fans in the arena were laughing (probably at the size difference between the two of us).

As it turned out, we got a deuce that end and took the lead.

After giving up a single in the seventh, we scored two more in the eighth to go ahead 6–4, and I thought we were cruising, but in the ninth it got ugly. I don't know if the BC team broke out some extra-dry corn brooms, or maybe Armstrong was motivated and sweeping harder, but there was crap all over the ice. We gave up a three ender to be one down, and that's when I started thinking about losing two straight Briers. I was worried, to be sure, but I told myself we had played a great game and that one bad end shouldn't cause us to lose our focus. One miss from BC in the tenth could be enough for our victory.

And in that tenth, Sparkes panicked. Tim made a hit and roll behind a corner guard we had up, and instead of peeling off the guard, they decided to chase us and attempted a freeze, to put their rock directly in front of ours so it would be very difficult to remove. Their shot was slightly heavy, and we were able to hit their rock out. We stayed to sit two. At that point, I'm sure Bernie felt committed to his strategy and tried to freeze again and again, but their rocks were always off a bit. With a couple of great shots from Glenn, we removed their stones, and Bernie was left staring at five Ontario rocks in the rings. Coincidentally, Bernie chose to play his shot down a part of the ice where we'd thrown five consecutive hits, which meant there was almost no straw there to help the rock curl. We'd swept it clean. As he always did under pressure, Bernie threw a good stone, but the BC front end anxiously swept the rock a little too soon, probably expecting debris on the ice to make it curl. The final BC stone bumped ours, creating some separation. Bernie's rock was shot, but as long as I hit it anywhere on the right side, we were going to win the Brier.

Of all the stones I've thrown in my curling career, that one stands out the clearest. It's almost as if I can put myself back there in time and experience it again. I remember releasing it and putting my head down so I could see down the line. I could see a slice of daylight between the inside of my rock and the outside of the BC stone. It was really straight in that spot, and I knew if the boys gave it one lick with the brooms, it would never curl, so I gave out a blood-curdling "Whoa," and I think Tim and Kent almost melted. For about half a second, my brain went, "Oh no, not again. Two years in a row." But the rock curled the way we envisioned, punching the BC stone cleanly past our five counters, and my shooter rolled out of the rings. We had won the Brier.

That shot was probably one of the best of my career. If I had missed it, who knows where I would have ended up—maybe in a rubber room somewhere. In the previous Brier final, I had played the same shot—a hit and roll out—in the ninth end to be the bum. This time, I hit and rolled out, and I was the hero. The next day I read that Sparkes admitted to playing that end as if he'd lost his mind, which I thought was a strange but possibly true statement. I certainly never expected him to play the end the way he did. We were nervous, but I could tell that he was too. He was probably having the same kind of doubts we were. He may have been thinking it was the end of his career—he was forty-seven—and that he'd never won the Brier as a skip. I could see the pressure take hold of him; I could see it in his eyes.

I looked down the ice and watched Glenn jump about three feet in the air, and then the four of us had a big group hug at centre ice. We were joined by our fifth man, Larry Merkley, who had vaulted the boards and beaten the security people to join us for the celebration.

In the midst of the celebration, I wasn't really thinking; I knew I'd won but that's it. There was no serious appreciation for what I'd done or how I did it; I just knew that we'd done it. The first thing I did after hugging the guys was look for Wendy, and I found her by the boards. Hugging her felt so good. She'd been there every step of the way, following me to big events and watching every end of every game, looking after things at home when I was away and being my biggest supporter. I think I was more relieved for her that we won and that there wouldn't be another summer of horror. It was a great hug.

This first Brier win was so special. As everything started to calm down, I felt euphoria wash over me. There was definitely a sense of pride, but also relief, because we'd come so far again, and this time gone the extra step. It was also nice to show the doubters that we were capable. All the bad things that had been said against us for the past year had been snuffed out. So there was probably sixty per cent satisfaction and forty per cent relief.

After I hugged Wendy, there was a bit of a frenzy. The CCA pulled me quickly into a scrum with about seventy-five media people. Cameras were everywhere and microphones were stuck into my face. I don't remember much about what I said, and after two or three questions the CCA pulled me out of the scrum and into a march down centre ice with my teammates. That was a wonderful moment, walking the length of the sheet as Canadian champions.

Then it was the closing ceremonies, photos and more media. Finally, after we completed a couple of hours of paperwork for the world championships, we were free to celebrate. One of the first people I met was Werenich. He had been in the stands watching and came over by the boards before we left the sheet and shook my hand. Then he offered up something I've never forgotten.

"Don't worry about the Worlds," the Wrench said. "You'll never win anything bigger than you won today." To the Wrench, the Brier was the pinnacle of curling. It had tradition, grandeur and importance that the World Championships couldn't match. In the Brier, almost every team had a chance to win, but at the Worlds that wasn't the case.

As I would find out a few weeks later, Werenich was right on. At that time, no one ever expected curling to be a full Olympic sport.

I've often been asked how we celebrated that first Brier win. Did we head to the Brier Patch, the massive bar that accompanies every Canadian championship?

Nope.

Did we head out on the town, stopping with the Tankard (the trophy awarded for winning the Brier) at every watering hole?

Nope.

Did we go out to some fancy restaurant for a big meal?

Not quite.

Wendy and I went to our hotel room and had hamburgers and milkshakes. It had taken about three and a half hours from the time I threw the last shot to when we walked out of the arena, and I wanted to share this special moment with my wife. We're partners and friends, and when I worry before big competitions, Wendy gets the brunt of it. It seemed right to share this with her. Also, I wanted her to know how much I appreciated her standing beside me.

The other part of winning was exhaustion. We'd won, and that gave use a big adrenaline high, but it had been a long, punishing week. Physically, mentally, every way, we were beat, and it all of a sudden hit us. Even the playoffs, when we had a day off and only one game a day, were draining, because we were under the microscope. The CBC wanted us to come early for this and to stay for that so they could add pre-game interviews to their broadcast. It seemed as if they interviewed us for hours. It all added up. When I get home from a Brier, I'm usually beat for a week.

We didn't get much time to savour our win, or even to recover. Three weeks after winning the Brier, we were in Vancouver for the

World Championships. I was absolutely overwhelmed when I saw our Canadian jackets. It was like putting on the Montreal Canadiens or Toronto Maple Leafs sweater or slipping on golf's Green Jacket. I had a hard time believing I was representing Canada.

We got off to a rough start in Vancouver. It started before we got to the West Coast. In the airport in Toronto, Kent decided to make a last-minute run to the bathroom and missed the final boarding call. We sat on the plane in horror as the flight attendant closed the door and we realized Kent wasn't on board. We tried to explain to her that this would be an international incident (at least in our minds), but to no avail. We were about to arrive at our first world championship without our lead. To make matters worse, when we arrived, we heard that Kent couldn't get a flight until Sunday. He would miss two practices and our opening game on Saturday.

As luck would have it, we were met at the airport by our driver who turned out to be a friend from Midland, Warren Wallace. (He was the same person who had curled for Jim Ursel and warned us how good he was before our first Brier contest, in 1980.) Warren was an Air Canada pilot; he made some calls and got Kent to Vancouver for the first practice. Kent had to travel through the U.S. on a milk run and pay $1,700, but he was there. He always took everything in stride, and he was ready to go for our first game against France.

Before the first match, we went through our ritual of checking out the conditions and examining the rocks. Our goal is to match all eight rocks in pairs so we each have two stones we're comfortable with. We start by throwing two draws each, always using different parts of the sheet. I might throw two inturns starting at the eight foot; then Glenn will throw two draws using the inturn aiming at the edge of the twelve foot, and so on. No matter where the first rock stops, I try to duplicate the same delivery with the second stone to see if it stops in the same spot. Then I retrieve the two stones and throw them in reverse order.

If they don't match, I grab a rock from Glenn. I repeat the process until I get two rocks that seem to run the same. In big events such as the Brier, this pre-game ritual is reassurance, as we've matched most of the rocks during our practice time. The same stones are used at every Brier, so we have a pretty good record of them. But at cashspiels there is no practice, so the pre-game time is vital.

If I end up getting two stones matched early in the ten minutes, I work on reading the ice by throwing rocks down different spots, seeing how much they curl...or don't curl. I also watch my opponents' practice and follow their rocks up and down the sheet. Any edge I can get on reading the ice can go a long way towards winning.

In the practice in Vancouver, we found the ice to be great and the rocks superb. We had no complaints; in fact, we were rubbing our hands in anticipation. The ice was fast, without frost, and we were able to easily match up our rocks.

That all changed, however, in our first game. It was as if someone had switched the rocks and turned off the chiller that keeps the ice from melting. The roof at BC Place acted like a greenhouse, and during the day, everything heated up as the sun beat down on the roof. This was Vancouver in April, not exactly mid-winter weather. In our opening match against France, we were cruising along, up 5–1 after five ends. At the start of the sixth, Kent uncharacteristically hogged both his rocks. Tim threw his first one through the rings, then hogged his second. In the next end, I threw a hit that didn't even make it to the rings. We hogged nineteen rocks in the second half of the game. At major events, there are officials who score the game, awarding points for shots made through a complicated scoring system. I was scored at eighty-five per cent through the first five ends, meaning I'd made eighty-five per cent of my shots, which is a pretty good mark. But in the second half, my mark dropped to thirty-nine per cent. We suffered one of the more embarrassing losses for any Canadian team. We lost to France. That's right, France—not exactly a powerhouse in curling. We were the first Canadian team to earn that distinction.

It became pretty horrendous. The air temperature in the building was above twenty Celsius—far too warm to keep the ice running well—and the icemakers weren't prepared for it. Every time I moved a rock, there would be a little puddle under it as the top level of the ice began to melt.

That had to be one of the most frustrating games I've ever played. Here we were, in our first game representing Canada, expected to win the world championship, and we lost to France. To rub salt in the wound, many of the BC fans chanted, "Where's Bernie?" The way we played the second half of that game, we couldn't blame them.

We thought the ice had broken down in our contest against the French, meaning the pebble had worn off and there were flat spots. On normal curling ice, there are little bumps on the surface. These bumps are called "the pebble." The rock rides across these bumps. Without pebble—when the ice goes flat—the bottom of the curling stone acts like a suction cup, and we have to throw it exceptionally hard just to get it to the other end.

I know it sounds like an excuse, but the rocks we were using were reacting totally differently than our opponents'. After the game, the lights were shut off, the crowd left, and the building cooled down. We changed and come back to try to figure out what had happened. We explained our problems to the CCA's Warren Hansen and Neil Houston, the main organizers of the event. Neil, a former Brier winner, decided to throw a few and see how bad the ice was. To our horror, he put two shots right in the four-foot circle and looked at us as if we had been drinking. I began to think it might not be the ice that was causing the problems, but the rocks. I took one of the stones Neil had thrown, lifted it off the ice and rested it on the backboards for a minute. I asked Neil to throw it again, and this time, his shot stopped halfway down the sheet. We realized that the sun's rays were coming in through the dome and heating up the rocks.

Hansen and Houston were sympathetic to our plight and convinced the ice technicians to put a foot-high Plexiglas barrier around each sheet. That was supposed to keep the cool air in.

In the car ride to the hotel, I bet Wendy we'd get a call from Shorty Jenkins. And sure enough, when I got to the room, there was a note under the door: "Call me. Shorty."

In machine-gun fire bursts of information, he told me that red rocks got hotter more quickly than the yellow, something to do with darker colours absorbing more heat. We had a preference for yellow rocks. And the icemaker had painted a yellow box at the back of each end of the sheet where we placed the stones that were not in play. The rocks were heating up from the top and the bottom. Shorty instructed me to keep the rocks off the painted box and away from the side boards, and to cover them when they weren't in use.

Before our next game, our driver devised some tin-foil covers to reflect the heat. We put the covers over the stones. Game 2 was at night, so it wasn't as big a problem—we beat Eigil Ramsfjell of Norway, a former world champion, which was a big boost to our confidence after that first game. A lot of other teams saw what we were doing, and the next morning, almost all the teams were covering up their rocks. Some used towels; others used different, homemade devices.

After our loss to France, I spoke with the press. I made sure not to blame the icemaker, because it wasn't his fault the building had a temperature of twenty degrees. I explained that the sun was the real culprit and suggested that perhaps it would be in the best interests of the competition to move the afternoon draw to 5:00 p.m. I didn't even think about the implications for television. It just seemed logical: it's a world championship and the sun is affecting the playing surface so let's not play when the sun's out. I didn't think I'd said anything too controversial, but the next morning, when I opened the paper, there in huge type was the headline: "Howard Complainer."

I knew the coming day was going to be tough. We'd defeated Bernie Sparkes in the Brier final, crushing the hopes of all the BC fans who wanted a home-province rink in the world championship in their city. And we were labelled as complainers. Sure enough, when we stepped onto the ice for the next game, we heard it from the fans.

"Where's Bernie?" they yelled at the most inopportune moments.

It was devastating. We were already under pressure as the Canadian team playing in Canada. Throw in the lousy conditions and the fans are starting to turn against us, and it was the perfect storm. As the week went on, conditions improved somewhat, mostly because the weather was cooler and overcast. We became Weather Channel junkies. Every morning we'd hope for a lousy forecast with lots of cloud cover.

We only had one more contest where conditions were as bad as they had been on the opening draw. That came against Rodger Schmidt and his German team, who beat us handily.

We ended up in the semifinal against Denmark and had a tremendous game, which we won on the very last shot. The crowd was behind us, which helped ease the pressure.

In the final, we played the German team and Schmidt, a transplanted Canadian from Saskatoon. We weren't as sharp as we hoped we'd be. We were down one playing the tenth end, and Schmidt got into a bit of a mess with lots of rocks in play. He started trying to freeze, which was tough with the ice conditions. My team played a perfect end and set me up for my final shot.

Just like at the Brier, I had a hit to score five. Glenn was trying to give me as much information as he could as he put the broom down. He was talking a mile a minute about the shot, but I looked at him and winked. This time, I had all the confidence in the world. It helped me tremendously that the shot was so similar to the one I had made against Bernie in the Brier final only three weeks earlier.

I made the shot, and we were world champions.

There was a big sense of relief at winning the Worlds. First, as Team Canada we were expected to win the world championship. Canada is the leading curling country in the world, with the most players and the top winning record in international play. Canadian fans expect their team to be better than any other. It's really a tough situation to be in. We were expected to win, and if we did, it was no big deal. But if we lost, it would be as if the sky had fallen. The top European teams were formidable opponents. Ramsfjell, for instance was a three-time world champion and had played in more than a dozen world championships. Such experience is invaluable, and even the best Canadian teams don't have it. Having to deal with the bad press—the first time we'd had that—and the fans was difficult. But we learned and adapted. It was almost as if we were becoming professional curlers in the way we dealt with everything that came along with the game. Until 1986, only the Brier final and semifinal games were televised, both on CBC. When TSN came on board, every game for the entire week of the Brier and world championships was shown. This added exposure helped the game of curling grow and increased the notoriety of the players. We'd need all of that in the years ahead.

We arrived at the Toronto airport, and I walked through the terminal with Schmidt, who had been on the same flight. Our team started down the escalator towards the exit, and we saw that a huge gathering of family and friends was there to welcome us home. I remember Rodger being kind enough to have his picture taken, with both of us holding the trophy. That wouldn't happen in many other sports.

After shaking hands and receiving plenty of congratulations, we were driven to Penetanguishene in a limousine. We were then put into a fire truck and paraded down the main street with hundreds of people waving and cheering. We ended up at the Penetanguishene Curling Club and watched the tenth end of the world final over and over.

Most years, the world championship ends the official curling season, but not 1987. In 1988, Calgary would host the Winter Olympics, where curling would be a demonstration sport. The Canadian Curling Association put in place an overwhelming and mind-numbing system to select Canada's men's and women's representatives. The process started in 1986 with a preliminary training camp, to which Glenn and I were invited. Forty curlers from the east and forty from the west had been identified as among the best. I wasn't happy that Kent and Tim hadn't been invited, but Glenn and I went with their blessing. In addition to on-ice testing, the CCA officials did a lot of measuring of our fitness levels. I'd spent most of the summer working my way into some sort of shape. I think I went from about eight sit-ups to forty-two, and from eleven push-ups to twenty-three. At camp they counted as many as we could do in a minute. Not bad for a thirty-year-old athlete. If only I had known then that at age fifty I would make it to the Olympics, I wouldn't have done all those sit-ups.

This was the famous camp where Werenich and Savage were humiliated and told they had to lose weight or they'd be excluded from the tryout in the spring. I still think that was wrong—hey, they'd won a world championship looking like that—but they were in pretty horrid shape. I watched Werenich fail to do one push up, and I think Savage managed one or maybe two sit-ups. Curlers weren't generally concerned with working out. A few were in good shape, but the benefits of being physically fit hadn't crept into the game. Curlers curled, and workouts were on ice, throwing stones. Today, just about every top player works out regularly. Curlers are certainly athletes these days. That probably wasn't true in the 1980s.

They put us through some psychological testing. They asked us all sorts of weird questions like, "When you were young, did your mother ever tell you not to cross the road in the dark?"

They also asked questions about other players. One question they asked was: "How would you feel about having John Kawaja as your third?" We were asked to rate him and other players on a scale of one to ten.

I quickly realized that if I put down a two on a scale of ten, and Kawaja got picked, I'd be out. So I gave a ten to everyone.

We also had a skills-based competition: all the eastern players competed for top skip, third, second and lead positions. I remember Denis Marchand from Quebec being the top skip; I was second, and Werenich was third.

Glenn and I were part of a hand-picked team, combined with Ian Tetley and Pat Perroud. They'd played front end for Al Hackner when they won the Brier and World Championship in 1985. Glenn and I were excited to be paired with this front end, and we played a number of games together in the camp.

At the end of that camp, eight eastern players—two teams—were invited to move on and compete in the playdowns in April 1987. Werenich's entire team was chosen, and so were Glenn and I. But we were paired up with Bill Fletcher, a solid curler from Ottawa, and Marchand, who'd won the Canadian Junior in 1982. We were joined by two hand-picked teams from the west, and a number of Brier-winning rinks were also invited to make up the field for the final playdown to determine which team would go to the Olympic Games.

From the time we heard we'd been chosen, we kept in close contact with Bill and Denis, calling each other and trying to co-ordinate a bonspiel we could play together. But, as fate would have it, when we won the Brier, our entire team—with Kent and Tim—qualified, so off to Calgary we went for another competition. I felt sorry for Fletcher and Marchand; they had to join up with a new skip and third, and they never won a game at the Olympic Trials.

We weren't much better, going 4–3 and missing the playoffs. We were so euphoric at winning the Worlds after a long and exciting season, the tank was empty. It wasn't a big disappointment. Curling was only a demonstration sport in 1988, and the curlers wouldn't be competing for officials medals. I had just won the Worlds; I didn't think there could be anything better. I also thought it was a poor way to choose an Olympic team, and the CCA has never used that system again.

I heard they spent $750,000 on those two camps, a huge amount of money. And I never understood why they picked individual curlers. I was quite upset that Kent and Tim hadn't been picked. Glenn and I were selected presumably because of our success in 1986, but why just the two of us? To blow all that money to come up with all-star teams didn't make any sense. As we'd learned in our year playing with Bob Charlebois, team dynamic and morale are important keys to success. Sticking four curlers together wouldn't necessarily work.

With the camp over, we found our way home and finally had some time to celebrate in Midland. It was great to return as local heroes.

Russ Howard (right) aged nine, with younger brother Glenn, three years old.

The brothers, although six years apart, were always close (here Russ is 14 and Glenn 8). They would be photographed together on the curling rink many hundreds of times, as they played on the same team for 15 years.

The Howard boys (Russ at right) with their proud Mum, at a reception in Midland after Russ's gold-medal win at the 2006 Turin Olympics.

From a young age, Russ loved the strategy involved in curling and was a natural skip.

Always happy to throw countless rocks for hours in practice, and coached by his father, Bill Howard, Russ developed a solid delivery at a young age. Here he is 16 years old, before he added the trademark yelling.

At seventeen years old, Russ skipped his junior team from Midland all the way to the final of the Ontario Junior Tankard, a province-wide competition. The 1972 tournament was held at the posh Toronto Cricket, Skating and Curling Club, and Russ's team felt like country bumpkins. Instead of the matching curling jackets each of the other teams sported, Russ's team wore big, mismatched fisherman's sweaters, hand-knitted by the boys' mothers—the runners-up looked like five young Charlie Farquharsons with brooms! From left to right: Bill White, Jim Clark, Bill Smith, Lindy Hurlbut, and Russ kneeling with the curling stone.

A highlight of Russ's early curling career. In the fall of 1977, Ragnar Kamp and his team from Sweden—the reigning world champions—came to Russ's local curling club in Midland to play an exhibition game against his rink, which ended in a tie. A week later, the boys beat the world champs in a bonspiel in Penetanguishene—a thrill that was a defining moment for the 21-year-old Russ, who from that moment on wanted to be a competitive curler. Ragnar Kamp's Swedish team stands behind; kneeling, from left to right, Kent Carstairs, Russ, Paul MacDonald and Carl MacAllen.

Born into a curling family, Russ came by his passion for the sport honestly. The sign in front of his parents' summer home on Georgian Bay.

As a child, Russ played hockey more than he curled. Bill Howard, Russ's Dad, seen at the Howard cottage on Georgian Bay with "the Binford, the Rolls Royce of snowblowers," that he used for years to clear off their backyard hockey rink in Midland.

Russ's "other" professional life. For 21 years, he was the club pro at Brooklea Golf Club, until he left to establish and run the Royal Oaks Golf Club in New Brunswick for five years, until beginning yet another professional life. He left the golf course in 2003 to join Wendy in forming Team Howard in a very successful real estate career with Re/Max Quality Real Estate in Moncton.

In 1981, Russ married Wendy Thompson in Midland. Wendy, a golfer and a curler, has always been Russ's number-one supporter and his best friend.

Russ (standing at left) and Glenn peering over the shoulder of their rival Jim Armstrong, third on Bernie Sparkes' BC team, at the 1987 Brier in Edmonton. After losing the 1986 final, Russ's team came all the way back to beat Sparkes to win their first Brier title.

From concentration to jubilation. The famous shot of Glenn Howard leaping three feet in the air after Russ's final shot to win the 1987 Brier. Tim Belcourt joins in the celebration. Note Jim Armstrong on all fours behind Glenn.

Three weeks after the first Brier win, it was off to the 1987 World Championships in Vancouver to represent Canada, and another happy ending as Team Howard defeated Rodger Schmidt's rink from Germany. Russ, Tim, Kent, Larry, and Glenn in a group hug immediately after the winning shot.

The newly minted world champions with their trophy. Left to right: Russ, Glenn, Tim Belcourt, Kent Carstairs, and Larry Merkley.

The celebrations seemed to go on for weeks. Brian Orser, from Penetanguishene, won the world men's figure-skating title the same week we won the Brier. It was an amazing story for Penetanguishene, Midland and Elmvale. From a total population of twenty thousand there were six world champions—Orser and the five of us (we always considered Larry, our fifth man, a part of our team in every way). The three towns held a joint banquet, which had to be located in the Penetanguishene Arena to seat everyone. It's one of my fondest memories.

Getting back home also reminded us of our real-world responsibilities. It's a tough thing for curlers to play well and have a decent career. I was lucky as a golf professional: I had part of the winters off when the course was closed. And Tim owned his own business, so that was a little easier. But Kent and Glenn had to beg, borrow and steal to get the time away. Glenn took an unpaid leave of absence from his job at the Beer Store, and I can assure you he spent the summer working most of the weekend shifts, making up for all the people who traded days off with him. Kent somehow managed to combine holidays and the generosity of his boss to get away from his work.

We didn't do a lot of out-of-town spieling in the first part of the year, so they banked almost all their holidays for the curling tours. Not too many employers will turn a person down if he says he needs a week off to play in the Canadian or World Championships. Kent and Glenn would tell their bosses, "Look, this is a once-in-a-lifetime opportunity. It's never going to happen again." Of course Glenn must have done that ten times!

Since all the vacation time was saved for curling, our young families had to be very flexible and understanding so we could follow our dreams. For many years, instead of warm southern vacations in the winter, our families travelled with us to many frozen parts of Canada.

These days, curlers who want to beat the Kevin Martins and the Randy Ferbeys have to play all the time. I think that was one of the reasons we were so successful with our Olympic team. The boys from Newfoundland and Labrador were in limbo between school and career, and everything was put on hold for the Olympic journey, first for the Trials in Halifax and then for the Games. For me, it was a different story. Wendy and I work together as a Re/Max real estate team known as Team Howard. We have an extremely busy business, and Wendy looks after it when I'm away curling. When we won in Halifax, it put a lot of pressure on her while I juggled practices, trips to Newfoundland and additional bonspiels across the country. From the time we won the Olympic Trials in early December to the end of April, I wasn't able to work in real estate at all. I can only imagine the lost wages for our coach, Toby McDonald, who is a very successful lawyer in St. John's.

The working-playing dilemma exists to this day. Curlers don't make enough to survive on curling, so they hold full-time jobs and are real people with real lives and family commitments. The curling bonspiels prepare me for the provincial, national and world championships. It's an honour to represent my province and country.

That year, all four of us paid a price, but it was worth it. We'd won it all. It had been a long climb up that mountain, but I knew I wanted to do it again.

New Rules, New Hope

6

COMING HOME AS A WINNER sure beat doing it as runner-up. Wendy and I had a fabulous summer that almost made up for the horror show we experienced the year before. My business at Brooklea was growing, and my notoriety helped. I taught more and more golf lessons as many people seemed to want to get instruction from a curling champion. And business in the pro shop increased as well.

As the summer moved on, curling called, and we received all sorts of invitations to play around the world and had to plan our year out accordingly. We took trips to Scotland, Switzerland and Germany, playing against the best teams in Europe and usually being feted at every turn.

Curling was a different experience in Europe, to say the least. I can remember our trip to Scotland. Just after getting there, we went to throw some practice rocks at the club we were to use for the bonspiel. I'd thrown two or three when the icemaker with a hose came out and asked me to leave because he was going to pebble the ice. I was standing on Sheet One and he was over on Sheet Seven. I told him we'd be finished by the time he got to our sheet, but he kicked us off right then and proceeded to pebble all seven sheets at once (in Canada, it's usually done one sheet at a time) by opening up the hose full blast.

The ice at this facility was not what we were used to. After getting back on the playing surface after the pebbling incident, I was throwing rocks on one sheet and found a spot where I couldn't make a takeout. Inturn, out-turn, lots of ice, no ice…it didn't matter where I threw it, my shooter would never get close to the rock I was trying to remove. The ice had all sorts of hidden falls and hills and would direct my shooter away from the stationary rock in the rings. I grabbed Wendy and made her try to hit the stone. She didn't have any more luck than I did.

The event we were playing was the very first Skins curling game. Skins curling was modeled after Skins in golf, and it's a highly entertaining format that I just love. In this format, each end represents a "Skin," or a point. To win a skin, a team has to steal a point (take a point without having last rock) or take two points. If a team takes a single point or blanks the end, the skin is carried over to the next end. Each skin is worth a predetermined value, so if there are a lot of carryovers, one end can be played for big bucks.

The format was devised by Doug Maxwell, a well-known curling entrepreneur, and Jim Thompson, the president of TSN. Not long after we played in Scotland, TSN aired a Skins event annually, and the Skins became a lucrative payday for the winner.

The Skins game in Scotland was the first, and the top eight teams in the world were invited to play. It was a lot of fun, partly because it suited our style of play so well. We liked to play an aggressive game and loved it when there were lots of rocks in play. That, I think, goes back to all the years of playing on quick, pure ice in Ontario. Because we got to play on great surfaces so frequently, that allowed us to play finesse shots more often than most teams.

I'm not sure the Scots and some of the other European teams knew what to make of the new format. It was certainly different for them. Most European teams played on straight ice, as opposed to the swingy stuff prevalent in North America, so aggressive play wasn't their forte, but this event was definitely competitive. Even the term "Skins Game" was new to the Scots. Wendy came to understand that "Skins" had more than one meaning in Scotland. While she was sitting in the crowd she got chatting with an elderly lady and her very distinguished elderly husband. Wendy told the lady she was watching her husband's team "play skins." The lady's jaw dropped, and she and her husband looked embarrassed and moved down a few seats. Wendy was dumbfounded. What could she have possibly said to upset them? Apparently in Scotland, "skins" is a slang term for condoms. No wonder the elderly woman was shocked.

That Skins Game was also the first time I'd ever played using time clocks, another Doug Maxwell innovation. When we were first told that our games would be under a time limit, we were horrified. I thought back to my famous four-hour and twenty-five minute game in the Ontario finals with Bob Charlebois. We didn't care about the time; we just played.

We were given eighty minutes, an eternity by today's standard of seventy-three minutes, but we were so worried about running out of time that by the halfway mark, we'd used twenty-two minutes. We'd been racing with just about every shot and constantly looking at the clock. We thought we'd need to save every second. As a result, we weren't making any shots.

The format was a round robin with four teams out of eight making the playoffs. We had to win seven out of eight ends in our last game to get fourth spot and sneak into the playoffs. We won the semi and the final, and I think we ended up winning $9,000 overall.

But probably the most exciting thing was that Wendy and I had a chance to sneak away and play a game at the famous Turnberry Golf Club, just outside Glasgow. We had never been in Scotland, and we wanted a chance to play one of the famous courses. Unfortunately, it was about three degrees Celsius and the windiest day I've ever played golf. I remember hitting a driver and a three-wood on a 400-yard hole. Under normal conditions, I'd be well long using those two clubs, but on this day, I still had to hit a full six-iron to reach the green. Two holes later, playing downwind, I drove the fringe with my tee shot on a 410-yard par 4. It was such a different game over there, I had to bump and run the ball, aim forty yards right of my intended target and trust the wind would blow the ball back, and I had to hold onto Wendy at the tee overlooking the ocean so she didn't blow away.

We came off the course excited, and I explained to the manager of the club that it was a big thrill because I was a golf pro. I added that it was too bad it was so windy.

"That wus noothing, just a wee breeze," he said in his thick accent. "Oon Wednesday, the pins were bent oover and touching the greens."

We went into the bar for a post-round drink and told the bartender we were from Canada. He relayed a story about twelve Canadian players who had been there a few weeks earlier. Eleven of the twelve golfers had rented a caddie, but the twelfth was too cheap and took a pull cart. The boys were having a big money game, and it was getting pretty serious as they came to the final holes. The cheap player had an important putt on the sixteenth hole and he turned to one of the other players' caddies and asked which way the putt would break. The old Scottish caddie replied, "Ask your pull cart."

The experience at the Scottish Skins Game really helped us in events in Canada. We were the only team in the McCain/TSN Skins Game to have played the format going into it, and we were the only rink to have used time clocks. A few years later the CCA adopted time clocks for use at the Brier.

It was around the same time in the late 1980s that Glenn and I came up with the Howard Rule, which eventually became the Moncton Rule, which led to the creation of the free guard zone. I'm probably more proud of that than just about anything I've done in the game. I think it's really changed the face of curling.

After our Brier win in 1987, curling took a huge turn towards defensive play, led primarily by Pat Ryan and his Ryan's Express. He had a team built for hitting and he used it effectively in winning back-to-back Canadian titles in 1988 and 1989. A lot of people criticized him for his style, in which he'd try to get an early lead and then peel everything. But he was only playing the hand that was dealt to him. His team's talents coupled with the improved ice conditions allowed for his strategy, and Ryan wasn't doing anything wrong—it was the rules that were wrong.

A lot of teams adopted Ryan's style, and curling got quite boring. We had Brier games with scores of 2–1 and 3–2, and fans started getting frustrated. We'd hear, "Borrr-innggg!" coming down from the rafters during almost every draw. And why not? It was like watching paint dry.

In about 1985, I started getting bored with all the hitting and, to spice things up, Glenn and I decided to try something different in our practice sessions. We used to play a lot of one-on-one games when we practised, and a game usually lasted six ends. I'd get three in the first end then start hitting all his rocks. Or he'd get two or three up and start peeling my stones. We weren't learning anything, because he'd throw up a corner guard and I'd peel it off. We also weren't playing many finesse shots in these practice games, and don't forget, the road to our Brier went right through the king of finesse, Ed Werenich. If all we did was throw peels, we weren't going to beat the Wrench. We had to learn how to play the soft shots.

In part because of that and in part because Glenn was starting to beat me once in awhile, one afternoon I said we wouldn't hit the first four rocks, no matter where they ended up, and see what happened.

That was the original rule—leads couldn't hit. It didn't matter where the rocks ended up—in the house or out in front—the leads were not allowed to play takeouts. That was the real appeal of the rule: if Glenn drew one into the rings with his first one, I might draw to the open wing. Then what would Glenn do?

The strategy implications were—and are still—much better with the rule as Glenn and I played it. Our rule allowed for a much more interesting game, and Glenn and I felt strongly we were learning to play more difficult curling shots and use a much more complex strategy.

We never thought our little rule would go any further than Penetanguishene Curling Club practices, but we told a few people about it, and there was a lot of interest. Then, at the 1989 Brier, everything changed.

We lost in the semifinal to Rick Folk and he went on to play Pat Ryan in the final. That game may have single-handedly done more to curling than any other. It was horrid to watch. It wasn't poorly curled, but nothing happened. Don Walchuk, Ryan's second, made a hit and roll in the fifth end, and that was the game. People were booing and a lot of them got up at the fifth-end break, went to the Brier Patch and never came back.

I was watching this mess, feeling sorry for myself because I wasn't in the final, when Doug Maxwell came by, tapped me on the shoulder and said: "Russ, I can brighten up your day a little bit. We're going to have this huge event in Moncton next year. It's going to be a bonspiel with the sixteen best teams in the world, playing for $250,000. It's Moncton's hundredth birthday and we want to make it special. It's a great chance to promote curling, and we want to try something different."

He asked me if I had any ideas, saying what was going on in front of us wasn't what they wanted. I told him all about the rule Glenn and I used in practice, and he was immediately intrigued. He left without saying too much more but a week later, I got a call that made me very excited.

"Russ, we're going to use your rule at the Moncton 100."

It was still more than a year away, but I couldn't wait. I was sure that once the rule got some exposure, it would be like trying to stop an avalanche.

Most of our year in 1988 as reigning champions of Canada was enjoyable and lucrative. In addition to the trips to Europe, we travelled to Western Canada a few times to play in big spiels, and most of the time all expenses were paid by the organizers of the events. We earned a lot of money, but when it really counted, we came up just a little short. We lost in the Ontario finals in a sudden-death extra-end game to Savage, who had convinced Werenich to trade places with him so Savage skipped and the Wrench played third. Graeme McCarrel was second, and the lead was Neil Harrison.

They won the Ontario final and headed to Chicoutimi, to one of the least memorable Briers in history. It was rare for Briers to lose money, but they managed to do so in Chicoutimi. The crowds didn't show up and the atmosphere was quite flat. The Georges Vezina Centre seemed quiet compared to Western Briers, and even the Brier Patch, the huge bar that accompanied every Brier, wasn't rocking as it usually did. Labatt invited us out for the week, and I carried the Tankard in during the opening ceremonies. That was a nice touch from one of the best sponsors curling has known.

I thought the week would be enjoyable. There we were, defending champions, all expenses paid, in a nice hotel, watching curling with our wives. But it wasn't that much fun. I watched about four ends of Savage's first game and left. He'd beaten us in the Ontario final a few weeks before. Every time they missed a shot—which didn't happen often—we looked at each other and wondered where that was three weeks ago when they were beating us in the Ontario final. I guess some psychologists would say we were bitter. Our rivalry with Savage and Werenich was in full bloom, and we wanted to be throwing the rocks, not watching. It wasn't anything personal; it was just the competitor in us.

Pat Ryan ended up capturing that championship, taking three points in the last end to win 8–7. It was a stunning defeat for Saskatchewan's Eugene Hritzuk, who hogged his final shot.

It was while we were at the Chicoutimi Brier that I first sensed a staleness in our team. We'd been together for some time and while there weren't any tensions, I could feel that our spark was fading somewhat. We didn't seem to have the drive anymore, the desire to win that was there when we were starting out. While I didn't know it at that time, the following year would be our last.

⊙

In 1989 we made it to the Brier, but not before getting through a very tough Ontario final. In the semifinal, we played Werenich and had to call in our fifth, Larry Merkley, after Kent came down with something. Larry had played earlier in the week, when Glenn got food poisoning. The round robin was one thing, but the semifinal was different, and Larry was pretty nervous.

I have to admit that I was a little scared too. We were without our exceptionally talented lead for a crucial game. Larry was a wonderful person with a heart of gold who would put a tremendous amount of pressure on himself and hope not to let down his friends. But he hadn't played competitively for five years. We were concerned about Larry being forty-five years old and playing in the semifinal. But Larry, as he had done in the past, came through big time. He played great. Our other concern in that game was Glenn, who still wasn't over his food poisoning. But in true Glenn fashion, he came out and played—besides, we were out of spares. Glenn made everything, as he usually did against Eddie, and the game turned in the fifth end when I made a long raise takeout for two. That put us up two points, and we never relinquished the lead. Once again, we were off to the final.

Our opponent was Dave Merklinger of Ottawa. Merklinger was best known as an icemaker and a darn good one. But he was also a solid curler and he had a strong team. Merklinger's third was Lovel Lord, who was wired tighter than a snare drum. Whenever I played an intense player, I tried to be intense too. So I was pretty worked up in that final, which added to the overall drama of the game.

The Ottawa team out-curled us for most of the contest, but we managed to tie the game coming home in the tenth end. Still, Merklinger had last rock. We had to steal a point. We went all out and pulled our goalie, as it were. With my last one, my only chance was to draw through a small hole between two guards and try to get partially behind cover on the button, as they were sitting five at the time.

Merklinger's team was one of the last to use corn brooms, and there was a lot of straw all over the ice. It had been a bit of a minefield throughout the game and as I slid out with my final shot, I could feel the rock grab—there was straw under the stone. Before I let go of the rock, I had the presence of mind to spin the handle, hoping the corn might fly out or, at the very least, that the corn wouldn't cause the rock to dig in.

Tim saw me spin the handle and yelled loud enough for just about everyone in the place to hear, "Shit!" He started sweeping furiously. Kent, Mr. Calm in such situations, dusted lightly, and before too long, it was clear that even with the spinning handle, the weight and line were pretty good. It hung for the longest time, then, just before it got to the hole, it curled ever so slightly and rubbed off the outside guard, which redirected the rock perfectly behind cover on the four-foot. I doubt I could have walked down and placed the stone in a better position.

Merklinger's only shot was a come-around tap. He let it go a bit wide, which wasn't the end of the world, since the chaff from his team's brooms made the rocks curl more than usual. But his front end jumped on it and started pounding it. One of the best things about corn brooms was the noise they made; it appealed to the fans. But it was also one of the worst sounds, because it was tough to hear the instructions from the third. As the Ottawa front end swept, Lord was screaming at them to stop. To get their attention, he slammed his broom on the ice, and as he did, the rock grabbed something and skittered off line short of the target.

Just like that, we were going to the Brier.

It was a very tough way for the Merklinger rink to lose, and in the locker room there was a heat-of-the-moment incident. While we were changing, Glenn overheard them talking in rather loud voices about how we were lucky to have won the game, that we didn't deserve it. Glenn has a much shorter fuse than I do and he let them know what he thought about their comments. It got tense for a few seconds, but eventually both sides backed off. I could understand their frustration, but it wasn't like we'd come out of nowhere to win. We'd taken the same route they had and beaten just as many teams as they had and earned our way to the Brier.

In curling, second really is disappointing. When we outplayed a team and lost by a shot, we felt like bums. It was a tough period for Ottawa teams. They hadn't won the provincial title since 1985 (and wouldn't again until 1999). Ottawa teams would grab all the cash during the competitive season but then flame out at the provincials. Werenich used to say that Ottawa teams would sleep, hit and lose while Toronto teams would drink, draw and win. That was in reference to the fact that the Ottawa teams didn't party as much at the big events and they liked to play defensively. Toronto teams were more likely to have a few beers after the game and employ a very aggressive strategy with more draws. For some reason, Toronto teams seemed to win more of the games against their Ottawa counterparts.

The Brier that year was in Saskatoon, one of the driest cities in all of Canada. Dry cities and my voice don't mix, and that led to one of the most infamous incidents in my curling career. After a couple of days of play and lots of yelling, I woke up Monday morning and couldn't talk. The other three guys may have celebrated not having to hear me barking orders to sweep, but having no voice was a big problem—I couldn't communicate with the sweepers.

The arena in Saskatoon didn't help matters. It was a small bowl and the seats were in quite close, which meant it was a lot noisier at ice level than most arenas. When a team on another sheet made a big shot and the crowd cheered, I had to yell extremely loudly to be heard. We tried to play a game, but it was a disaster. We thought we'd be okay with hand signals, but the signals didn't work, and we lost primarily because of the communication problem. After the game, I recalled years earlier my old skip Paul MacDonald told me about some headsets he thought would be great for communication between the sweeper and the skip. They were voice-activated so there was no need to press any buttons, and they wouldn't interfere with the sweeping. I was worried about the next game, against Saskatchewan, which would be loud because of the home-province fans. So off to Radio Shack we went, and we got the headsets and took them to the hotel to test. I put one on, and Tim put the other one on, and we went to opposite ends of a long hallway. I barked out orders in my little squeaky voice, and he could hear me clear as a bell.

We thought we were pretty ingenious and we never even gave a second thought to asking any officials if this was allowed. We just wanted to curl and be able to communicate.

When the game started, I felt like a blind man who could see again. There was only one hiccup, which nearly cost Tim his hearing. On one of Glenn's rocks in the first end, I yelled, expecting a muffled peep to come out. Unfortunately, my full voice kicked in, and I think I nearly blew Tim's head off. He looked as if he'd been hit by an electrical shock.

Throughout the game, I noticed officials pointing at our sheet and speaking into their hand-held walkie-talkies. As the game neared its end, it was clear something was up, and right after I shook hands with our opposition, the CCA officials descended. I was escorted off the ice and into a room—Brier jail! Claude Bergeron, a director from Quebec, was in charge and he wasted no time in telling me that the walkie-talkies would have to go. "This can't happen," he said. "It's against the rules."

I apologized and said I wasn't aware of the infraction. I thought about it and added, "What rule is it against?"

"Well, it's jamming the walkie-talkies of the officials so you can't use them."

When I was a little greener, I probably would have shelved the headsets. With a few Briers under my belt and a knowledge of how the CCA worked, I fought back. "Is there a rule against them or isn't there?"

They conceded that there wasn't anything in the book specifically to deal with someone using headsets. "If there's no rule, what are you going to do if I use them?"

They refused to answer and refused to show me anything official that prevented me from wearing the headsets. Back and forth it went. It was draining to deal with these guys without a voice. In my opinion, they didn't have a leg to stand on. Every time I asked what the penalty was, the comeback was, "It doesn't matter, just don't do it."

I went to the hotel room and met with the team. They were as incredulous as I was. Kent was adamant that we keep using the headsets, and the more I thought about it, the more I knew he was right. I couldn't see how we were getting any kind of advantage by using them. All we were doing was trying to create a level playing field.

If we didn't use the headsets, we were probably going to lose. We saw the remarkable difference in our play between the games in which we used them and the ones we didn't. The more I thought about it, the more upset I became. This sort of approach from the CCA made me furious.

So out we went for our next game, walkie-talkies in place. Before we played, I explained the situation to the Quebec skip, Pierre Charette, and told him I hoped there wouldn't be any incident but to be prepared. He gave me his blessing, as did all the curlers. In the warm-up, Pat Ryan came over to find out what was going on and I told him. He asked how the headsets worked. Tim was at the far end and didn't know where I was. Without raising my voice, I spoke into the headset. "Hey Tim, how big is your thing?" Tim immediately spun around to face me, and held his hands up over his head about three feet apart.

Ryan howled. "What a great idea," he said. "Good luck with it."

He knew, as I did, that trying to fight the CCA was a never-ending battle, and I was sure that after the game I'd be in Brier jail again. Without any rule to stop us, we played the game with just about every official in the place giving us dirty looks.

We won the contest and the circus started all over again. Off we went—this time Kent came with me—and things got hot.

Again, Bergeron led the discussion with Warren Hansen backing him up. We always felt Hansen was the unlucky front man for the directors—he had to do their dirty business. They wanted us to stop using the headsets, and we kept telling them that unless there was a rule preventing us, we were going to keep using them. They never gave us a reason we couldn't use them. That may have been the most frustrating part.

They suggested we use a whistle but I shot that down immediately. I knew as soon as I came out with a whistle, it would be open season for anyone in the crowd to start blowing whistles, making it impossible to determine who was calling the sweeping.

After a while, it was pointless to keep talking. Kent and I left, saying unless there was a rule in place, we'd be wearing the headsets in our game later that day.

When we arrived in the locker room before our next game, we were handed a memo that said the CCA had made an amendment to the rule book and, as of that moment, no electronic devices were allowed on the ice.

Between games, the CCA board of directors had met and passed the amendment to the rules. Part of me was furious and the other part amazed. The CCA had changed the rules halfway through a national championship. It was so stunning it was almost laughable. Then Kent read the wording of the new rule and said this wasn't over. The rule said no electronic devices were allowed.

"I guess that means Rick Folk can't play," Kent said. "He uses a stopwatch, and that's an electronic device."

Brilliant, I thought. I left the locker room to find Hansen or Bergeron. I was stopped by a reporter and I told him about all the skips who wouldn't be able to use their stopwatches. That lit a fuse, and the CCA became even more irate. Once again, they had to amend their rule to make it specific to headsets.

The CCA was trying to win the media war, but wasn't having much luck. When Hansen was asked to explain the situation, he told the press that the CCA was worried someone in the stands might be passing information to me on the ice. The reporters did not buy this line of reasoning. "And just what is someone in the stands going to tell Russ Howard?" asked Tom Slater of the *Toronto Star*.

The reporters found me. "Russ, the CCA seems pretty worried that your mother in the stands is feeding you information," said a reporter.

"Well she's a pretty good strategist," I replied.

By this time, everyone but the CCA was laughing. I would have dropped the whole thing if a competitor had said it was a distraction. But none of them did. Instead they were right behind me on this one. I used the analogy of Folk's eyesight; he used glasses because he has bad eyes. I had a bad throat. Where was I going wrong?

The CCA said it was a precedent-setting incident. They agreed that there probably wasn't anyone in the crowd giving me tips, but what if my son was playing and I was in the crowd? That angle had a little bit of teeth. But Kent had the perfect comeback: "Let's worry about that after the Brier is over."

Once the story got out into the press, it became almost comical. Three different people faxed me (this was before e-mail, of course) saying they could hide a device on my body that couldn't be found even if the CCA put me through one of those airport metal detectors. One of the Mounties said he'd get me two units the CCA wouldn't even be able to see.

And every time I went anywhere, these old ladies gave me secret concoctions that would clear up my laryngitis. When I walked into the rink, people would throw Fisherman's Friends and Halls throat lozenges at me by the bundle. We ended up with a big basket of stuff.

I wasn't as knowledgeable about laryngitis as I am now; I'd never gone to a throat specialist. I've since learned that the candies and lozenges are loaded with sugar, which would cause the vocal chords to thicken, which would make the laryngitis worse. The ideal solution was plain old water, and lots of it, to keep everything lubricated. I haven't lost my voice since about 1994.

We used the walkie-talkies for two games, and maybe because I didn't have to yell during those contests, my voice had improved when I woke up the next morning. It was at about eighty per cent, so we didn't even need the units any more.

The next morning when I arrived at the rink, I was asked to go to a formal press conference. That's a rarity at a Brier. At the start of a usual week, eight to ten reporters scrum teams after a game. By the end of the week, that number might grow to twenty-five or thirty, but there's no formal sit-down—there is a circle, and reporters stick a mike in front of the curlers.

But this was different. I walked into the room and there had to be 150 media people in there, and a dozen or so television cameras. I sat at a podium with all these microphones in front of me, and I felt like Richard Nixon saying, "I am not a crook."

I couldn't believe that this story had drawn that big a crowd. There were sports guys and news people. We had a little fun with it, partly because the reporters were sympathetic to my side of the story. The CCA was cast as Big Brother. I benefited because I got to sit there with all my sponsor logos showing, which I couldn't display when I was on the ice. (The Brier organizers had strict regulations about what curlers could wear on their uniforms. Only the event sponsors, such as Labatt, were permitted. Coincidentally, that regulation would bring me into conflict with the CCA later.)

In all my years, I never saw a bigger media gathering at a curling event—including the Olympics.

With so much going on off the ice, my curling suffered, especially as the round robin concluded. I was extremely tired, and all the talk about the headsets took a lot out of me. To add to that, Wendy was about three months pregnant with Ashley, and she was pretty sick most of the week. Neither of us was getting much sleep, and I was worried about all the commotion affecting her health.

Somehow we managed to make it to the semifinal against Folk. We got two in the first end and then they out-curled us the rest of the game. I hated to lose and was disappointed, but at the same time, I was questioning everything. It seemed we were fighting with everyone. I began to ask myself what I was doing wrong.

On the ice, I questioned whether I was in control of the team. I probably brought a lot of this self-doubt on myself. When I skip,

I like to get input from the rest of the team. I ask what they think of certain calls. Should we do this or that? In some games, I'll ask about ice, in other games I'm confident and don't ask. But I began to sense the team giving me input without me asking for it. They started calling the game on their own. I know Kent was trying to help, but it felt like he was calling three-quarters of the shots. I started to shut down. It bothered me that he called everything.

I was tired and cranky, and every second shot, he questioned what I was calling. I spent so much time with those guys—from the start of the season to the end, I saw more of them than my family. I felt we were stale.

I've learned over the years that every curling team has a lifespan. When the players join up, they're full of energy. If they start to win, it goes well. If they manage to win a Brier, they're on top of the world, but it takes a lot of energy to accomplish that. It becomes tough to gear up again. Every time the players step on the ice, the opposition is gunning for them, which means they have to be at a high level all the time. It becomes tiring, and after they've accomplished everything, they begin to feel as if they've been there, done that. A malaise can set in on the team easily, and very few rinks last more than seven or eight years.

In some cases, once a team wins, the players start to look for their own roles. That happened when my team with Wayne Middaugh and Peter Corner ended. Middaugh wanted to skip, and who could blame him? But in 1989, it wasn't so much the four players who weren't meshing; it was that I had had enough. I was burned out. I had problems with the CCA, which had become a huge distraction at the Brier. I had a team that was starting to question my skipping abilities, and Wendy and I had two young children and busy jobs, and I think it all came together. The bottom line was that it had stopped being fun. Everything seemed like it took a lot of effort.

I bounced my feelings off Wendy. She listened for a few weeks and then offered up a straightforward piece of advice.

"Russ, you've had enough. Walk away."

Deep inside, I knew that was probably the right move, but I was scared to admit it. But once Wendy said it, I knew she was right. I had to end it and get away from the game.

I phoned Kent first. I knew that would be the toughest call because we'd been together the longest, and he was my best friend and had been the best man at our wedding. Glenn would probably say, "Whatever," and not believe me. Tim would say something like, "No problem, man." But Kent would want me to sit down and talk about it. I told Kent how I felt and of my intentions. At first, he understood. He said he was in the same boat and that he was going to scale back too. It had been a long few years and he needed to commit time to other things besides curling.

My next call was to Tim, and he was also understanding. He too felt the pressure of family and business. Glenn was the most shocked of the three, and he couldn't believe I wasn't going to curl. I told him that was how I felt but if I changed my mind and did go back onto the ice, it definitely would be with him.

There was a sense of relief when I had made the three calls. I was glad the team understood and accepted my decision. Kent did talk to the newspaper after our breakup became public and told them he really didn't understand my move, but I wasn't surprised. I knew Kent well, and I wasn't offended that he questioned my decision.

For the first time in years, I felt free. I wasn't thinking about next year, the team, the travel schedule, the entry fees. It was as if a big weight had been lifted off my schedule. Curling was a long way from my mind, and I was looking forward to having a winter without rocks and brooms.

How soon that would change.

New Directions

MY DECISION TO STEP AWAY from the game following the 1989 season freed me up from curling, but I still had a business to run. Being the head professional at Brooklea was a big job. In the peak of the summer, I was working pretty much seven days a week. I had managed to make a nice business for myself. I ran the pro shop and owned the inventory; I taught lessons, organized tournaments, wrote golf tips in the local newspaper and worked closely with the owner to set marketing and pricing plans.

In 1987, the course had expanded to twenty-seven holes and added fifty carts to the six we had before. The golf course was doing exceptionally well as was my business, and I'm sure the notoriety of my curling success was part of the reason for the success.

In early April, just as I was planning the golf business for the year and almost forgetting about curling, I got a phone call. It was Wayne Middaugh.

In 1984, the Midland Curling Club asked me to be honorary chairperson for the Ontario Junior Championship, which was being hosted by the club. Wendy and I had just purchased our first home in town. I was on the committee, so I volunteered to billet a team. Coincidentally, that team was from Brampton and was skipped by fifteen-year-old Wayne Middaugh. His cousin Peter Corner played third.

The boys, with some backseat coaching from me, came second in the province. It was easy to see that these kids were going to be around the curling scene for a long time. But from 1984 until he called, I'd only run into him once or twice. I'd always kept track of how he was doing in junior curling, watching his results in the curling papers. One year he and his team won a trip to Switzerland to curl in a big junior bonspiel, and we ran into them in the airport when we were leaving for the 1987 Brier. He couldn't stop talking about curling. Actually, he just couldn't stop talking period.

I think he held me in high regard because I was from Ontario, had won a Brier, and he'd stayed at our house.

Wayne and Peter had a great junior career. When they left the junior ranks after turning twenty, Wayne decided to skip his own men's team, and he found the competition a little stiffer. In his second year of skipping, he made it all the way to the provincials but finished 2–7, which was very disappointing to him. I had followed his play and Peter's too. They were excellent shooters and competitive players, but they weren't winning. And that's why he was calling.

"Russ," he squeaked down the phone line, "I hear you dumped your team."

"No, no," I replied. "I'm just tired and I want a year off."

As only Wayne could express it, he said, "Listen, you're the best skip in the world, Glenn's the best third in the world, and Pete and I would be the best front end in the world. I think we should curl together." In the matter of about forty-five seconds, Wayne had proposed we form a team. There were no niceties, no "how's your summer?" It was pure Wayne. The direct, slam-bam, in-your-face approach to life.

I told him it was a nice offer and I'd certainly run it by Glenn and get back to him. I hung up the phone, stunned. I didn't know what to think of this steamroller offer. My first impression was that news sure travelled fast. The old team hadn't broken up more than a few weeks before, and already the buzzards were circling, ready to pounce on the remains. The second impression was that this was a pretty good offer.

Wayne and Peter Corner were an attractive package. Here were two kids who were unbelievable curlers, who could play all kinds of shots, and who had lots of drive and enthusiasm, and certainly believed in Glenn and me. They were a bit green, but suddenly, I had energy just thinking about the possibilities. I decided the best way to think this over was to go for a walk. I went down the street and kept walking faster and faster and faster. I ended up walking all the way to the hospital a few miles away where Wendy was working and told her about Wayne's phone call.

Wendy could sense the excitement in my voice. That excitement had disappeared when I talked about curling in the past year. "Do you think you would enjoy curling with the boys?" she asked. "I think it would be great," I replied.

After I talked with Glenn later that day, we decided we'd try an end-of-the-year spiel in North Bay. It was known as the Jamaica Spiel because first prize was a trip to the Caribbean island. The event was also traditionally where new teams for the following year got their first spin, and we were in that group.

There were a lot of adjustments to make with Wayne and Pete. That was apparent early on in the spiel. In the first end of the first game, I had to throw a peel with my last rock to blank the end. As I sat in the hack, cleaning off my stone, I told the boys I was going to throw peel weight so they might want to get a head start. I let the rock go and looked up to see them halfway down the sheet, waiting for my rock to dribble down the ice.

They were laughing so hard, they almost forgot to sweep.

"That was peel?" chuckled Wayne.

Wayne and Peter were of a different era. They had grown up on perfect ice, never knowing the difficult conditions we had to play under, never knowing corn brooms and what their litter did to the ice. They were used to throwing hard, accurate shots if they needed them. Their deliveries had been grooved to include a powerful leg drive combined with perfect accuracy, so their peel weight was almost twice as hard as mine. That was a definite asset to our team. But they also had the ability to play finesse shots, in large part thanks to their years playing skip and third. They were the complete package and a perfect front end.

To make up a good front end, players need to be good sweepers and shotmakers, but the exceptional ones have more than that. They can read ice, so they can react with sweeping if necessary. Many average front ends sweep only when the third or skip yells at them, but the best—like Neil Harrison, who played for Ed Werenich for many years and with me for a brief period—know the ice almost as well as a skip. When one of their players releases the rock, they can tell immediately if sweeping is needed. They know how the rock will react on a certain part of the ice, and that comes from focusing on the game. The best front ends also reassure the skip when he's about to throw an important rock. When I come down the ice to play a key draw, I might say to the lead and second, "Has the ice changed speed?" A good front end player will know how to answer that, by affirming that it is the same or by saying that it might have changed a bit, but saying it in a positive manner. "It might have slowed up just a touch, Russ, but throw it the same and we'll sweep it." That's the type of response I like to hear, as opposed to, "Oh, it's so different than the first end." The last thing a skip wants the front end to do is put some confusion in his mind. Pete and Wayne learned to do all this very quickly.

I learned a lot from them, but they learned a great deal from me too, especially about matching rocks, which they had no idea about when we started out. Although they look the same, every rock is unique and has different characteristics that can cause it to curl more or less, or require more or less force to get down the sheet. If you play with two that are different and don't realize it, you're at a huge disadvantage. Even if you throw the two stones exactly the same playing the exact same shot, you'll get different results.

We picked up on this much earlier than most teams, and it was a big advantage to us. It took Wayne and Pete some time to understand that all rocks were not created equal. I remember one spiel out west when Glenn threw a draw and it over-curled drastically. He came down to the far end and said to the rest of us, "That had to be a cutter." He was referring to the fact that his particular rock curled more than normal. Wayne looked at me and rolled his eyes. He didn't believe it. It took the best part of a year to convince Wayne and Pete that each rock was different.

We lost in the semifinal at the Jamaica Spiel in our inaugural run, but we had a lot of fun, and I could see the potential in this new team. I was raring to go once again.

When the next season started, we jumped out of the gate...and promptly fell flat on our faces. We went to five spiels and didn't win a nickel. It was horrible. Not only were we struggling on the ice, but there was an uneasy feeling among the four of us that maybe we'd made a big mistake. I wouldn't call it tension because we were all still friendly and getting along, but I could tell that doubt was starting to creep in. Every time we got knocked out of another spiel, the feeling of uncertainty grew. I was beginning to think this was another Bob Charlebois experiment gone wrong. I was on the verge of packing it in but elected to go until Christmas, primarily because there was no other route to go except take the rest of the year off, which wasn't an entirely crazy idea, considering where I'd been at the end of the previous year.

Our sixth event of the year was a big one in Calgary, the World Skins Game. There were twenty-four teams, and we got the final qualifying spot, finishing eighth. To do that, we had to win nine of ten ends in our last game, and somehow we managed to sneak through. In the semifinal, we got past Doran Johnson, the first self-billed curling professional. He proclaimed that curling was his full-time job and that he always played for money, something like a professional poker player. He loved to gamble in his curling games, playing each one for money, which is quite rare. There really isn't much in the way of gambling in big events.

The semifinal game was tied after ten ends, and under the rules, that meant a draw to the button. Johnson went first and managed to get his rock to bite a piece of the button. He was positive he was going to win, and he was beaming behind the ice. It was going to be tough to beat. But we managed to cover the pin and advance to the final.

We shook hands, went in and changed, and headed up to the lounge for a refreshment. I was about halfway through my drink when someone pointed to the ice. There was Johnson, still sitting there, stunned that he'd lost. He finally came up to the lounge, and the boys decided to have a little fun at his expense. Big Jim Armstrong, whom we'd played in the Brier final in 1987, was betting anyone in the room that he could lift three guys up with one arm. He was a huge man, and looking at him, I almost believed he could do it.

The crowd in the lounge, mostly curlers from the event, found three volunteers, one of them Johnson, who had to be goaded into the role. The three men lay down, with Johnson in the middle. Following Armstrong's instructions, the two guys on the outside linked arms and legs with Johnson. Then Armstrong huffed and puffed, putting on a great show as if he was an Olympic weightlifter. He reached towards Johnson's belt, saying that was the balance point where he was going to try the lift. He had difficulty getting his hand under the belt, and convinced Johnson to let him loosen it a notch or two. He then grabbed the belt and lifted up Johnson's pants, and while he was pretending to struggle to lift, another fellow came from out of nowhere and threw a bucket full of ice right down Johnson's pants.

It was a beautiful gag, made that much better by Armstrong's antics. Johnson, despite being upset at his loss on the ice, took the gag well, laughing at his own expense.

The next day, we went out and won the final and took home $24,000. It was amazing how a win changed not only the whole complexion of the team, but also the year. We went from falling apart to being hungry for the playdowns to start.

Our next spiel was with our old team, which had qualified for the Moncton 100, the richest bonspiel curling had ever seen. The purse was a staggering $250,000 and there were only sixteen teams. Doug Maxwell, Bud Gerth and a group of organizers decided to hold the big event and break all the rules doing it. The entry fee was $1,000, which included airfare and accommodation. And the organizers elected to pay out after every game—even if a team lost its first two games, they won $1,500. How could we lose?

Best of all, to combat all the defensive strategy in the game, they'd elected to use the Howard Rule, where leads couldn't play takeouts. The lineup was remarkable: Ed Werenich, Ed Lukowich, Al Hackner, Orest Meleschuk, Rick Folk and Pat Ryan were among the Canadian rinks, along with Europeans Eigil Ramsfjell and David Hay. Two women's teams—skipped by Linda Moore and Heather Houston—also received invites.

We received the invitation based on our 1989 third-place finish at the Brier, so I felt that was the team that should go. Wayne and Pete wanted to go, but Kent and Tim were the ones who came third, and therefore they earned the right to play. We'd planned to get a couple of games together before leaving for Moncton, but that never happened; we arrived having not played together since the end of the Brier.

I was excited about going to the Moncton 100 but also a little apprehensive. We were heading to the richest bonspiel in history with a team that hadn't thrown a rock together all year. I'd heard through the grapevine that Kent thought I'd dumped him and Tim for Wayne and Pete. I wasn't sure of the reception I'd get.

The two had been playing together in the Elmvale Major League and enjoying life without the bonspiel-crazed pace. When we finally met up to head to Moncton, there was a good vibe; there didn't seem to be any hard feelings whatsoever. As we headed east, I rubbed my hands in anticipation. There was a huge purse and they were using our rule, the one Glenn and I had practiced for years. We would have a huge advantage over the teams from around the world that would be using it for the first time.

In our first game, we played Orest Meleschuk. He won the Brier in 1972. As we suspected, Orest struggled with the strategy of the new rule, and we jumped out to an insurmountable lead and posted our first victory.

Our next game was against Jack MacDuff, who won the '76 Brier while playing for Newfoundland. He'd moved to Moncton and was the local talent. Jack had a game under his belt and had started to figure out the rule. He gave us all we could handle. He had a tricky hit and stick to win but missed, and we won in an extra end. Then we faced two-time Brier champion Pat Ryan and his famous Ryan Express team, which had made a name for itself playing a strong takeout game. They were probably the best hitting team I ever witnessed. Their third and second, Randy Ferbey and Don Walchuk, never seemed to miss. But they were playing by our rules now, and we had very little trouble with what was probably the hottest team in the world at the time.

The format was one I had never seen before or since. It was a double knockout, but teams were paid for every win and loss. If a team stayed on the A side of the draw (if it kept winning) it was paid more than those in the B side (the teams with a single loss). Each win meant an increase in the payout. With this sliding scale, we had won approximately $18,000 for three wins, and we were at 3–0, so we had the luxury of knowing we would be paid $10,000 if we happened to lose our next two games, meaning a guaranteed cheque of $28,000. Our next game was against Ed Werenich. He was a master at the aggressive game, and if anyone in the field would thrive on the new rule, it would be the Wrench. If we happened to beat him, we'd earn an additional $10,000, and a win against Werenich also guaranteed us another $13,000 even if we lost our last game. So the game against Werenich was worth $23,000.

Games between the Wrench and our team were always aggressive. Even playing under the old rules, we had lots of rocks in play, with both teams trying to create offensive opportunities. At the Moncton 100, we needed a front-end loader to remove all the rocks at the completion of an end. About halfway through the game, Eddie said to me: "If the ice had a little more curl to it, the crowds would never have sat in their seats."

As usual, our game came down to the last shot. We were one up in the tenth, and Eddie had last rock advantage. They had one frozen to our shot rock at the top of the four-foot. We had no choice but to guard it. Just short of the hog line, my guard picked up some debris and stopped right on the line. We had to remove it from play. I turned the stone over to see what had slowed it and found a tiny piece of fluorescent orange tape, like the kind on the handle of an 8-Ender curling broom.

With my rock pulled off, Werenich only had to hit his own rock, which was frozen to ours, and stay for two points and the win. Werenich's shot seemed perfect. He hit two-thirds of his rock and rolled to the edge of the eight-foot. The stationary stone he hit spilled out of play. But our stone was driven at a much different angle than either team expected and jammed on another rock at the back of the eight-foot. To everyone's surprise, our stone was shot rock, and we won.

It was a stunning result, mostly because nobody anticipated the drastic angle change when Werenich's rock hit the two frozen in the four-foot. Right after the shot, John Kawaja, Werenich's third, turned and looked at me, obviously stunned.

"Did you burn that rock?" he asked, knowing full well I hadn't been within five feet of the stones, but no one was able to explain how the two stones didn't leave the house. Werenich's team walked off the ice as if someone had shot them.

We weren't sharp on the angles because we'd never had a game with so many rocks in play. Later, teams were forced to play in crowded houses because of the free guard zone, and understanding angles became a necessity. Today that shot could be easily explained, but at the time, it was mystifying.

We qualified for the final and the money was really piling up. Unfortunately, that was where it ended. We had been on a roll and just when we thought we had the game figured out, the curling gods brought us back to earth.

The final was against Ed Lukowich of Alberta. The game was really close until about halfway through the first end. We lost 13–2, and all I can remember is waving a white flag on national television after yet another spectacular shot by the Calgary foursome. Then, mercifully, I got off the ice. The loss was tempered when we were handed a check for $51,000. I hadn't even worked up a sweat! I had only one question for the organizers.

"When are you having another one of these?"

The Moncton 100 was the best bonspiel I ever played in. The Maritime hospitality was overwhelming. Maybe that's why our family moved to Moncton eight years later. As my mom would say, things happen for a reason.

Aside from the money, there were a couple of other positive notes to this event. The first was that it was a fitting way to say goodbye to the old team. We had a great week, and everyone walked away with a nice piece of change. The second, and perhaps most important, was that it showed how exciting curling could be. In 1989, 3–1 games were the norm, and it wasn't unusual for half the ends to be blanked. We'd just come off of a Brier in which there were more than 120 blank ends. It was like bowling on ice out there. The Moncton 100 proved that a minor change such as the Howard Rule could improve the game remarkably. Thank goodness Doug Maxwell decided to put the rule in place for that event. It was a perfect showcase for fixing an ailing sport. I don't think it was any coincidence that the World Curling Federation put their version—the four-rock free guard zone—into play in its championships the next year. The strong support of the top European teams such as Ramsfjell and Smith, who were at the Moncton 100, no doubt fuelled the decision.

Unfortunately, we didn't get the same result in Canada. The CCA, in its infinite wisdom, decided to remain with the old rules. Canada was the only jurisdiction in the world that didn't switch and continued to play a boring, dull game. Of course, the fact that Howard had come up with the rule, that someone other than the CCA had put it in use, and that the World Curling Federation had adopted it pushed the CCA in the other direction. "If it's not our idea, then we won't be told to implement it," seemed to be the attitude. The CCA didn't like to be told anything, it seemed.

That year the Howard household had a very good Christmas. With the $24,000 we'd won in Calgary and the $51,000 from Moncton, we had earned $75,000 in two weeks. We were full of confidence and ready for the playdowns. We sailed through the zones and regions and played exceptionally well in the round robin at the Ontario final. I don't think we gave up ten points in all those games combined. Our only loss was to Werenich, who beat us in the round robin. Our team and Werenich's finished with 8–1 records, but Werenich's victory over us meant he received the bye to the final, and we played a semifinal against Bob Fedosa.

And that's where our year ended. Fedosa, who used a Manitoba-type tuck delivery—he slid out with his body balanced on his toe—beat us with a fabulous across-the-house double from which we never recovered. I remember that shot as if it was yesterday. The loss was especially disappointing to Pete and Wayne, who were hungry for a Purple Heart and their first chance to curl at the Brier. They played so well in the weeks leading up to the Ontario final and then ripped through the round robin, so it was tough for them to take the sudden loss.

I didn't like it either, but I knew it was what happened in the big leagues. A team could play great for an extended period of time, lose the wrong game and be down the road with nothing but its broom bag. Sometimes it happened against a team we'd beat ninety-nine times out of a hundred; other times it happened because of a bad break: a rock caught some debris, or someone missed a sweeping call. I've always been of the opinion that if I played enough games, the breaks—good and bad—eventually evened out.

In many ways, that's the beauty of curling. I can never be sure of what's going to happen. I don't know of another sport where so much time elapses between the time I throw the rock and the time it comes to rest. A baseball pitch occurs in a split second. A slapshot or wrist shot in hockey is also measured in tenths of a second, but a curling shot can take twenty-five or thirty seconds from the time it starts until it comes to rest, and in that time, it's travelling on its own with throwers and sweepers almost helpless to affect its outcome. Sometimes it's torture for the thrower to watch, but it's also what makes curling great.

If 1990 was our year to gain experience as a team, then it paid off well the following season. We were a much more mature team, and we were all learning our roles. The front end started to learn how to be a front end. As remarkable as this may sound, Wayne couldn't sweep from one end of the ice to the other when we started playing together. That's how out of shape or out of practice he was. He'd go hard and then quit at about the hog line. In 1990, he became this strong kid and an effective brusher, and, just as important, he knew when to sweep. So many leads and seconds are powerful sweepers, but judging a rock's progress and knowing instinctively when to sweep and when to lay off is a real asset. It's the difference between good and great. Wayne was starting to learn that, as was Pete, too.

A lot of people don't believe this because of the success Wayne has had in his career, but back then, Pete was a better curler. Pete could slide straight at the broom, whereas Wayne would slide out five inches wide and get the rock back on the right path by feel. Back then, if I came out five inches wide, I couldn't correct it.

In terms of mechanics and fundamentals, Pete was better, although he had to learn how to miss, something he caught on to very quickly.

Both young men continued to learn to match rocks and finally started to believe what Glenn and I had been preaching for some time. This allowed them to be consistent with shot after shot.

I was coming to understand their personalities and what made them tick. I think many skips overlook that part of team-building. Understanding who is throwing the rock can be as important as how they throw it. I got to know certain tendencies and whether or not they were capable of throwing a big shot—whether they would even know it was a big shot—and how their nerves would affect things. I learned how to talk to them, what I could say and couldn't, almost like a caddie's relationship with a golfer.

Wayne and Pete were almost exact opposites in this department. Wayne was a high-strung, in-your-face type of player. He wasn't afraid to offer any opinion on any topic. Our team was better than everyone else, he felt, and he took that attitude onto the ice every time. He also hated to lose, which got him a reputation as a bit of a whiner, but it was something that I came to appreciate. What would a skip rather have? A guy who didn't mind losing?

Because of that, Wayne was often misunderstood. When he banged his broom on the ice, people got the wrong impression of him. They viewed him as temperamental. I can assure you every curler at that level felt the same way after a missed shot or a bad break. Wayne gained a reputation for taking his emotions a little bit further. At times, Wayne was difficult to curl with. If I'd miss a shot, he'd look at me and say, "Come on, Russ. That was easy." He loved to hit and I was more of a finesse player. I remember one game making a really nice triple take-out that Wayne had to talk me into playing. I thought it was a tough shot, but the way he saw it, I was supposed to make shots like that. I remember him saying, "You only have to hit half a rock."

He was really the antithesis of the guys on the Gushue team. Their whole mantra—drummed into them by the psychologists—was to keep everyone up and positive. If I missed a shot, they would have said, "Don't worry, Russ. Let's get the next one."

Pete, to most people, seemed much calmer than Wayne and almost laid back, but that wasn't accurate. He was as intense as Wayne but he carried it in a different way. We didn't see a lot of broom banging or facial expressions or anything else that indicated his feelings, but the feelings were there. He was every bit as forceful in his beliefs but not nearly as opinionated. But he had a short fuse. It didn't take much to put him over the top. In the early days, he came with an attitude: "We're going to make everything, and if we don't then I'm firing a broom somewhere." But his attitude changed considerably over the years. Pete probably became more a friend to me than Wayne. To this day, he calls me Skipper, and even though we're on different teams, we always find time to have breakfast together when we're at the same spiels. He was a great team player a real honest, dependable, hard-working guy.

Together, they were phenomenal. The Randy Ferbey team was probably the most successful team in my era. I could be a little biased, but I truly believe that Glenn, Wayne, Peter and I made up the most talented curling team ever assembled. We went to four consecutive Briers, played in three Brier finals, won more than $500,000 in five years and individually accumulated thirty-three Purple Hearts. All four team members skipped at the Brier at one time or another.

We got a lot of attention for our play, and I began to get noted for something else: my sweeping calls. Although I'd been yelling out sweeping instructions for as long as I had been skipping, I think our four consecutive trips to the Brier with this team brought the notoriety to a wider audience thanks to television. I got the nickname The Wounded Moose from Tom Slater of the *Toronto Star*, who thought my yelling sounded just like that injured animal. I've had all sorts of comments and quips about the yells from fans and players. And I get asked time and time again why I yell the words, "Hurry hard." The answer is simple. In the late 1970s, all the competitive teams started to use synthetic brooms. There were two very popular brands. One was the Rink-Rat, which was made up of three plastic fingers covered in foam and nylon and joined together. The other was the Cat, which Kent Carstairs, my faithful lead, used before he switched to the push broom. It was composed of one large plastic section, also covered in foam and nylon. These brooms were very popular. They replaced the dirty corn brooms, which caused havoc for the rocks and icemakers by leaving debris all over the ice. The synthetic brooms, however, were also very loud. When four or five sheets of front end curlers were hammering these brooms on the ice, it was absolutely deafening.

In those days, everyone yelled "sweep," and it became nearly impossible for the sweepers to distinguish my instructions from the instructions of other skips. Out of necessity, I came up with a different phrase to distinguish me from the other skips. It was, "Hurry Hard." Quite often, people would only hear the last part of the word hurry, and often thought I was yelling, "Reee," but one way or the other, it worked. When we played in front of large crowds in arena settings, I could communicate over the crowd noise.

I know not everyone likes to hear me yell—I've heard from lots of those folks over the years too—but if you think I'm annoying, try yelling "Sweep" at the top of your lungs and holding it for four seconds. And most fans only have to hear me for a few games a year. Imagine my teammates, who get it all year long. Wayne Middaugh got so used to hearing it, his license plate reads "HURREE."

Heading into the 1990–91 season, our machine was starting to roll. We were winning cashspiels and qualifying in every event.

We began the playdowns for the 1991 Brier ranked tenth in Ontario, even though we had finished third in the previous year's provincial. But for once, we managed to get there via the direct route of winning our zones and regions; we didn't need to take the long road through the Challenge Round.

Again we steamrolled through the provincials, which that year were in Owen Sound. We kept the momentum going with a 7–1 round-robin record with one game left. Only one team stood between us and a first-place finish—Ed Werenich. Eddie was 6–2 and if he beat us in the last round-robin game, he'd get the bye to the final. The draw was supposed to be made randomly, by pulling names from a hat. But If I had a dime for every time I played Werenich in the final round-robin game at an Ontario final, I would be a rich man. I think the organizers wanted that marquee match-up late in the week to draw crowds.

We had another classic game with Eddie, this one with an unpredictable ending. We were one up coming home but Eddie had last rock. He had the opportunity for a delicate tap back for two, which was the kind of shot he thrived on. When he released the stone, I had some hope because it looked a little narrow, and with Eddie's out-turn, I was never quite sure how a shot was going to come off. That wasn't his strong turn. But right out of his hand, the front end started to sweep, and the rock caught what must have been a hair from a broom. It veered sharply off course, ending the game. In a blink of an eye, we had beaten Werenich and finished first in the round robin, escaping the semifinal and gaining last rock in the first end of the championship game. When Eddie's rock took its left turn into the boards, Glenn instinctively raised his arms for a second, as if to celebrate the win. It was a knee-jerk reaction but it upset Eddie, although he didn't say anything. It wasn't until later that I found out how upset he was.

Werenich dropped into the semi against Kirk Ziola, a transplanted Westerner living in London and, as so often happens after a big loss, the underdog shot the lights out and ended Eddie's season. We came out as we had all season and played as good a game as our young team had ever played and defeated Ziola for the provincial title.

It was exciting to see Wayne and Pete get their first Purple Hearts. Not only were we representing Ontario in the Brier, but I really felt this team was the complete package and we had the opportunity to win it. But Wayne and Pete hadn't been there before. I wanted them to realize we hadn't accomplished our goal yet. They had to stay focused.

The 1991 Brier was in Hamilton. Because Copps Coliseum was built to international ice hockey standards, the organizers were able to put six sheets on the ice surface. With a twelve-team draw, all the rinks played at once, and the organizers eliminated the dreaded morning draws. That was a plus as was the fact we were the home team; at least, I thought this was a positive. I drove down a day early to do some interviews to help launch the Brier, and when I met the press, all the reporters wanted to know my reaction to an article that had appeared in the papers that day. Werenich had been quoted calling us a "classless bunch of guys who didn't deserve to go to the Brier." It was in response to Glenn's reaction at the Provincials. I tried my best to defuse the situation, but after repeated questions, I responded that if Werenich had a problem with this, I had a phone and he could call me. The media had a field day with the story. For me, it was frustrating. In 1989 I almost quit because of external pressures, and now it was starting again.

This isn't the way I would handle things now; I have a great deal more experience under my belt. Going through such situations paid dividends later. For instance, when we arrived at the Halifax Olympic Trials, the first thing Brad Gushue did was hand me a faxed article that quoted Manitoba's Jeff Stoughton saying our young/old team had "no chance" of winning the Trials. The boys were upset and offended at Stoughton's comments, and Brad wanted to defend his team in the press. But I told him to laugh it off. I was able to defuse the situation, and we developed a strategy to handle the hungry media. Nobody knew better than I did that distractions can hamper a team's performance.

We didn't play well in the 1991 Brier, and I missed a lot of big shots. I think that may have been my worst performance at any Brier. Of course we had a little help in having that bad week. We lost to some teams we'd never heard of—teams like Kevin Martin, Jeff Stoughton and Randy Woytowich. A lot of people thought that Brier had a weak field, but there was a lot of talent. The skips just weren't household names as they are now.

If there was any benefit to our mediocre performance at the 1991 Brier, it was that it fired up Wayne and Pete. They knew they were capable of winning a Brier, and they knew what it was going to take. I

think the attitude—win, win, win—that Glenn and I shared was starting to rub off on Wayne and Pete. They were also learning how to
throw the finesse shots, and they were becoming comfortable with
lots of rocks in play. They were also teaching Glenn and I how to
throw big weight, and we learned about the benefits that could come
from throwing big weight.

For me the best part of the team was that I realized the weapons
I had. Pete would make unbelievable finesse shots, and Wayne was
becoming one of the most accurate hitters in the world, but he
was also very capable of being the set-up man for Glenn, who had
all the shots. Thanks to our dad, Glenn's delivery was very similar to
mine, which gave me a huge advantage in reading the ice.

With all that going for us, not to mention a healthy dose of youth-
ful confidence, we put together a dream year in 1991–92. We only
played seven spiels that year and won six of them.

One of our biggest wins came at the TSN/McCain Skins Game.
The annual made-for-television event brought four of the best teams
in the land together to play for one of the richest purses of the year.
McCain Foods and TSN put up the money. The rules were the same
as at the Skins competition we had played in Scotland years earlier.
Each end was a "skin" that had a dollar value. To win the skin, you
had to take two points or steal the end. If you took one or blanked the
end, the skin carried over. If you blanked the end, you lost control of
last rock. Every end was filled with rocks and great shots. There were
triple raises and quadruple takeouts and draws to the button for tens
of thousands of dollars. When most curling in Canada was still using the bland traditional rules, the Skins Game was revolutionary and
appealing. It drew huge television audiences and became one of the
highlights of the curling year.

I played in the first version of the TSN/McCain Skins Game in
1988 in Thunder Bay. That year, the organizers invited the four most
recent world champions from Canada: Rick Folk from Saskatchewan,
who won in 1980, Werenich, the 1983 world champ, Al Hackner from
Thunder Bay, the 1985 champion, and our 1987 rink.

Next door to the Skins Game in Thunder Bay, there was a full cashspiel in the curling rink. It was a wonderful atmosphere, and the organizers sectioned the crowd into quarters; each quarter of the building had to cheer for one of the four designated team. There was lots of cheering and healthy back-and-forth between the crowd as the rooting heated up.

One of my fondest memories of the Skins Game was the draw. Rather than make a random draw, the organizers decided to have the four skips throw a draw to the button, and the winner got to choose his opponent and whether he wanted to play in the afternoon or the evening. The draw took place at 9 o'clock the morning of the first game. When I arrived, the Werenich and Folk teams were already there. A few minutes later, in walked Hackner with what could only be described as a bad case of *bonspieling*. He must have had an allergic reaction to something that Labatt, the sponsor, had so generously provided the evening before. We all threw, and Folk was the closest, virtually right on the pin. Werenich and I were a close second, and Al's rock ended up exactly between the two hog lines, halfway down the sheet. He was quick to point out that the line was perfect. Folk was no fool, and he picked the afternoon game and Hackner as his opponent.

Anyone who knew Hackner knew his ability to combine late-night adventures with on-ice performance. His teammates popped him in the shower, poured him a few strong coffees, and they managed to win nine of the ten available skins, to the delight of the hometown crowd. That was the only year the organizers let the winner of the draw to the button pick his poison.

After that year, the organizers also changed the way teams got into the Skins Game. There were four paths to get in: win the Brier, win the Skins Game the previous year, or win one of two McCain-sponsored cashspiels held annually in Portage la Prairie, Manitoba, and Florenceville, New Brunswick. We made it into the 1991 Skins Game through a long and winding road that started when we won the 1990 Florenceville spiel. That got us into the 1990 Skins Game where we won our semifinal and lost a real close game to Eddie in the final.

That was a tough loss because the Skins Game was the biggest cash event of the season. The winner usually took home a cheque three or four times bigger than any other first prize. Our team made it one of our goals every year to reach that shootout.

Because we won the eastern qualifier in 1990, we were given an all-expenses-paid trip to Portage La Prarie for the 1991 western qualifier. When we arrived, we were told that if we won the western event we would receive the $10,000 first prize, but we would not receive an entry to the Skins Game. The organizers wanted to ensure there was regional representation, so only a western team could win the Portage la Prairie spot, and only an eastern team could earn the spot from Florenceville. We went through the event undefeated and played Jim Armstrong in the final. I spent four ends explaining to Jim that he and his team had already qualified for the TSN Skins Game, win or lose. We beat Jim and earned an all-expenses-paid trip to the qualifier in Florenceville two weeks later. We had now won 2 consecutive qualifiers, but still hadn't qualified for the Skins Game!

It became a quest for the team to get into the Skins Game. We won the eastern qualifier, and made it. All the hard work paid off: we won $42,000 in that event and by winning the TSN Skins Game we had qualified for the 1992 TSN Skins Game. We won again, this time $37,300. We made it three in a row in 1993 with a payday of $37,000.

The 1991–92 year stands out for more than our big Skins Game win. We played well all season in every event. The three guys in front of me were so good, it was almost like cheating. I never had to play many tough shots. It was only the elite teams we had any trouble with, and we won most of the games we played against them. We played so well that every time we stepped onto the ice our mentality—right or wrong— was that we deserved to win. We only lost six games all year. We went through the zones and our regions undefeated and were favoured to win the provincials in Ottawa. But the ride wasn't quite as smooth on this trip. We were 3–0 and sailing along when my dad called Wendy to tell her that our son, Steven, was in the hospital. He had appendicitis and was going into surgery. Wendy was snowbound in Ottawa and couldn't get a flight until the next day. She was able to talk to my mom and Steven just before the operation started. Understandably, she was quite upset. She managed to find Larry Merkley, our fifth man, the father of four girls. He's a pretty emotional guy and he spent a great deal of time talking to Wendy. As I was comforting her, I suggested that Larry go in and play the next game, which was about to start. I looked at him, and his eyes were filled with tears. He said he couldn't curl for me and he'd be better staying with Wendy. So out we went, trying to keep our minds on winning one for Steve. Wendy kept running out to a pay phone to get updates on Steven. Just before I threw my rock in the fifth end, Wendy signalled that everything was okay. There were a lot of tears and hugs at the fifth end break, including ones from a teary-eyed Larry. Wendy got a flight the next morning and was relieved to get home to Steven.

At the Ontario final, we went 8–1, our only loss a meaningless game at the end of the round robin. Mike Harris defeated the Wrench in the semifinal and faced us in the final. We found ourselves trailing by one coming home against a young team in the sudden-death final. In the last end, Glenn managed to make a great shot around a wide corner guard, which resulted in a miss from the Harris team. I drew to the other side of the rings to split the house for two, and Harris had no option but to try to freeze to the one I had just played. He was slightly off line, and I had an open hit for the win.

Steven was still in the hospital, and Wendy stayed in touch throughout the game, thanks to a wonderful volunteer who gave her and Steven a play-by-play of the final ends over the telephone. The volunteer got me to the phone right after we won. Emotions were definitely running high in that game.

It was going to be different going into the Brier. We were a much more mature team. The front end had one Brier under their belts, and I had experience dealing with the media. But there was a more important matter to deal with first. The morning we were to fly to Regina, I rushed Wendy to the hospital. After tests, she was going to be transferred by ambulance to the Orillia Hospital, thirty miles away, for emergency surgery. All I can remember is giving Wendy a big hug as they put her into the waiting ambulance. I raced home to pack some personal items for her, phoned my mom to tell her what was happening and drove to Orillia. I parked the car and held the door open for Wendy's stretcher, which arrived a moment after I did.

Wendy went into surgery that evening, and I stayed at the hospital. My parents were leaving for the Brier the next day; I talked my father into going that night with the team. If all was well with Wendy, I'd take his flight the next day. Wendy was fine and I limped into the Brier. I missed only one practice. Three days later, Wendy got on a plane and arrived in Regina. It was early to travel after the operation but we felt if we were together, we wouldn't be worried about each other.

The team continued to play as we had all year, aggressive to get the lead and then hitting everything in sight to protect it. We ended the round robin with an impressive 9–2 record, tied with Vic Peters of Manitoba. We were relegated to second place because of our round-robin loss to him. That meant a semifinal, and it was a wonderful game against Kevin Martin and his Edmonton foursome. I made a come-around raise double takeout in the sixth end to score three points to break the game open...until the hog line official ruled that I was over the line. That great shot was nullified, and we went from an insurmountable lead to a tie. Two years earlier, this might have been devastating, but the team had come of age. We had played too well all year to let one incident stop the momentum, and we managed to defeat Martin.

This put us in the final against Manitoba's Vic Peters. He was one of the nicest guys in curling, a classy competitor, win or lose.

Maybe we would have won that game if we had found a way to dislike Vic and his team. Glenn and I had a wonderful success rate over the years when we were motivated by the opposition. Against Vic, though, there was nothing. We wanted to take him down to the Brier Patch and buy him a beer.

The key to that final came in the ninth end. We were down one with last rock and played a great end. We were sitting two and I was throwing my first rock. If I made it perfect, it would be game-set-match. As it crossed the hog line, it picked and went off line and wrecked on a guard, opening things up for Peters. Vic threw a good freeze that gently tapped our shot rock and sat a couple of inches off the corner of our stone.

That left me with a fairly tough come-around tap for three. I slid slightly narrow then redirected the stone back to the broom, causing it to run straight. It was a straight spot in that part of the ice, and the rock never curled back, jamming the Manitoba rock. We got one, but if I'd made it, we would have scored three. Instead, we went to the tenth end tied. Peters gave us life by hitting and rolling out with his last one to force an extra end, but the second time around, he made no mistake, scoring one and winning.

It was a crushing defeat because our great year came up one game short. In the locker room after the game, Wayne was in tears, and the rest of us were devastated. We all felt helpless. We'd curled so well all year and then not played our top game in the final.

How could the curling gods have been so cruel? A year like we'd had was snuffed out a foot short of the finish line. No matter how many spiels we won, how much money we took to the bank, how many great shots we made, a loss in the Brier final wasn't the finish we had dreamed of. I had more incentive than winning the Brier that year. Wendy had me scheduled for a vasectomy the same week as the Worlds! All I had to do was beat Vic, and I could have postponed that painful operation. Now I had a reason to dislike Vic Peters!

On Top Again

THE SUMMER OF 1992 was not a repeat of 1986. Although we'd lost the Brier finale, we were prepared for what was ahead. We knew what people were going to say, how they would react. Glenn and I told Wayne and Pete what they could expect, and I think that helped them keep their perspective. As well, Glenn and I had a Brier and a world championship, and our new team with Wayne and Pete had completed an extremely successful season, so it was easier to accept the loss. And there was the exposure the game was getting on television. TSN was broadcasting every draw at the Brier, and viewers were better educated about the game and had an appreciation for the competition and our team's potential for the future. We had a positive outlook for the next season. We weren't just the team that had lost the final.

There was also the sense of knowing what a great team we had. In 1986, we had no idea whether we'd make it to the Brier again. It had taken us six years to return after our 1980 Brier, and it had been tough to get back. In 1992, six years later, we'd been to the Brier five times in seven years. We knew we'd be back. Given the chance, we thought we could win.

Confidence is a funny thing, the way it comes and goes. But Wayne and Pete brought a new measure of it to our team. Wayne was so confident he convinced his fiancée to postpone their April wedding, which would conflict with the World Championships. Now that's confidence!

This is not to suggest that it wasn't hard to get over the loss. I'd lie awake at night and run through the game, think about the shots we missed and what we could have done better. We spent a lot of time together that summer. Most of our meetings took place at a golf course. I only managed about fifteen games a year, but I could still get it in the air once in a while. Wayne, an assistant professional at St. George's Golf and Country Club in Toronto, played a lot of golf at some of the best courses in Southern Ontario. Glenn was extremely busy in the summer, burning up all his holidays to curl in the winter. He only played golf ten or fifteen times a summer. Pete, a police officer, worked shifts and played in spurts, but not that much. He was the highest handicap on the team, at five.

Anyone who didn't know us would think we were playing for our lives with the passion we showed on the course. Wayne was the most fun to play with because of his intensity. He could hit the ball a mile but was a brutal putter and could get extremely frustrated if he was off. The first time I played with him was at my course, Brooklea. It's a short layout and the greens are quite small, putting a premium on accuracy. He hit seventeen greens in regulation—which was very impressive—but he shot seventy-four. I hit nine greens and shot sixty-eight. Wayne immediately requested a rematch—in Toronto.

We played at Beacon Hall, an exclusive club with a course consistently ranked as one of Canada's top five; I was intimidated by the exclusive facility. I got to the club at 9:30 and there wasn't a car anywhere. I figured the course was closed. I later learned that there were only 150 members and the empty parking lot was standard. (It wasn't unlike the first time I arrived to curl at the Toronto Cricket, Skating and Curling Club as a junior.) I was also nervous when I learned that the other two members of our group were pros as well—one from

Glen Abbey and another from Angus Glen, two more high-profile Ontario courses. On the opening nine, I was all over the place and shot forty. I wasn't comfortable. Wayne shot thirty-seven, as did one of the other pros, and the fourth was even. I didn't care about the other two—but I couldn't let Wayne beat me. I was three back and I was going to catch him on the back nine. By the time we got to fifteen, I'd caught the other two and was one back of Wayne. The fifteenth was a par three, and I hit my shot so far right that getting it on the green and making par was almost impossible. Wayne hit a great shot and was inside ten feet. I used a lob wedge and managed to get the ball to within about twelve feet of the pin, then drained the par putt. Wayne charged his ten-footer and ran it about four feet past, then missed that one and had to settle for a bogey. We were tied. I won the sixteenth hole to go one up, and on seventeen I hit my shot into a fairway bunker. Wayne was about forty yards past me, right down the middle. I have a tough time getting out of fairway bunkers on most occasions, but not this one. I hit a six-iron out of the sand and landed the ball on the green about fifty feet right of the flag. The ball spun some forty feet sideways and came to rest ten feet from the pin.

I looked at Wayne, and he was surprisingly calm. He set up to his shot, took a couple of practice swings and made a mighty lash. Remarkably, he shanked it. The ball went straight sideways and disappeared into a lake that hadn't been on the radar screen as a hazard for this particular shot.

I figured I should duck to avoid flying clubs, but to my amazement, there was no reaction. He calmly reached into his bag, took out another ball and, looking very composed, walked to the edge of the pond. That's when the fuse reached its end. Staring into the pond, he threw the ball in the air and took an angry swing with his club, as if he was hitting a baseball. A stream of swear words followed as he realized I was going to beat him.

After the round, Wayne was his normal self, although the other two players took delight in teasing him over a beer.

That was the way our team was—we were the greatest of friends but ultra competitive. We were invited to play in Japan once by the Japanese curling association. Between games, we found ourselves at a gym with a badminton court. My team constantly teased me about my age—the boys would call me "Old Man" and ask me when I was going to start playing senior curling. I decided a game of badminton might show them I wasn't over the hill just yet. I played quite a bit of badminton at Georgian College (instead of going to class). I knew Glenn hadn't played much, and earlier in the week, Wayne had let it slip that he wasn't a badminton player. I had a big advantage. (Pete, a police officer, had gone to visit a Tokyo police station.)

I said I would take on Wayne and Glenn—two against one—and they gladly accepted. Glenn was playing in his big Kodiak boots, and I think he almost had a heart attack, he was trying so hard. He tried playing in his socks and eventually his bare feet. I managed to beat them but not before Glenn's feet got badly blistered. We lived to compete.

Another time, in Grindelwald, Switzerland at a big curling event, we had the opportunity to toboggan down the side of a mountain. It was no bunny hill—we had to take a bus to get to the top. We all knew this was going to be a great race. As usual, I was looking for an edge, and I decided I could get it by finding the faster sled. So while the bus driver patiently waited, I pushed two sleds back and forth to find the faster one—like matching curling rocks.

The course was groomed for toboggans: there was a wide track with snowbanks on both sides. On our first run down the hill, my sled work paid off—I was the fastest. But on the second and third trips down the mountain, the boys found that if they went head first, they would go faster.

On the fourth trip, I convinced Glenn I needed a head start. Off I went, with Glenn in hot pursuit. I cut him off on the left, then on the right. He managed to get a lane and started to pass me. I knew I'd never catch him, so I "accidentally" shoved my left foot onto the back right corner of his sled, which caused him to take a quick turn. He shot off the course and disappeared from view.

I stopped my sled and ran to the place where Glenn had exited the course. I located his sled...but not him. His moaning indicated his whereabouts, and told me he was still alive. Glenn and his sled had hit a tree, which stopped him from travelling off the edge of the mountain. Still, it was pretty tough to convince Glenn that the ten-inch bruise on his leg was a good thing.

That wasn't the end of this little adventure. As Glenn and I got back on course, Pete went past and turned to laugh at me. He didn't see the bus making its way up the hill with another load of sledders. Its path cut right across the toboggan hill. Pete was travelling at about forty kilometers an hour; the bus was going about three. It looked like a collision was imminent unless Pete took one of three courses of action. Turn left and go over the two-foot snowbank and hope he didn't roll in front of the bus; turn right and go over the two-foot snowbank and hope he didn't fly off the edge of the mountain; or hope his body and sled would fit underneath the bus.

To my astonishment, he took Option Two and tried to ride the bank on the right without going over it. He managed to stay on top of the bank, get past the bus and come to a stop.

Such competition got us through the off-season after losing the Brier final. We stayed together and focused on our goal.

Of course, some events helped put everything in perspective. That summer, Geno Reda, a well-known broadcaster on TSN, and I were invited to the Special Olympics fundraising dinner in Charlottetown, PEI. I was fortunate enough to meet Joey, a Special Olympian, who spoke as the ambassador for the athletes. Joey's sport was curling, and he was the skip of the PEI Special Olympics team. I sat with Joey after dinner and talked curling with him and his coach. I told them we would be in PEI at least once for a bonspiel, and if he would like to have an exhibition game with our team, we would be very happy to work that into our schedule. That October, Joey's coach gave me a

call, and we set it up at the Silver Fox Curling Club in Summerside. I
talked my teammates into going a day early so we could play Joey and
his rink, and when we arrived, the curling club was jammed. We were
stretching in the change room when Joey came in. I went and shook
his hand and said hello. I could tell Joey was really pumped for the
game. "Have you done any curling this year?" I asked. He responded
with a huge smile and said, "We played in a bonspiel last Saturday."

"How did you do?" I asked. He smiled again and told me, "We
came second," Then he added, "We came second—*three times!*"

I've been associated with Special Olympics ever since. When the
Special Olympians compete, it isn't about winning or losing; it's for
the love of the game.

That summer, we received news that gave us another reason to be
optimistic about the upcoming curling year. The Ontario Curling
Association, in its wisdom, had elected to adopt the free guard zone
for the provincial playdowns—the first Canadian association to move
away from the old rules. The decision showed how progressive curling was in Ontario. The administrators knew it was a matter of time
before the rest of Canada switched and decided it was time for Ontario
curling to make the move. The change was applauded by fans and
curlers. It put more rocks in play, it made for more exciting shotmaking and it also meant a better chance for a team that was trailing to
make a comeback. It made the end of the game the most exciting part.
That hadn't been the case under the old rules, where a team would
get a lead and then play takeout after takeout until the opposition was
mathematically eliminated. It really put the fun back in the game.

The rule Ontario decided to use wasn't quite the Howard Rule,
which we used in Moncton; it was a variation called the three-rock free
guard zone. A takeout couldn't be played on any stone sitting outside
the house between the tee line and the hog line (the area designated as
the "free guard zone") until the fourth stone of the end. The Ontario

version wasn't nearly as good as the original. It was complicated, for one thing, and it had a limited effect on getting rocks in play. But I wasn't about to complain too loudly—at least the OCA was moving in the right direction.

Almost every major cashspiel was using some version of the new rule. The world championships had adopted a rule in which a takeout couldn't be made on a stone in the free guard zone until the fifth rock of the end—the four-rock free guard zone.

The only missing piece to the puzzle was the Canadian Curling Association, which wanted to keep studying the rule. In my mind they were getting left behind. It was so frustrating to wait for the change at the national level. It seemed the CCA wasn't moving because the rest of the world was pushing the rule. The CCA didn't want to be seen as the follower. It wanted to be the leader. The result was that Canadian curlers and the sport had to suffer. The CCA was anything but a progressive organization.

For example, in 1992, Vic Peters won the Brier using the traditional rules of curling. Then, in the most important curling event of his life, the Worlds, he had to adapt to the four-rock rule, which the Europeans had been using for a couple of years. Peters was at a disadvantage; his team struggled and didn't win the world championship.

I knew the new rule in Ontario would benefit two teams the most: ours and Werenich's. A realignment of the zones meant his club and ours were in the same starting group; we'd likely have to knock heads in the Brier playdowns a lot earlier than usual. It didn't affect the rest of the season—we played our regular schedule of cash events across the country—but when it came time to play down for the year's biggest prize, the Brier, we were on a collision course almost out of the gate. The OCA and curling fans would have preferred seeing us play at the provincial final in an arena with a trip to the Brier on the line, not in a curling club where the loser would be eliminated.

Both teams lost their first game and faced off in the second game. It was a double knockout competition, which meant the loser was relegated to the Challenge Round.

In the first end of that game, Werenich scored five on us. I thought our chances were pretty slim after that. But the new rule showed how exciting—and unpredictable—the game could be. About two ends later, we scored five, then won the game 10–9. Werenich was gone after just two games.

Although we won our zone, we lost in the regional playdown and had to go back to our favourite bonspiel—the Challenge Round. It was a long slog to the provincial final. But we managed to do it. The team was too good not to get there, and our determination and confidence carried us through. We got through the round robin without any bumps, then played Mike Harris in the final, as we had the year before. Harris wasn't well known outside of Ontario, but he and his team were solid players. A win was anything but guaranteed.

After nine ends, Harris was up two. Against a team as good as his, it would be extremely difficult to score two in the final end. Under the old rules, I think we would not have had a chance; they could have hit every rock we put in play. But playing with the free guard zone gave us a little hope. And at third rocks, we got a big break when Richard Hart, Harris's third, missed a crucial shot. We managed to score three and turn what looked liked defeat into a stunning win.

Harris and his teammates were devastated, but they grew into one of the best teams in Canada. At the first Olympic Trials in 1997, they surprised many people, who didn't know them. I was playing Kevin Martin late in the week, and he asked, "Who is this Mike Harris guy?"

"Kevin, he's really good, and I think everyone's about to find out just how good," was my reply.

Sure enough, Harris won those trials and captured a silver medal in Nagano in 1998. He later became the CBC's colour analyst.

The provincial win in 1993 sent me to my seventh Brier. I was getting up there in terms of Brier participation and wins as a skip. I passed Paul Savage, my boyhood idol, in appearances, although I didn't think about that at the time. I was more concerned with winning another one and I was confident our team had a good shot.

The 1993 Brier was in Ottawa, another home-province competition. Lots of friends and family made the trip to the nation's capital, which made the Brier more social. The socializing was good but time-consuming. Every trip from the hotel to the rink and back took longer with all the handshakes, hellos and short chats, and we had to plan accordingly.

We knew the routine, and we weren't going to deviate from our plans. We knew which appearances we had to make and which we could miss. We focused on our curling.

There was some disappointment with the conditions. The provincials had great ice with lots of curl everywhere on the sheet, and it had the three-rock free guard zone. The competition had been a real treat for fans and players. In Ottawa, the rocks were very straight, and we were back to the old hit-everything-in-sight rule—there was no free guard zone here. A defensive style was necessary because of the conditions. On straight ice, trying to get rocks behind guards is tough, so they can be removed quite easily. I had the team that could play a hitting game—Wayne and Pete were phenomenal bangers. Our plan was simple: go aggressive early, get up a few points and then do the old Rope-a-Dope and hit everything the opposition put up. It wasn't our favourite style of play, but it worked.

In one memorable contest (or maybe not so memorable) we beat PEI's Robert Campbell 2–1—in an extra end to tie the lowest score ever recorded in a Brier. The straight ice may have been beneficial to us, but it wasn't making the CCA happy. The conditions created a mundane game style. The fans were yelling "Borrr-innggg" from the stands, and folks at home were dozing off in front of their television sets. The CCA decided to bring in Shorty Jenkins to work his magic and get some swing into the ice.

This was a momentous step. For years, the CCA had refused to hire the best arena icemaker in the business. No one knew why; it seemed the CCA officials wouldn't use Shorty because everyone was telling them they should. We certainly thought he could improve the conditions. My first introduction to Shorty came at the 1977 provincial finals, where he was doing the ice. Not long after that, my father, who had retired from Loblaws and become manager at the Midland Curling Club, contacted Shorty to ask how to improve the ice at his club.

That was the way my father was—always trying to improve by asking the experts. He called Shorty from time to time to ask for tips. Shorty was only too happy to help; once in a while he went to Midland to have a look.

Shorty was easily the best icemaker the game had ever seen. He did a lot to improve ice conditions, especially in large arenas. He would go to great lengths to make great ice because he knew the curlers could shine. He studied rocks and tested them to compare arena ice to ice in a curling club. He learned how the conditions of a building affected the surface and considered everything from humidity to the PH of the water to the heat of the lights to the effect of a large crowd. His attention to detail allowed him to provide great conditions.

In Ontario, we were spoiled: Shorty made the ice at the provincial finals. We'd get twenty-four- or twenty-five-second ice that was swingy. On a scale of one to ten, the ice at our provincial final was an eleven, and the stuff at the Brier was about a four.

Shorty's ice gave Ontario teams an advantage in a finesse game—lots of draws, freezes and delicate taps. With good conditions, world-class players felt they could make anything, and most often did. That made for good curling and great entertainment. It wasn't until the late 1990s that the ice at the Brier got to this level.

Icemaking wasn't Shorty's only forte. He became an expert on rocks. He'd match them up and knew how to sandpaper the bottom of them so older rocks would curl again. He was truly a magician. Shorty contributed as much as anyone to the growth of the game. And he always passed on his information and techniques. He was willing to try new things, too. In the early 1990s, he became the first icemaker to run lines down the sheet from the edges of the four-foot. He did that at the TSN/McCain Skins Game. It looked like a runway down the middle of the sheet, but it allowed viewers to see the rocks curling. It's pretty much standard in curling clubs these days.

Shorty was one of the first to use an infared gun. The infared beams could tell the temperature of an object or a surface. He studied the temperatures of the ice, the rocks and the building so he could avoid or repair problems with the conditions.

About half way through a game in the Canadian Mixed championship in Lethbridge one year, the ice was getting flat—the pebble was wearing out. The icemaker, who had worked with Shorty, asked me if I had any solutions. I suggested a few things, but the problem persisted. I offered to call Shorty, and the icemaker said please.

Before I could tell Shorty anything, he asked: "The ice is getting flat, isn't it?"

"Yes," I said, "but how did you know?"

"I've worked in that building before. I know exactly what your problem is."

He told me to take the icemaker's infrared gun to the middle of the ice and point it at the ceiling. I thought maybe he'd lost his marbles, but I did it. The gun displayed a temperature of twenty-seven.

"That's your problem right there," Shorty said. "Your roof is too low. The hot air can't escape."

He made about nine different suggestions, such as opening certain doors, turning on the air-conditioning system and turning off the lights between draws. By the next morning, the ice was perfect.

After I moved to Moncton, I called Shorty for some expertise. On the opening weekend of my first season in New Brunswick, I went to the Beausejour Curling Club to throw some practice rocks. I stepped into the hack, threw four down the ice, then walked to the other end and kicked the rocks back. The ice was so bad, I packed up and left. It was slow, it didn't curl, and it was hard to slide on the surface.

I switched to the Beaver Curling Club, where the ice was marginally better, but it wasn't what I was used to.

I decided to phone Shorty. His response was predictable: "I'll be there Wednesday." When he showed up, he was on the verge of

pneumonia. I wanted to take him to my place, where Wendy had prepared a nice dinner. But he wouldn't have any of it.

"I came down here to fix your ice," he said. "Take me to the curling club."

He met our volunteer icemaker, who gave him the particulars
about the facility, told him a few things, then went to work, scraping
and pebbling the ice over and over to try to work his magic.

Finally he looked at me and said: "Twenty-seven."

Shorty and I had a special code. Before I stepped on the ice, he'd
tell me the speed it was running. I'd try to throw at that speed, timing
the rocks from tee line to tee line, to see if my speed matched up. He
was telling me he'd turned the ice in the Beaver Curling Club into
twenty-seven-second ice—nothing short of a small miracle. I stepped
into the hack and delivered the rock, and it barely got across the hog
line. Shorty looked as if someone had shot him. I threw another one
and it wasn't much better.

Without hesitating, he wiped two fingers across the ice, brought
them to his mouth and licked them. "What kind of water are you using?" he asked the volunteer icemaker.

"We were told it was really hard so we have a softener downstairs."

Down we went into the bowels of the building, to the big water-
softening unit. Beside it were several big bags of salt. The icemaker
had been putting salt in the unit, and the salt was causing the problem.
When the salt was eliminated, the ice got better almost immediately.

That's the type of individual Shorty is: hardworking, never satis-
fied. He's also extremely hyper, running all over and going a hundred
miles an hour in ten different directions. He is intense in just about
everything he does. He has upset icemakers at rinks where he's gone
to try and improve the conditions, but it's out of his love to make
things better. I love the guy. He's one of a kind.

So did a lot of other curlers. Shorty became an icon. As his
name suggests, he isn't very tall, about five-foot-four, and most often he wears a large cowboy hat, usually a bright shade of pink. He
would go up and down the ice between draws at big events, checking

temperatures, working with a scraper, supervising his ice crew, talking a mile a minute along the way. Shorty got to be such a character that Tim Hortons made a television commercial featuring him.

And in Ottawa, he finally had a chance to get his hands on the Brier ice. Between games, word reached us that Shorty had been called in. We started the week 6–0 with straight rocks, which wasn't our strength. Imagine what we could do with Shorty's conditions. We practised before our seventh match and found four feet of curl on the outside-in shots, which was about three and a half feet more than it had been bending before. We started smiling. It would be a lot more fun to play with rocks that curled, or so we thought.

At that practice, none of us threw a rock from the centre out to the wings, maybe because we were so excited about the curl into the middle of the sheet, or because Shorty was at the helm. We assumed it would curl both ways.

In the first end of a game against New Brunswick I had a wide-open hit and missed it by a foot and a half. The ice was dished—it was higher on the outsides of the sheet and fell towards the middle. On the inside out shots, there was a big fall, so the rocks did the opposite of what they were supposed to do. We struggled with the ice, growing more and more frustrated with every shot. We gave up three in one end, then allowed the other team to steal two more. We ended up losing 13–9. When I walked off the ice, I knew something had gone drastically wrong. The ice was not typical of what Shorty delivered. The press asked me what had happened, and I was frank: Shorty had come in and dished the ice but had overdone it.

Shorty was nowhere to be found. The CCA gave him his shot then fired him on the spot. He heard some of the comments made by curlers and took them to heart. I knew Shorty was a very sensitive person, and would have a strong reaction to the mistake and the comments about the ice. I had to speak to him, and I spent two hours between games trying to contact him. For years, Shorty had wanted nothing more than to make the ice at the Brier and the CCA had never let him do it. When he finally got his chance, he messed up. The last thing he wanted to do was

ruin the Brier. When I finally got hold of him, Shorty explained what
had really happened. Before the Brier started, and again when they
asked him to come in halfway through, Shorty told the committee the
rocks they were using were far too straight to be used in an arena. Most
people blamed the ice, when the rocks were more often the problem.

Shorty wasn't allowed to bring in swingier rocks, so he did the
only thing he could do: he carved a trench down the middle of
the sheet. That would at least let rocks curl to the centre. He wasn't
given enough time to make things subtle. To correct the problem, the
organizers decided to flood the surface, but they couldn't do it until
the end of the next day, and we lost our second straight that day.

When the smoke cleared at the end of the round robin, we were
in a four-way tie for first place at 8–3. Vic Peters of Manitoba, BC's
Rick Folk and Rick Lang of Northern Ontario joined us atop the
leaderboard to create the biggest mess the Brier has ever seen.

Heading into the last game of the round robin, all four teams
knew there was a potential for a big logjam, but Manitoba believed it
had an edge. John Loxton, the fifth man for Manitoba, read the rule
book and believed that in the case of a four-way tie, Manitoba would
earn first place because it had defeated the other three teams in the
round robin. He talked to an official from Manitoba to get clarifica-
tion of this rule. Before the final game, he told his team they would
be awarded first place if they won. That was huge because first place,
then, meant a bye right to the final.

When the four-way tie materialized, Manitoba was all smiles, believing it was in the final. But the CCA officials gathered us together
and told us that no team could be moved two games in front of any
other team. Instead of Manitoba getting a bye to the final, all four
teams would play tiebreaking games. Unfortunately for Manitoba,
there were two sets of rules—one the official rule book and another
called the competitor's guide. There were rules for regular curling and
rules for the Brier, but none of the rules anticipated a four-way tie.

As soon as they heard they would play tiebreakers, Peters's team
went nuts. "This is crazy," yelled the skip. "There's absolutely no credit

for beating those other three teams." Dan Carey, the team's third, was even more upset. In front of the media, he stomped across the backboards yelling, "This is shit!" When the press asked me for my opinion, I said I hadn't read the rule book—I admit I was brutal for that; to me it was like school work and I left it to Glenn—but that if we were all tied and Peters had beaten us all, he should get some reward.

The officials decided Peters would get first place, but he still had to play in the tiebreakers, which didn't mean much of an advantage.

They lined the other three teams up and had each throw a draw to the button to decide who played Peters. We were allowed three practice shots, and on every one of those, I put my stone right in the centre of the rings. But when it counted, I came narrow, and my rock got into a flat part of the ice—this was well after the game was over, and they hadn't re-pebbled the ice—and stopped at the eight-foot. I came third out of three and ended up facing Peters.

For a second I was disappointed, but then I realized it was probably the best thing that could have happened. We were going out onto the ice to play a team that was spinning out of control. If I'd thought about it at the time, I should have taken that shot for the draw to the button and hogged it to ensure we played Peters. The playoff system that had been set up really didn't seem to make a lot of sense either. We were playing Peters and Folk was playing Lang. The two winners would meet on the A side. The two losers would play each other on the B side, with the loser of that game eliminated and the winner facing the loser of the A side to get a berth in the Brier final. This made matters worse for Manitoba; it was like rubbing salt in their wound. Their situation had changed from being one game away from winning the Brier with a day off to rest and a bye to the final (with hammer in the first end, on straight ice with the old rules), to potentially having to win three more games to win the Brier.

On the ice, I could tell Carey was still steaming, and his mood affected his play. Peters was probably still mad, but he was so respectful of his opponents he'd never dream of throwing them off with his problems.

Our game was close, but I was fortunate enough to make a long raise double for two in the sixth end, and our team made everything the rest of the way. We won 6–4 and moved on to the A final against BC, which had defeated Northern Ontario.

There was still more fun to add to this mess. The CCA called the four teams into a meeting. They informed us that the CBC had come in to set up for their weekend coverage. They put a track used for a rolling television camera across sheet one, and placed technical equipment on sheet four. The Brier ice had been reduced from four sheets to two. I had played Peters on sheet two; Lang and Folk had played on sheet three. There were two games left to play, which meant two teams would play on the same sheet they'd just played, giving them a distinct advantage. They would know the intricacies of the sheet, where it curled, how much it curled and how certain spots would react.

The way it had been drawn officially, I was to play Folk on the sheet I'd just played, sheet two. Folk refused to move from sheet three. If the game was on his sheet, I wasn't going to move either. Peters said he sure as heck wasn't moving, and Lang made it four. Stalemate.

There was no animosity between the skips, but no one wanted to be at a disadvantage. The officials weren't prepared to make a decision. I told them to get Warren Hansen, the head of the event. I was informed that this situation was Neil Houston's responsibility.

I said we needed to see Hansen; he was the guy running the show.

The first one to offer to break the stalemate was Lang.

"Listen, I'll make you a deal. You give me Russ Howard's rock book and I'll move sheets so everyone can be happy."

"Nice try, Rick," I said.

We kept a little book where we recorded all the good and bad rocks wherever we played, and we noted which rocks should be paired up. We were definitely ahead of most teams: we were known as rock experts. I took Lang's offer as quite a compliment; he had been to nine Briers and won three of them. In the end, Lang, a real gentleman, agreed to move, and the matter was settled.

This was another example of the frustration of working with the CCA. Why wouldn't they have something like this covered in the rule book? But there was a silver lining: the Ottawa tiebreakers were the forerunner to the Page Playoff System used today.

Peters lost his game to Lang 6–5 and was eliminated from the Brier. We got past Folk in the A final in a well-curled, defensive battle, one of the best games our team had played all year, which gave us the bye to the final. Folk played Rick Lang in the true semifinal of the 1993 Brier. Folk's win set up the final a lot of people had predicted.

I was worried going into that game. Folk's team had been the class of the western curling circuit all year. His third, Pat Ryan, stepped down from a very successful skipping career and joined Bert Gretzinger and Jerry Richards. They formed what the western media had called the Dream Team. Folk was a tremendous strategist and reader of ice, one of the best in the game. He was unafraid of throwing the big shot. I had played against Ryan for more than a decade and thought he was about the best hitter I'd ever seen. We were playing against a tough team on their type of ice—very straight—using rules that favoured their style of play.

In the final, we blanked the first end. We were forced to one in the second end, and I managed to make a timely hit and roll to the button behind cover in the third when Folk was heavy on his draw. We stole another one in the fourth to go up 3–0. After that, the boys hit everything in sight, leaving the BC team very little opportunity to get back in the game. My teammates left me a wide-open hit on my last rock to win the Brier.

There was some irony in that final: we played a great hitting team on straight ice using the old rule, and we won. A year later, we played them in the Brier final on swingy ice, with the free guard zone, and they beat us. Go figure.

We were back on top. It was a second Brier win for Glenn and me, a first for Wayne and Pete. It was great to see them get that win. They had worked hard and played well. The win was the culmination of four great years for the team; the last two years had been spectacular.

We won lots of money, lots of titles, and we won the Brier. We had gone from a very good team to a great one.

We celebrated our victory at the Brier, but we knew there was one more mountain left to climb.

A World of Difference

9

A FEW WEEKS AFTER our Brier win in Ottawa, we jetted off to Geneva, Switzerland for the World Championship. And for the third time in the same season, we were using a different set of rules.

We'd won the Ontario championship with the three-rock version of the free guard zone, the Brier with the old rules, and at the World Championship we would use the four-rock free guard zone, which was closer to the original Howard Rule. Before we left I told the press we were probably the only team in Canada that wouldn't be at a disadvantage.

I was amazed the CCA didn't go to the four-rock free guard zone. It's a much better rule than the three-rock, and the rest of the world was using it. Talk about putting a country at a disadvantage.

But we were confident. We were coming off two tremendous years and at the top of our game. The men's championship was held concurrently with the women's, and the Canadian women's team that year was Sandra Schmirler's rink from Saskatchewan. We didn't know their team—eastern boys and western girls. But our team leader, Jim Waite—the same Jim Waite I'd played against in my first provincial final—did a great job of bringing the two teams together. The first two nights we all had dinner together. There was a lot of great curling talk, and Waite impressed upon us that we were one big team, that we needed to stick together and share information, which we were all more than happy to do.

Glenn and I tried to help the women with some of the subtleties of the four-rock rule, since this was their first competition using the rule. Schmirler was very confident about the way her team would approach its first world championship. So we helped them with rock matching. Once we told them about our read on the rocks, they were a little more receptive. We picked up information from them on ice conditions and other things. Overall, we got along famously. We watched their games, and they did the same for us, which was a huge boost. At a Brier ten thousand people cheer a team on; it was a little lonely in Geneva, where attendance at our event was sparse. For our Thursday morning game, as the national anthem was playing, I counted nineteen people in the stands of the twelve-thousand-seat arena—and I was related to most of them. We needed each other's support.

The arena was a big problem; it was built for hockey, and the floor was put in on a tilt so to take the ice out, they shut off the compressor. The melted ice ran out the low end.

At one end of the arena, the ice was twelve or thirteen inches thick, while the other it was only a couple of inches. At the deep end, so to speak, the pipes were so far from the surface that the ice was quite warm (as far as ice goes). At the other end, there was frost. It was probably the strangest ice I've ever played on.

If we were delivering at the frosty end, we had to resist the urge to really push it down there. The ice felt very slow as we were coming out, but as the rock travelled down the sheet, it hit the fast stuff and just kept sliding.

One game, with my last rock, I needed to draw into the house to score two points. I had a rock in the top of the eight-foot and I was playing down a path that would have me come right to that stone. All the way down, Wayne and Pete were lightly sweeping, keeping the path clean more than anything. At the hog line, Wayne lifted his broom and yelled down the sheet, "Nice shot, skipper." Then we all watched as the rock kept sliding and sliding and sliding. It hit the one in the top of the eight and pushed it all the way through the rings. We scored one. It was almost as if the rock was on a downhill ramp. Coming the other way was no bargain, either. The rocks would slide and slide and then hit the frost and almost stop, as if they had brakes.

We advanced to the sudden-death semifinal with a record of 7–2. The semi, against Scott Baird of the United States, was one of the most nerve-racking games I've played. It was one of those contests in which we played great but the other team wouldn't go away. We were one up playing the tenth end and had last rock. This was the first time we had used the four-rock free guard zone was used in national or international competition, and it made the tenth end anything but certain. Baird and the U.S. were far from out of this game.

The Americans threw up a guard with their first one. We had a decision to make—play defensively and chip the rock to the side of the sheet (under the free guard zone rule, it couldn't be removed, but it could be moved out of the way) or play offensively and try to get rocks in the house. The second was the more dangerous play, but with my team, I was confident. I elected to have Pete draw around the guard, which he did perfectly. The Americans threw up another guard, and Pete drew around again. We were sitting two buried and frozen together on the four-foot. The Americans tried to draw down to that, but came short, adding another guard out front. We elected to put up a guard of our own to prevent a raise, and very quickly, there was a tangle of stones over the sheet. When Baird came to throw his last one, there were fourteen rocks in play, and he was left with an extremely difficult double-angle raise with draw weight to push a stone to the side of the button. Yes, it was nearly impossible, but if he made it, we were probably going to an extra end.

Baird didn't make the shot, but it was a memorable game. (Thirteen years later, Baird was the assistant coach of the U.S. Team at the Torino Olympics. The head coach of the American team at the Games was Canadian Ed Lukowich, who defeated us at the 1986 Brier. Old curlers rarely disappeared from the game.)

The final was against David Smith of Scotland. He was the toughest of all the Scots I played over the years. I was always surprised he didn't have more success internationally; he won only one world championship. He played a good game, knew the strategy well and always seemed to be calm. We knew we'd have a battle on our hands; the Scots wouldn't fold.

I was a bit nervous. I'd been around the frozen block long enough to realize that no matter how good a team I had or how good a year I'd been through, playing one sudden-death game against a world-class team was like flipping a coin.

The organizers decided to have the men's and women's games on the same afternoon, but staggered the starts. The women's game began an hour before the men's. After we got a big three-ender in the fourth, we headed into the fifth-end break, the halfway point in the contest, just as the women's game was wrapping up. We watched Schmirler and her team seal the win for Canada. I slid over to her as we were about to start our sixth end and gave her a big hug of congratulations. She looked at me and said: "You know what you have to do now." I smiled and said, "I'm trying."

Glenn, Pete and Wayne were phenomenal in the second half. They were on a mission, but Smith refused to go away. He got to within one playing the ninth, but we had last rock. Pete set up two perfect corner guards, and Wayne and Glenn managed to get a couple of rocks behind them. Smith had no choice: he had to play the always difficult freeze. I picked out his first one, and he tried it again, trying to come down to one of ours on the button. The ice was so crazy he set his broom down about three inches outside our rock, then watched his stone curl ten inches—past our rock—and then fall backwards seven inches. He managed the line all right, but was just a little heavy, and bumped our rock about a foot. On most ice conditions, to hit half a rock would be a pretty simple shot, but this particular shot was anything but simple. I had to hit the right half of the Scottish stone while the broom was about six inches outside the mark, playing the wrong turn. In other words, the stone would fall in the opposite direction it would curl on regular ice. When I threw an inturn, I expected it to curl from left to right. At the Worlds, the stone moved from right to left. Glenn reassured me to trust what we had seen, that the rock would fall back into the Scottish stone.

I can remember that shot as if I had let it go a few minutes ago. Once I knew it was close, the boys swept it as hard as they could all the way down to stop it from falling too far. It was perfect: it removed the Scottish rock and allowed us to score three for a four-point lead coming home.

Like all Scottish teams, Smith's team didn't give up. He was sitting two buried when I threw my first rock of the tenth end. The boys swept it out of my hand from the greasy end all the way to the frosty end, and it snuck past a guard to push one of their rocks out, mathematically eliminating them and giving us the world championship.

The feeling was sensational. I'd made it all the way to the top of the curling world for a second time. A number of curlers have won a single crown, but only a few have multiple wins. I was honoured to be in that group, thrilled to have won with my brother and glad to have been a part of Pete and Wayne's first world championship.

Another great part of the win was to have our parents there to witness Glenn and I on the podium as the national anthem was played. As Wendy and I watch our two children, Steven and Ashley, compete, I have a better understanding of what my mom and dad went through all those years. It is so much easier to play than to watch. My mom has said to me many times that I'm the cause of her grey hair, to which I always reply, "Things happen for a reason."

This had to be one of the most incredible seasons for our curling team. By capping off the season with our second World Championship victory, we were dubbed in the press as the only team in the history of curling to win the Grand Slam—the writers felt the Grand Slam was made up of four events—the TSN Skins Game, the Player's Championship, the Brier and World Championship. This, to me, was even more special with the fact we played three different curling rules to win the provincials, the Brier and the Worlds.

With two world championships came more demands on my time. I was invited to speaking engagements, television appearances and celebrity charity golf tournaments. At one of those, my career took another turn.

I was playing in Toronto at a big celebrity event and found myself in the buffet line behind Brian Williams of CBC fame. We started talking, and he asked me if I was going out to Banff for the big celebrity ski challenge. I said no, that no one had asked me.

"What do you mean?" he asked. "Doesn't your agent have you filled in on that?"

My reply consisted of one word. "Agent?"

Williams couldn't believe I didn't have an agent. He asked for my card (I didn't have one of those either) so he could call me with information. I wrote my phone number on a napkin, never expecting him to call. But he did, and gave me all the time in the world. He told me I should have an agent and that there were three ways to go. The first was the biggie, the International Management Group (IMG). But he warned that they were so big, I could get lost. Then there was the small guy, for less commission. Then there was something in the middle, which he recommended, and suggested Elliott Kerr.

I met with Kerr, and we hit it off right away. I liked his relaxed and honest style. His company, Landmark Sport Group, had done a lot of work with Olympic athletes, and he thought curling—or more precisely curlers—would be a good fit. Kerr set me up with one of his agents, Randy Paul, and after a couple of meetings, Randy was off and selling. I was really excited about the opportunities Paul laid out for the team. A short while later he called to say that Ford was willing to give us four free Ford Explorers. Not a lease—free cars. All we had to do was wear Ford logos on the backs of our curling sweaters.

This was unbelievable. I was ecstatic, and so was the rest of the team. Curlers were finally getting recognized, getting some respect. This felt like the big time. But the feeling was short-lived. Ford had taken the deal to its ad agency, and the ad agency told them we weren't allowed to wear the logos during the Brier.

Paul couldn't believe it. I explained that after a team wins the provincial final, before they were even allowed to have a celebratory beer, they were required to sign a contract with the CCA. That contract effectively handed over all rights, without compensation.

The CCA could use a curler's image in ads to promote the event, feature curlers on television and tell curlers what they could and could not wear. All year long they could wear their sponsors' names on their sweaters, curl in big cash events and in the playdowns leading to the provincial final, but once they got to the Ontario final and the Brier, everything changed. Curlers had to wear the uniform provided by the CCA, which had only CCA sponsor logos. Curlers got free room and board, and the association got millions of dollars.

"What's wrong with your sport?" questioned Paul.

Elliott Kerr went a step further. He looked into the CCA contract and told me exactly what he thought.

"Let me explain this to you, Russ," he said. "It's legalized prostitution."

Kerr was shocked. In all his years of dealing with sports organizations, he'd never seen anything like the CCA contract. I had played in enough Briers to understand what Eddie Werenich had complained about for many years: curlers performed in front of 175,000 people during the week of the Brier. All those people paid for their tickets and refreshments and souvenirs. Curling also had television audiences that rivaled hockey audiences. There was a lot of money generated at the Brier, and the curlers never saw any of it. Curlers who competed at the top level travelled across the country to national and international events. Travel was expensive, and the only way curlers could offset costs was through sponsorship dollars. Sponsors requested exposure in return for their investment; they asked athletes to wear their logos at all events, especially those that are televised.

I told Kerr how frustrated I was at the entire situation, not to mention losing the four cars. He asked me if I wanted to take a stand. He thought we had a case to challenge the CCA's contract, possibly in court.

"Golfers can wear logos—all the athletes I represent wear sponsor logos."

Kerr took the matter to a lawyer, who told him it was a slam-dunk case, that we couldn't lose, and so we decided to take action. Kerr said the next time we won Ontario we should refuse to sign the contract and see how they reacted.

Ontario was one of the more progressive associations in the country; before 1994, curlers were allowed to wear sponsor logos while playing at the provincial final. A few weeks before the '94 championship, we received a letter saying Labatt was the exclusive sponsor of the event, and no other sponsor logos would be allowed. We were getting five or six thousand in sponsorship, which wasn't big money but which helped defray our costs.

I was big on loyalty, and had told the sponsors we'd be wearing their logos and names at the provincials. Now that was no longer allowed. Goldline, which ran a couple of curling equipment stores and manufactured their own clothing, was our primary sponsor, and I felt I should be promoting their lines.

When we showed up for the provincials that year, we were told to put duct tape over the logos. It looked horrible, all these curlers with big strips of tape on their sweaters. Most of the curlers got together in the locker room before one draw and talked about putting tape all over their sweaters, to make a mockery of the entire thing.

We managed to find a way around the new rules. Goldline had a booth in the arena where they were selling sweatshirts with little curling bears all over them. The sweatshirts didn't say Goldline on them, so we were allowed to wear them. We wore them for the entire week as our on-ice jackets, and Goldline couldn't keep them in stock. We defeated Axel Larsen in the '94 Provincial final in a well curled game. We wore the curling-bears sweatshirts for our official picture as provincial champions, and the photo was used in the Brier program.

We had promoted our sponsor and received way more exposure than if we'd worn sweaters that had Goldline written across them in three-foot letters. At every interview we did that week, the reporters asked why we were wearing the cute little bear sweatshirts.

We made the OCA's rule look silly, but to their credit, most of the officials laughed when we managed to get one past them. They weren't smiling a few minutes later, when John MacRae, the longtime general manager of the association, handed us the CCA's contract to sign. We all refused. MacRae was dumbfounded.

I told him I respected their association but I didn't think it was right to give up all our rights. That set the officials into spin cycle. They hit the phones to the CCA to ask for advice, then told us they'd be in touch, and we left. I expected it would take a day or two for them to sort things out, but when I walked in the door that night, the phone was ringing. An official told me that unless we signed the contract by 5:00 p.m. the next day, the second-place team, skipped by Axel Larsen of Guelph, would go to the Brier.

Larsen's team had never been to the Brier and that worked against us. I'm sure if it had been Ed Werenich who finished second, there would have been some solidarity. He probably would have told them to go and ask the third-place team. But I'm sure Larsen would have jumped at the chance of going to his first Brier if they'd offered the spot to him.

This was our first line in the sand. I phoned Glenn, and we decided we were prepared to sit out the Brier to further our cause. Wayne and Pete were in a different boat. They'd only been to a couple of Briers and weren't as definitive in their stand. They brought up a good point: we had won the last Brier, so we were throwing away a good chance at becoming a repeat winner, something pretty rare.

Finally, after lots of phone calls between the team and the officials, we came to a compromise. The team would go to the Brier and agree to the contract demands, and immediately after the Brier, we would be invited to sit on a committee with Elliott Kerr and come up with solutions for the next Brier. In this decision and others that came up in the future, I always tried to think about what was best for the game. The sport was much bigger than Russ Howard. We based a lot of decisions on that belief. For us not to represent Ontario at the Brier wasn't right. We'd won the province, and we had a good chance to win Canada. That's how we made our decision.

After the Brier, the CCA kept its word and created a committee that included Pat Ryan, Anne Merklinger, Randy Paul, Glenn and myself. We met in Ottawa and the curlers tried to get the association folks to understand our position: this wasn't about making money for the curlers. We described the out-of-pocket expenses over the course of a successful season. I told them our 1993 world championship team spent $25,000 for expenses to represent Canada at the world final in Geneva. Pat Ryan said he disagreed with me; his team had spent $30,000 at the world championships that year.

The CCA said it was thinking of putting prize money into the men's and women's national championships. Would that make us happy?

I told them I don't curl for money at the Brier; I played for my province and tried to win the national championship. I want to represent my country. If I made $4,000 at the Brier, it wouldn't make any difference in my life.

They said they were thinking of making first place worth $10,000.

"What's that going to do for the Territories?" I asked. That region had never made it to the playoffs, let alone won the Brier.

In the end, the CCA agreed to increase the amount teams received for expenses. The association was telling the press how generous it was with expense money, but it cost teams to go to the Brier. If a team went once, it wasn't a big deal. But teams were making it back time and again. The elite teams were beginning to tire of having to spend their own money while the CCA announced million-dollar profits.

I tried to explain it to Dave Parkes, the CCA's chief executive officer: "Dave, you give me $5,000 to go to the Brier and it's great. But if you let me wear a Ford crest I can get four Explorers."

The $5,000 they were offering the twelve teams at the Brier came out of money that went to the local Brier organizing committee. A thousand-plus volunteers worked three years to make a profit for their curling community, then the CCA would walk in and grab $60,000 for the curlers. I didn't think that was right. Give that money to the local clubs, and give teams the right to wear one non-conflicting sponsor logo. Every team could benefit from a relationship with a sponsor.

His comeback was predictable. "We can't let that happen. Labatt has an exclusive." The CCA wasn't going to budge one inch. The only concession the association made was to run a scroll of the team sponsors on the broadcast. It wasn't much, as far as I was concerned. I left the meeting in Ottawa still very frustrated. I felt the curlers were getting the short end of the stick. I talked to Kerr about it, and he said it wasn't fair that we had to give up our rights. He constantly tried to impress upon me that our image as athletes had a value and that we should be compensated accordingly. "But what can we do to get them to see that, Elliott?" I asked.

The answer was to take the association to court. I phoned a lot of curlers and tried to get the top names to join our cause. One of the first calls I made was to Ed Werenich, and he was onside right away. "Let me know what you need," the Wrench said. "I'm there."

I was pleased. Eddie easily could have hung me out to dry. But like all the other big-name curlers who joined the cause, he and his team realized that a fight was the only way curling was going to come out of the dark ages. We weren't trying to get rich from our sponsorship endorsements; we were all just looking to offset our expenses and create exposure for our sponsors.

We had won lots of money curling over the years, but we weren't able to make a living playing the game. A few have tried, but there are no professional curlers. I knew it wasn't going to happen overnight even if we won the court case. But a win would be an important step in the right direction.

One lawyer told us it was illegal for the CCA to restrict teams from making a profit through sponsorship. Unfortunately, the CCA lawyers found a loophole: the CCA was a not-for-profit organization. Competitive curlers paid membership fees to play in the competition organized by the CCA, which technically made us members of a non-profit organization and as such, we were not allowed to generate income from any events hosted by the CCA.

That was definitely disappointing, but the bigger picture was positive. Our group of curlers showed the CCA we were no longer going to roll over. From all of this came a lot of good things. For example, the CCA did move to get the curlers at the Brier more money, largely at the urging of Al Gilchrist, head of Nokia, which took over from Labatt as sponsor. He'd been a curler, had heard the complaints from the grassroots and suggested putting a Nokia crest on every curler's sweater and paying them for it. His idea continued when Tim Hortons took over. It's a small amount—about $7,000 a team—compared to what we could get if we were allowed to work our own deals, but at least it shows we have some value. This never would have happened without the support I had from the top curlers.

On the ice, we were still rolling. The 1993–94 season was another good one for our team, and as defending Canadian champions, we received a bye directly into the Ontario finals, another progressive move by the OCA, which was really listening to the curlers.

After defeating Axel Larsen in the final we were off to Red Deer for our fourth consecutive Brier. It was quite an accomplishment. We were the first team to win four consecutive Ontario titles.

Rick Folk, whose team we'd defeated a year ago, was back as well. Folk started off 7–0, and we were 6–1. Only three teams would make the playoffs; the first-place team would have a bye to the final as well as last rock and choice of stones. The game between our team and Folk was tremendous, and close the entire way.

During the contest, a couple of hecklers started to get a little boisterous in the crowd. Heckling is rare in curling. I guess they were folks who'd spent a little too much time in the Patch and had come to watch the last part of the game. I was in the hack getting ready to throw and they yelled things like, "Don't throw it wide," or, "Don't be heavy, Russ." Glenn took it upon himself to deal with them. He turned to the crowd and put his index finger to his lips, politely asking for quiet. The next time he was in the hack, there were fifteen people going "Shhh. Everybody be quiet. It's Glenn's turn." He glared at them, which only delighted them.

Every time Glenn went to throw, more and more people said, "Shhhh." When it came down to my last shot, I had to draw a piece of the button to either win or lose the game, and my rock slid two inches too far, which delighted the biased western crowd who were cheering for the great Rick Folk and Pat Ryan, who'd played for so many years out of Alberta.

After the last shot, I went to the far end, picked up my jacket and started toward the home end. I noticed a scrum of about thirty report-ers. I figured it was Folk talking about his win, but as I got closer, I could see Glenn's head. My first thought was, "Great, he's handling all the media. I can go right to the locker room." I was almost past the scrum when Robin Brown of CBC Radio stopped me.

"Russ, would you care to comment on what happened out there?" she asked.

"Well, I thought the ice had tightened up a bit there and so I gave it just a little extra and it was too much," I answered.

"No, would you care to comment on what happened with your brother?"

"I'll tell you what," I said to her. "You explain to me what you're talking about and I'll see if I can comment on it."

Brown explained that things between Glenn and the crowd reached a climax, and Glenn had given them the finger.

I knew immediately this was going to be an ugly situation. We'd just lost to Folk, our nemesis. Glenn had the crowd on him all game, and then he had to deal with the media. I tried to defuse things; I said the fans were really knowledgeable and it was nice that they were getting into the game. I added that the fans hadn't been that distracting and that Glenn was just trying to help me out.

I went into the locker room and saw that Glenn was still pretty hot. Pete and Wayne didn't give him an inch—they were howling with laughter at the situation. I figured after a cooling off period, everything would blow over.

How wrong I was.

When I went down for breakfast the next morning, I saw Glenn's wife, Judy, reading the paper. She looked at me with a glare that would stop a stampede. Without a word, I knew I'd better read the paper. There in big type was a quote from Glenn: "This is the worst bunch of fans I've ever curled in front of." My comments made it seem as if I was agreeing with the crowd, effectively cutting the legs out from Glenn. And that's the way he took it.

By this point in the week we were all a bit tired and on edge. We went out and lost our next game to Saskatchewan, and Glenn gave us the silent treatment. He didn't talk to us or even accompany us anywhere. We didn't handle it well, either. Wayne was still laughing at Glenn, as only Wayne could do, which was like pouring gas on the fire. Glenn could be bleeding to death and Wayne would find something funny about it—that's just the way he was. It was really the way we all were with each other—we never cut each other any slack.

The next day we were all sitting at a table, having breakfast, and Glenn was still hot. Judy was equally upset.

Poor Glenn had to deal with a lot of reporters that day. The tension didn't enhance our play. The team dynamic was strained, and we weren't very focused. Gradually, the matter became less important, and towards the end of the week, we all realized we had to pay attention to what was happening on the ice. Glenn still seemed a little distant for the rest of the week; he wasn't enjoying himself as he usually did at a Brier.

We managed to finish second in the round robin with a mark of 8–3 and went into the semifinal against Manitoba's Dave Smith. That's when there was another fiasco, thanks to some poor planning from the CCA. Under the rules, Folk had first choice of rocks for the final. He could select any eight rocks from any of the sheets used that week. If he selected red, the winner of the semi would take yellow, and vice versa. After Folk made his selection, Smith would get first choice for the semi, and we'd pick last.

After our last round-robin game we were told the only time we could match rocks was right away, which would make us late for the big closing banquet, a tradition at the Brier. We knew, however, that matching rocks was more important than the dinner.

I called the head official, who was in charge of the arena, and he agreed to have a sheet prepared for us, but when we got to the rink, it was dark and there was no one around to scrape and pebble a sheet of ice. We finally found a CCA official, my old friend Jim Armstrong from BC, who told us to go ahead and throw. I said there was sup- posed to be a sheet of ice prepared for us. If the sheet wasn't prepared, matching rocks would be impossible. Jim managed to find part of the ice crew to get the sheet ready. I asked him if he could tell me what colour Folk's BC team had selected, since they had first choice. Jim said they had elected not to pick.

Folk was paranoid about rocks. If we took yellow in the semifinal and won, he'd take those eight rocks and use them against us. We were still known as the best at matching rocks. I knew that, and so did Folk. Armstrong told us we were paranoid.

I asked the team if they thought we could beat Smith using bad rocks. We knew if we were successful Folk would use those bad rocks against us in the final. We decided against that strategy. The semi was too important. We all found the rocks we wanted to use in the next game.

After we defeated Smith in the semi, Pat Ryan was at the end of the sheet, writing down all eight rock numbers and the order we had thrown them. Folk picked all eight stones we'd used, knowing he had the best eight stones in the building. We had to match another eight.

In the final, Folk's team beat us fair and square. In the fourth end, they had us in trouble, and I elected to try a tough double takeout. It curled more than I thought it would, ticked a guard, and we gave up three. That put us down 4–2. In the next end, I decided to go aggressive, and we played a bad end, allowing them to steal two more. They went on to an 8–5 win.

While it was disappointing to lose, I was still proud of our record. I had been in five Brier finals in nine years. Folk beat us pretty handily in 1994, but we had lost to Lukowich and Peters on the last shot. We were close five of the six times.

Our team was close to running its course. We'd had an amazing run, earned $500,000 in four years and won a Brier and a world championship. We went to a spiel in Calgary late in 1994, and as we were going home, Wayne told me that unless we could get $20,000 in sponsorship money, he was going to leave the team.

He left it at that. Then, in June, I got a call at the golf course, and Wayne said he wanted to buy me lunch. I knew right away that was it. I called Glenn and asked him if he knew anything, but he said no, adding that he thought Wayne would be silly to quit since we were doing so well.

Wayne was really good about it, although I had to laugh because he said he wasn't sure what he was going to do for the next year. I think we all knew he was going to team up with Graeme McCarrel; he'd played with McCarrel in a league in Toronto for about five years, and McCarrel was an exceptional talent. He added Scott Bailey and Ian Tetley to form a solid team.

Wayne told me he'd had enough, that he wanted to skip his own team and that he felt it was time to move on. I was disappointed but I couldn't fault his decision. I'd met him when he was fifteen and I'd seen him grow into one of the best seconds in the world. I think he and Pete and Glenn and I had formed the best team ever.

And then he was gone.

After that sentiment passed, I wondered: what was I going to do now? In a strange way, it was like I was back in the 1970s. Most of my curling had been either in Europe or Western Canada at that time, and I would know about a great second from Saskatchewan or Manitoba, but I wasn't familiar with the top players in Southern Ontario. The competitive circuit in my province had slipped considerably. Many of the big cash events had disappeared as sponsors left. Many of the big events were sponsored by companies that had a curler in a prominent position. The sponsorship was often due to the personal involvement of the president or marketing director rather than because it made good business sense, and when the curler left the company, the sponsorship evaporated. In Ontario, the big events at the Royal Canadian Curling Club and Whitby Curling Club ended. Molson had backed the event at the Royal Canadian Club, while Whitby had Sun Life Insurance as a sponsor. The sponsors were gone and so, too, were the bonspiels.

It made more sense for our team to travel west, where events still attracted big sponsors and large prizes. Curling was much more popular in Western Canada, and large crowds would turn out to watch the big events. It was expensive for us to go there, but the potential payoff was greater.

I was out of touch with curling in my own province. It was almost ironic, considering how I'd started my competitive career, not venturing much outside Midland or Penetanguishene.

While we hunted for Wayne's replacement, our notoriety was translating into more appearances at special events, especially celebrity golf tournaments.

I played a lot of those that summer. One was the Toronto Raptors golf tournament. As my mom would say, things happen for a reason, and she was right. My foursome managed to win the tournament, and after the trophy presentation, my agent, Elliott Kerr, introduced me to his friend Bruce Bowser, the CEO for AMJ Campbell Van Lines. Bruce and I seemed to hit it off immediately, and four days later, Kerr phoned and said he was working on an endorsement deal between AMJ Campbell and Team Howard. It's been one of the best relationships I've ever had, one that exists to this day.

In some ways, it was ironic that my deal was with a moving company because in the next phase of my life, I'd need their services.

WHEN WAYNE LEFT, I knew he would be tough to replace. His talent was extraordinary and the pool of players at his level wasn't that deep. The first year AW—after Wayne—we signed on Ken McDermot as lead and moved Pete to second. Ken was a good player from Brampton who had competed around Ontario for a number of years. He was close in age to Glenn and Pete, but he was coming in to a tough spot and being compared to Wayne. We had a pretty good cashspiel year and we really started to roll during the provincials. We made it right to the final and early in the game had a four-point lead, against, guess who…Ed Werenich. Eddie and his team worked their magic and managed to sneak out a one-point victory with a tough finesse shot in the extra end to finish our season.

It was much the same thing in 1995 when Noel Herron, a former Canadian junior champion from Kingston, replaced McDermot. We qualified for the Provincials, made it through the round robin in first place and received a bye to the final. Eddie had to play Bob Ingram of Ridgetown, a small farming community near Windsor, in the semi. Bob had been around for years and had a good solid team, but a betting man would have put Werenich as his choice to make it to the final. But curling is a slippery game. We sat in the crowd and watched Ingram and his team make everything to defeat Eddie in a close game. Our team felt a little more confident playing Bob and his team, rather than the Werenich squad. That confidence evaporated in a hurry the next day when Ingram stole four on us in the first end of the final. The ice was very straight and Ingram's team could throw bullets. We did a wonderful job of staying composed and working away at the nearly insurmountable lead but lost a tough 8–7 decision, and Ingram was off to the Brier.

The Ingram victory ended an incredible twelve-year run for our team and Werenich's. The Wrench's team won Ontario four times and my teams won it seven times. From 1980 to 1997, I won the province eight times, and Eddie won it seven.

Neither McDermot nor Herron provided the perfect fit, so in 1996 I was still looking for a replacement for Wayne. For two seasons, Pete had played second, but he wasn't as well suited for that position as he was lead. Pete was an incredible lead, and Glenn was the best vice in the world. We just needed that world-class second again.

I got a call from Phil Loevenmark, a talented player from North Bay. He asked if I was looking for a player, and I thought I'd finally solved my problem. Phil was a second, and a good one.

Phil had played most of his career with Scott Patterson, another good player from Northern Ontario. The two had played third and skip for Northern Ontario in a couple of Briers and played very well. So closely knit were the two that when Phil told Scott he was leaving, Scott tried to follow. He called me and asked if I wanted a package deal.

I wasn't sure what to do. If I just took Phil, he wouldn't have anyone to practice with up north. Putting Scott on the team meant those two could practice and travel together. It seemed to make sense, so I parted ways with Pete, a terribly difficult decision for me to make. Sometimes, however, decisions about team lineups have to be made at the expense of friendships.

Playing with Phil and Scott, we had a good year on the cash circuit and managed to come third at the provincial playdowns, not exactly what we had hoped for, but a good year all the same.

There was one more carrot that year, a chance at the Olympic Trials, which would determine Canada's representative at the 1998 Games in Nagano.

Curling would debut as a full-medal sport, and I was anxious to try to be Canada's team. I was forty-two, and, this was probably my first and only chance to get to the Winter Olympics. Or so I thought.

The CCA had set up the Trials, a system of qualifying so that ten teams that would play down in a Brier-like format. The winner would go to the Olympics in Japan. There were different ways to get to the Trials, but we were quickly running out of opportunities. By the start of November, we were down to our last two chances. Our second-last chance was to win a big sixty-four-team event in Halifax, which the CCA had designated as a qualifier. The final Olympic Trials spot was awarded to the winner of the Players Championship, the grand finale of the World Curling Tour. The Tour was still a fledgling operation, but the Players Championship was one of the most competitive events of the year and offered one of the biggest purses, as well. All the best teams would be there, meaning the winner would have earned the title and the Trials berth.

In Halifax, we won a hard-fought battle against Pat Ryan in a quarterfinal game. We met up with Ed Werenich in the semifinal. That was a huge game. Both Werenich and I thought the two teams on the other side of the draw were beatable; the key was going to be winning the semi. The winner of our game would likely be off to the Trials. In a close match, we lost to Eddie, who managed to win the final, and we were down to one life, the Players Championship.

When that event rolled around in April, we weren't sharp. We suffered two losses in our first four games and were on the verge of being eliminated. We'd have to rattle off six in a row against increasingly tough competition to win, starting Saturday morning at 9:00.

Scott and Phil must have felt our chances were beyond hope because they disappeared into the night Friday. The next morning, ready to head to the club, Glenn and I knocked on their door, but there was no answer. We pounded a little more and finally Phil came to the door, looking somewhat worse for wear. Scott was asleep in the bed, still wearing his boots from the previous night's adventure. The two weren't exactly game ready, and it looked as if they'd enjoyed the night and most of the early morning, too.

We raced to the club and arrived just in time to miss our practice. In the first end, Scott and Phil—to no one's surprise—didn't make many shots, and we were in trouble. Glenn had a chance to correct things with his second shot. Halfway down the ice, it was right on target and that was about the point where the boys got tangled up and burned the rock. Looking back on it now, I can laugh, but I wasn't chuckling much then. I was livid. That was my last chance at getting to the Olympics, and we were not making it easy on ourselves.

Thankfully, our opposition wasn't sharp that day either, and somehow we managed to beat them. We continued on, rolling through teams, and eventually got past Saskatchewan's Randy Woytowich in the final to earn our place at the Trials.

At the end of the 1996–97 season, we parted ways with Phil and Scott as a regular team although we were still committed to playing together in the Trials. I managed to convince Pete to return to the lineup, and we added Steve Small, another former Canadian junior champion who had played around Ontario for a few years. He was a solid curler, but it didn't prove to be the right fit for our team.

We played the early part of the season and then briefly separated with Pete and Steve to play in the Trials in Brandon, Manitoba, in December with Phil and Scott. The Trials were a new experience for all the teams competing. Although it was set up like a Brier, it was far tougher. The field wasn't based on regional breakdown like the Brier. There were no provincial champions—just ten very good curling teams. Although we played well, it was clear we weren't prepared to take on this field. All the other teams had been playing together all year and were in a groove. We were playing together for the first time since winning the Trials spot in April, and it showed. We ended up at 3–6 and were never a threat. My Olympic dream was over.

Glenn and I continued on with Pete and Steve, and qualified for the Provincials. We ended up third that year. Not long after the 1997–98 season ended, we parted ways with Steve. As it had been with McDermot and Herron, it was tough to tell Small we were moving in another direction. It was always difficult to split with players; they were all good people. I tried to break the news in a nice way, sort of an anti-Donald Trump "You're Fired." We needed something different, and that came out of left field when I got a call from Neil Harrison asking if I was looking for a lead. He was probably the best lead to ever play the game, and I was floored. He'd played with Ed Werenich as part of the Dream Team when they won the Brier and World Championship, and had been to a number of Briers after that. With him and Pete and Glenn, I would have a magical team. I was excited again and with good reason. But that was about all that I was excited about. Life outside of curling was not so rosy. I had left Brooklea following the 1997 golf season and was earning a living in 1998 by teaching at a driving range in Midland. It wasn't exactly the ideal situation.

Leaving Brooklea was a hard decision, but I had little choice. I had worked at Brooklea since 1980, becoming the head pro at age twenty-three and then slowly helping build the golf business. By the early 1990s my pro shop business and the golf course were far more successful, thanks to a lot of hard work by the owner, Mike Sherloski, myself and the other staff. It was a real team effort, and I was proud of where we had brought the course. Unfortunately, in that era owners were taking back all their profit centres and reducing pros' wages, putting them on straight salary. I'd be lying if I said I didn't feel a bit like the rug was pulled out from under my feet. I worked hard to grow the golf course as a business, then lost the ability to generate income through shop sales and golf lessons. The cut to my income—about $40,000—was drastic. Financially, I had no choice but to move on.

Finding a job wasn't going to be easy. I'd been looking but my past was catching up with me. I was forty-one, and all the prospective employers wanted a pro with the CPGA designation, which I had never acquired. I'd apply for jobs, they'd be all excited because of my notoriety through curling and because of my experience, but when they found out I didn't have the CPGA designation, it would end right there.

I contacted the CPGA and looked into getting some sort of grandfather exemption (I had apprenticed for seven years under a CPGA pro), but was told that I'd have to start from step one. I would be a trainee for seven long years.

I toiled away that summer at a driving range up the road, teaching many of the clients from Brooklea who came to me for lessons. The owner of the range, John Webber, thought I would help draw people to the facility, and he also knew that having a good teacher might mean golfers would hit more balls. He even allowed me to put my old stock from Brooklea in his pro shop, which helped bring in some money. I enjoyed teaching, but it was a steep drop in income and resulted in a lot of belt-tightening; we had to watch every penny. My curling teams were also winning less, which didn't help. We'd gone from earning $100,000 a year, when I was with Wayne and Pete, to $50,000 a year. I never counted on that money, as I never knew if I'd win anything, but when we picked up a nice cheque, it certainly made life easier.

As my mother would say, things happen for a reason, and the teaching job gave me a more flexible schedule, which allowed me to travel to some of the celebrity golf tournaments around the country. Before, I had to turn these down because of work commitments. One tournament was in Toronto, where I played with my good friend and the sponsor of my curling team, Bruce Bowser of AMJ Campbell Van Lines.

As the round went along, I told Bowser of my situation, and he asked what I was going to do. I said I was hoping to land a head pro job. I'd been to a couple of interviews at courses in Muskoka, but so far nothing had panned out. Bowser asked if I would consider moving Down East; he had a friend who was building a course near Halifax. One phone call later I was on the interview list. As only he could do, Bruce arranged for Wendy and I to fly to Nova Scotia the next week, when he was opening his company's new office in Dartmouth. So off we went, with rower Silken Laumann and Michael Smith, the decathlete. The three of us took part in the ribbon-cutting ceremonies, and Wendy and I checked out the eastern hospitality and the possibilities of a job. We loved our visit, the hospitality was infectious, and it was an area that would meet the needs of our young family.

Bruce tipped me off that another course near Peggy's Cove was looking for a pro, and I went down to check it out. The manager was a big curling fan and was impressed that I was willing to move to Nova Scotia. He verbally offered me the job of head professional. He wasn't at all worried about my lack of a CPGA designation. It was a relief to know that I could work in my desired profession again. But a week later, I followed up with the manager to see how my job opportunity was shaping up. To my dismay the man who offered me the job no longer had a job of his own—he had been let go. My opportunity was gone.

The celebrity tournaments continued. I received an invitation to an event in Digby a month later. This event was famous and used to be sponsored by Canadian Airlines. I had been asked to play in the event for years, and had been told by many celebrities that it was the best event they had ever been in. After a great day on the golf course, I met up with a fellow named David Murray. After a few beers, David told me all about this exciting new golf course that was being built in Moncton, New Brunswick. "It's going to be a world-class golf course," he said.

With enough help from Labatt, I was able to counter, "Do you need a world-class golf pro?" Murray had heard that I was willing to move east and asked if I would consider Moncton. He told me all about the new place, that it was to be designed by Rees Jones, a famous American golf-course designer, and that it had a large real-estate component. It was called Royal Oaks Golf Estates and sounded like a dream come true.

About two weeks later I was on a plane to Moncton to play in a pro–am event alongside a Canadian Tour tournament. The night before the event, I met Ron Gogeun, the principle behind Royal Oaks Golf Estates, at a reception at his house. Two weeks earlier, Goguen had run a charity event that had raised $100,000 for minor football in Greater Moncton. He flew in some of the biggest names in NFL and CFL history. All the greats had signed a football for Goguen, and at the party David suggested I sign the football. Ron turned to David and said: "Why would he sign it?" That should have been my clue that he didn't follow curling. I still had a lot of work to do to impress him. My fears were reinforced the next morning when Ron's chauffeur drove right by my hotel and left me stranded. By the time I grabbed a cab and found the club, it was three minutes before the tee-off. I was told that I wasn't playing as part of the scramble team, I was playing against the top Canadian Tour pros. As usual, I slashed my way around, hitting my customary seven greens in regulation and shooting a 71. Ron was impressed.

The next morning he called me into his office and gave me a choice: head pro or director of golf. I was no fool, director of golf sounded more lucrative. He told me he'd be in Toronto a week later and asked if we could meet to finalize matters.

I talked to Wendy but there really wasn't much of a choice to make. I was earning peanuts teaching at the driving range, and Wendy had left her job at the hospital in 1993 to work with me in the golf business, so our income was not great. We had an opportunity to start over in a new city, and after a bit of discussion, we made our decision.

I met Ron on a Tuesday night in August at the Royal York Hotel, and two hours later, I was on board. Wednesday we told our families about the opportunity. Steven was about to enter Grade 9 and Ashley Grade 4. School was starting in a week, and we decided it would be best to have both kids start at their new schools on the first day back after summer break. Four days later, AMJ had us packed up, and the Howard family was in the car, starting the twenty-hour drive to Moncton.

Emotionally, the relocation was difficult. Moving was tough for the children, and Wendy and I had lived in Midland most of our lives, with both sets of parents. The children were very close to their grandparents, they had many friends, and moving was quite a shock to them. With the promise of a dog at the other end of the trip, we managed to get them in the car. We talked at length about our need to stick together throughout the move, that it would be a team effort for the family. Even with a bright future ahead of us, Wendy still cried every hour on the hour during the trip east.

I continued to curl with Glenn, Pete and Neil, making the commute from a little farther east to the big spiels we had put in our itinerary. It was worth the extra travelling. We curled in six events and won five of them, including two that Wild Bill Hunter, a noted Saskatchewan entrepreneur, had created with first prizes of $40,000 each. By the end of the year we had won the money title by a wide margin and set a new single-season record with $142,000 in earnings.

But that would be as far as we'd go. Because I had moved to New Brunswick before September first, I was ineligible to curl in the Ontario playdowns. (Each province has residency rules.) Ontario was out, and I had no inclination to play in New Brunswick. I was busy with the new job, and playing with the Ontario-based team was taking a lot of time.

But the New Brunswick curlers found me. Right after signing on with Royal Oaks, Goguen said he wanted me in Moncton as soon as possible: there was a huge press conference to welcome Rees Jones. Jones was the son of another famed course designer, Robert Trent Jones. He had made his name as the person who remodelled courses for the U.S. Open. He'd also designed courses all over the world. This was Rees Jones's first design in Canada. Goguen elected to surprise the reporters by announcing me as director of golf at the same press conference. The next morning the newspapers carried several articles about me and my move to Moncton, which had created quite a stir in the community. Goguen was quite impressed with the publicity.

That morning the phones started to ring. The first call was from Jack MacDuff, the legendary Newfoundland curler who was living in Moncton. (Jack had won Newfoundland's only Brier in 1976 with Toby McDonald at vice, and thirty years later Toby became the coach of our Olympic Team.) Jack welcomed me to the province and kindly offered to give me the lowdown on the competitive curlers in New Brunswick. The first name he gave me was Grant Odishaw. Over a beer, Grant asked me to curl in the regular men's league on Tuesday nights, with no strings attached in regard to playdowns or anything competitive. He thought it might be a good way for me to get acclimatized to Moncton's curling scene. He was trying to help me find three players I would be comfortable with. I decided Grant would be one of those players.

Grant already had a competitive team, comprised of Wayne Tallon (the ex-Ontario curler who I'd beat in the final of the 1986 Ontario playdowns), Rick Perron and Jeff Lacey. They were highly ranked in the province. I played with him for a few months, and Grant asked if I'd consider joining them and playing with a five-man rotation; players would take turns sitting out. After a few games, however, the other four decided I would skip all the games and they would rotate in and out of the lineup.

Because I was still playing with Glenn on our competitive team in the cash events, I could find time to fit in only two small bonspiels with the New Brunswick team. At one point, at a bonspiel in Florenceville, I played with Glenn and Pete and Neil against Grant and my New Brunswick team.

Our five-man rink found our game in time for the 1999 playdown. The playdown system in New Brunswick was new to me. It wasn't any easier to win the province than in Ontario, but it was easier to get to the provincial finals. The zone playdowns were thirty-two-team triple-knockout competitions that led to an eight-team provincial final; the top three teams went into the playoffs. I'm not sure either the

Ontario or New Brunswick system is easy. Of course, getting to the Brier shouldn't be a simple task.

We ended up winning the province. It was Wayne Tallon's first trip to the Brier, and he said that since I'd cost him a chance to go in '86 by beating him in the Ontario final, it was fitting I helped him finally get there.

Our five-player rotation helped us at the provincials and the Brier; during such gruelling events, it was nice to have a break once in a while. Too many people decide they must always be the skip, or the third, which spoils many a good team. It was the unselfish spirit of my four teammates that made this team work.

For this Brier, the CCA instituted a new playoff procedure, called the "page playoff." Four teams (instead of the traditional three) advanced past the round robin. The first-place finisher played the second-place finisher; the winner moved to the final. The third- and fourth-place teams played each other; the loser was eliminated, and the winner moved to the semifinal against the loser of the first-place, second-place game. It was complicated, but it created an additional playoff berth. We made it into a tiebreaker and beat Paul Flemming of Nova Scotia, then lost to Saskatchewan's Gerald Shymko in the page playoff three-vs-four game.

After that year, Jeff quit the team, and I couldn't blame him. Although our rotation was supposed to be equitable, he wasn't getting the games he deserved. I was sad to see him go, but relieved to be playing on a four-man team.

In 2000, I was asked to be the honorary Chairperson of the Canadian Junior Championship, which was being held at our Beausejour Curling Club in Moncton, New Brunswick.

As Chairperson, I gave a speech on the Wednesday evening of the event, and as fans, my family and I watched as many games as we could.

Brad Gushue's talented young team from the Rock was playing in the Championship final against British Columbia. Although I didn't know the boys, I was very impressed with their performance throughout the week. As fate would have it, Brad had to draw a piece of the 8 foot to win the Canadian Championship. Brad's rock came up short, and British Columbia won the Championship.

As I filed out of the building with Wendy, I could see Brad slump over on the side of the sheet in tears. I watched, who I assumed was his mother, come over to comfort him, but to no avail. I felt compelled to talk to him. Since I had survived four Brier Final losses, I was probably the most qualified in the building to give him a pep talk. As I approached Brad, he recognized me, and I simply said to him "Congratulations on a great week." which didn't seem to console him at all! I then asked him how he felt he had thrown his last shot. He responded with "I thought I threw OK and our split time was great." I responded with "then there's nothing to worry about." I went on to explain to Brad that as long as he feels he threw the rock well, that's the best he can do. I then said my mother always told me that things happen for a reason, and as tough as this loss feels, there must be something bigger and better in the future for this team.

Who would have believed that six years later I would be part of that bigger and better future.

Later in 2000, we had a chance to get a few games together. We played great all through the playdowns, finished first in the round robin, then won our final game against Jim Sullivan. We got to the Brier and continued to roll. The boys from Down East really believed in me, and that gave me a tremendous amount of confidence—the way I felt in my college days. Our team didn't have the marquee names I had curled with, but we bonded and became great friends. It was probably the most comfortable I felt as a competitor, and I had my best Brier. We won seven in a row in the middle of the week and played Quebec's François Roberge in the semifinal.

It was a well curled game, and both teams were very aggressive. In the sixth end, I gave Wayne negative ice—where a bad slope in the ice causes the stone to move opposite to normal—on an out-turn hit. The ice was particularly straight in that spot, and Wayne could throw the rock hard. We needed to hit the inside of the stone, so two inches of negative ice made sense. But when Wayne looked at the broom he felt it was the proper ice for an inturn; he threw a shot that over-curled and jammed out our shot rock. What looked like a peel weight double to sit three suddenly became a draw against five on my last rock. We managed to survive that scare but tormented the life out of Wayne by calling him "Wrong-Turn Tallon."

We defeated Quebec and entered the Brier final—uncharted territory for this team. We had won nine games, a record for New Brunswick at a Brier. We wanted to make it one more.

In the final against BC's Greg McAuley, both teams played strong games. The turning point came in the eighth end. Our team was leading by a single point. I faced two BC stones, but there wasn't an opportunity for a double, so I played a hit and roll fully buried behind a centre guard. McAuley made a delicate come-around tap for two points, which appeared to be narrow when he let it go. I thought there was a good chance he was going to wreck on the guard. The front end from BC swept it from one end to the other, and I swear it went through the edge of the guard, making the shot perfectly for two points. We gambled in nine, and McAuley stole three to end our hopes of New Brunswick's first Brier title.

Although we didn't win the Canadian title, the city of Greater Moncton treated us as champions. We had a huge reception at the Moncton City Hall, which poor Wayne, who lived in St. Stephen, had to travel four hours through a snowstorm to attend. He showed up a few minutes late, and I covered for him by saying he would have been fine timewise but he made a "wrong turn" in Sussex!

It's funny how experience helped me put my losses in perspective. My first Brier loss in 1986 was devastating. In 1992, it was difficult but easier to accept. My defeat in 1994 was much easier to swallow because we were two-time world champions. In 2000, we were the toast of the town because we finished with the best record in New Brunswick history. When I left Ontario for my new job in New Brunswick, I thought my curling career was over. So to me, this was all gravy.

We climbed the mountain again in 2001 and made it all the way to the provincial final. I made a tough double in the tenth end to send our sudden-death game with Jim Sullivan into an extra end. Jim made a difficult takeout in the extra end to win.

There was a silver lining to this runner-up finish. I was asked to serve as a commentator for TSN at the Brier. I hesitated because I was still stinging from the loss at the provincial final. Then I thought this was an indication that people were telling me I should start looking for a post-curling position—so I accepted. That Brier week was an unbelievable experience. TSN was an amazing organization, and I was treated exceptionally well in my rookie attempt at colour commentary. John Wells and I did all the morning draws at the Brier so Ray Turnbull could get his beauty sleep.

Although we missed the Brier in 2001, my New Brunswick team was compensated with a trip to the Olympic Trials. In 2000, we once again came down to our last chance to qualify—the Players Championship in Calgary. We fought our way into the playoff and made it to the semifinal, where we were up against an old friend, Pete Corner. In a good game, we ended up coming out on top, and as we shook hands with Pete's team, we looked over and saw Kevin Martin, who had already earned a Trials spot and would win the Trials, then a silver medal at the Olympics. Kevin won his semi, so the qualifying berth was ours. We were so excited we promptly went out and lost the final.

We had the whole summer to prepare for the Trials, but early in the fall of 2001, we were dealt a sudden change. On the way home from a small spiel in Nova Scotia (which we won), Rick Perron was obviously in pain. He had bad knees and had been hurting a great deal throughout the spiel. In the car he said he wasn't sure how much longer he could keep playing. A week or so later, he showed up at my office and let me know he was quitting. Rick was a team player and worried that his wonky knees would let the team down at the Olympic Trials.

We began to hunt for a replacement for the Trials, and Grant suggested my brother Glenn. My brain was thinking we needed a

New Brunswick curler, but there were no geographical restrictions for the Trials. I called Glenn and he agreed to be our fourth. With Grant at lead, James Gratton second; and Glenn, I thought we'd have a chance. The thought of qualifying for the Olympics with my brother was a thrill.

My hunch about Glenn was right. In the first game at the Trials in Regina, he curled 100 per cent, and we got sharper and sharper as a team, winning our first three. Our fourth game was against John Morris, one of the best young skips in the game. We were on the wrong side of the inch for most of the contest, and after a poor ninth end we found ourselves three down with the hammer. We had our two corner guards up but needed some help. With one rock partially buried, Morris elected to peel out our rock in the rings. Their rock came fast but only hit the thinnest sliver of our stone, moving it about an inch sideways. It was still in the rings, now completely buried behind the guard. Glenn buried another one around the same guard and we were sitting two. Morris tried to run the guard back onto our two stones in the house. His shot hit the guard, but the rock missed our two counters. We were still sitting two buried. Glenn's next shot came down a hair heavy, and Grant and James instinctively relayed the message; we changed the call and swept it enough to bury it behind one of the stones in the house. We were sitting three, all behind cover. Morris played the run back again, but his luck continued to be all bad. He hit the guard but drove it through a small hole between our three stones, missing everything. I threw a perfect guard on the three rocks, and John, frustrated beyond belief, had no choice but to throw the freeze against the three buried rocks. It was a really tough shot, but John threw a good one, which just bumped the back rock a couple of inches.

We had a choice to make. We could hit Morris's stone dead-on with normal takeout, which was partially buried, then jam out our back rock, score three and hope to steal the extra end. Or we could play soft weight and try to squeeze the Morris rock out without touching any of ours and play to score four. Glenn and I looked at each other and agreed that since we had come this far, we should go for the win.

As I released the rock, I thought the weight was close to being right, but it started to bend early. The boys swept as hard as they possibly could. As the rock neared the guard, Glenn was on his stomach, calling the sweeping through the handle of the Morris rock. To our amazement the sweeping was enough: the stone barely passed the front guard, then tapped the Morris rock just enough to sit four and win our fourth consecutive game. The dream was alive, and our momentum was building. With a 4–0 start we were thinking playoff spot.

But we hit a speed bump and lost a great game to Kevin Martin. Then we lost another to Jeff Stoughton, when a crucial rock of Glenn's caught some debris. A third defeat came when Bert Gretzinger pulled off a truly remarkable shot to beat us. All of a sudden we were playing Randy Ferbey to stay in the event. We gave up a four early, and that was it. I was probably too old to think about qualifying for the 2006 Olympics. My chances of going to the Olympics were done.

The New Brunswick team regrouped a year later to go to the 2002 Brier in Calgary, and we started on the right note, beating Ferbey 10–2 in the opening round. We made it to the playoffs but couldn't go all the way. In the first page playoff game, I threw one of my best games against Scott Bitz of Saskatchewan (I was scored at ninety-nine per cent). I had to make my last shot to win, but I thought if we continued to play like that we might have a chance. Unfortunately, Ontario's John Morris took us out in the semifinal 9–5 to end our dream short one more time.

In 2003 we went to the Brier, this time in Halifax. It was my twelfth trip to the Canadian men's championship, but the first time I'd been to a Brier in Eastern Canada. I didn't arrive in the best of mental states. Things at work were not going well. Then an incident in our round-robin game against Mark Dacey of Nova Scotia set me off. In the last end, tied coming home, we put up a centre guard, and they elected to try to split it. They pushed both stones far to the side, almost but not all the way out of play. When their rock hit ours, I started sweeping it, knowing that if I could get it to hit the boards, I'd get to replace it because of the free guard zone rule. I swept and swept and swept, and just as it was coming to a rest, it spun and grazed the foam barrier at the sideline.

I turned to Dacey and said it hit the boards, and he said fine. Then the Nova Scotia third, Bruce Lohnes, disagreed with my call. I was about ninety-nine per cent certain it had hit; I wasn't sure Bruce could have seen it, because he'd been at the other end. Lohnes asked for an official to be called, but we couldn't find one. It was the tenth end in a tie game, and our official who was supposed to be stationed behind the sheet was missing.

An official finally arrived and determined the rock had not hit the wall. I'm not sure what he based his decision on. In my opinion, it was a bad call that got me so upset, I wasn't able to concentrate. Not surprisingly, we lost the game, falling to 0–2. As the week went on, we continued to struggle. By midweek, we were 2–4. As I was watching the opposition warm up before game seven Ray Turnbull came up and put his arm around me.

"What's the matter Russ?" he asked.

"Oh, we're just not playing that well, not getting any breaks," I said.

"No, that's not what I mean. You're not yourself; there's something wrong. You're not confident. The boys are calling the shots for you. That's not the Russ Howard I know. I'm here to give you a kick in the arse."

Ray didn't realize the culmination of events that had led me to this low point. My bad attitude at that Brier was in large part a result of my day job. At first, it had seemed like a dream. Royal Oaks was a world-class facility, designed by a top golf-course architect. I started in September 1998 as head of golf operations, but the course wouldn't open until 2000. For the first year I sold the real estate that surrounded the golf course. I sold building lots, town homes and condominiums. At first, I didn't mind doing it. In fact, I enjoyed it, and I did quite well. In year two, 1999, I juggled two positions, director of sales and director of golf. In 2000, the course was playable, and I was in my element, running the golf side of the business. At that time, real estate sales slowed down dramatically, so the decision was made that I would wear both hats again, the thinking being that I could get the sales moving again.

My salary moved more and more into commission sales from the real estate side. But sales were slow. In 2001 and 2002, I slowly bled to death financially. Thankfully, in 2002 Wendy's career in real estate was taking off as she developed a good reputation in the city.

The years 2001 and 2002 were difficult for us as a family. Wendy's dad and my father suffered heart attacks. Both survived, but in early 2002 my dad was diagnosed with cancer, and Wendy's father was told he had pulmonary fibrosis.

Both of them passed away in 2002, within three months of each other, and their deaths took a huge toll on our family. I had known Wendy's parents all of my life, and was very close to them both. Wendy and I surely couldn't have enjoyed all the Briers, world championships and trips to Europe and Japan together if they hadn't been there to look after our children.

Over the years, my mom and dad had followed Glenn and me across the country as we curled, and I'm sure Dad was my biggest fan. He was so proud of Glenn and I. After we beat Werenich to win an Ontario title one year, he came into the locker room with tears in his eyes to tell me how happy he was for me. Of course, he followed that up with, "What happened to that shot in the fifth end?" That was my dad. Although he never said anything, I know he was saddened by our move to New Brunswick. It was not that he wasn't happy for us getting a fresh start, but that we were now so far away and he'd see us less. When he passed away, it left me with a big hole in my heart.

After Ray's pep talk at the Halifax Brier, we rattled off four straight victories. One more victory in the final round-robin game would take us to the playoffs; it would also be the one-hundredth Brier game I had won. That game was coincidentally against Ontario, and it came down to a delicate board weight takeout in a spot we hadn't played. It wasn't the toughest shot in the world, but I wasn't sure where to put the broom. I can remember making the hit and my kids in the crowd raising a sign with "100" boldly displayed. I pointed toward heaven, and my thoughts went to my dad. He must have known the ice for that last shot.

I'm extremely proud of that record of 100 wins especially when I look at marks of the greats such as Ernie Richardson (45), Ed Werenich (55) and Bernie Sparkes (43).

We were in the playoffs, but we came up short in the page playoff game against Dacey.

I had another off-ice dilemma during this period. One day in 2001, I got a call from Chad McMullen, a competitive curler who stopped playing to help the powerful International Management Group (IMG) start up a curling division. He told me the company wanted to start the Grand Slam, a series of four events that would be played by the top twenty teams in the country. Each event would have a purse of $100,000. They wanted a commitment from the skips that they'd play all four events.

I was intrigued. The only information, though, was that there would be four new, rich bonspiels. I said I couldn't commit my team to all four without some discussion, but I would love to play a couple. Chad told me I was one of the top names in the game, and they wanted me to be there, especially as a draw for television. I ran it by the boys, and they were a little worried about the expenses: flights, accommodations, meals and time off work. There was no guarantee we'd win anything. Then, while I was talking with my team, I heard that IMG had scheduled the events opposite the playdowns for the Brier. We could play one or the other, but not both. IMG was trying to draw a line in the sand.

I called Chad and he confirmed that the Grand Slam would happen at the same time as the Brier playdowns. If all the top curlers went to the Grand Slam, it would grow, and television ratings would rise, meaning bigger purses. But it was being done at the expense of the Brier. The roots of this went back to my old fight to wear sponsor logos at the national championship. The curlers felt they weren't getting proper compensation for playing in the Brier, an event that was earning profits in the millions. Instead of going after the CCA to change the rules, they were going after the biggest event in curling.

That didn't sit well with me, despite numerous appeals from McMullen. Soon the lobby group grew. My brother called to try to get me to come on board; then Wayne Middaugh called, then Kevin Martin. It became a bad situation and I felt really stuck. I wanted to help people put more money into curling and make more big events, but I couldn't see doing it at the expense of the Brier.

As well, my old agent, Randy Paul, was working with IMG, and he told me that the company didn't do anything unless there was a way to make money. It was clear to me they weren't in this because they loved curling, not that there was anything wrong with that. The story I was being told had lots of red flags. I was also worried about the effect of taking the top twenty teams out of the Brier. If two unknowns made it to the final, what would happen to the television ratings and the ticket sales? Would this help the game? All the guys who were standing against the Brier had become household names by playing in it. Now they were ready to boycott it.

Some curlers hurled insults at me in the press. A year later, when I was playing in a Grand Slam in Gander, a reporter named Robin Short from the *St. John's Telegram* wrote a scathing article about me, saying I had screwed my fellow curlers by not standing beside them, and that I was trying to grab a portion of the riches they'd created. I was outraged. I told the organizers I wanted a word with the reporter at the end of the next game. I took Short into the locker room and tore a strip off of him. He listened to my logic, realized there was more than one side to the story and printed a follow-up story.

The incident split the curlers into two camps. Teams like Martin, Stoughton, Middaugh and my brother Glenn were on one side, and Ferbey, Hemmings, Morris, Gushue, and I were on the other side.

Kevin Albrecht, the head of IMG Canada, contacted me and asked me what they had to do to get me to play the Grand Slams. I said there was nothing; it was a financial problem for our team. To commit to four events in Western Canada was going to set us back roughly $20,000. He said he could get me free entries, if that would help. I said I would try to get to two of the events to show our support for the Players' Association, but I reiterated that I was not going to boycott the Brier.

After I told Albrecht I would play only two events, I got a letter telling me I was suspended from the Grand Slams for two years. The letter came after I had booked flights and reserved hotels in Gander for the first of the events. I was trying to appease Albrecht and show some support for the cause and now I was getting stabbed in the back. I couldn't understand the logic behind this move. But it solved my scheduling problem; I entered the Brier playdowns.

The Grand Slam events were good and still are, but the only truly big event in curling is still the Brier. The boycott ended after two years, when the CCA and the Tour agreed to meet and work out their differences. All the teams that supported the boycott returned to the playdowns. And Brier curlers entered the Grand Slams, making them stronger events as well. While it was an ugly battle and no one really won in the end, the fight did a lot for curling in many ways, such as better organizing the players as a group. I felt proud that I took my stand. Both the Brier and the four Grand Slam events are doing well and guess what? They don't conflict.

With all this happening and our family debts mounting, the stress became too much. I ended up in the hospital with chest pains. My job at Royal Oaks had started out as a great opportunity, and I never for a minute regretted leaving Ontario for New Brunswick, but the job I had dreamed about wasn't there anymore. The vision of the course had changed, and it wasn't for me. I left Royal Oaks on great terms:

Goguen offered me a lifetime membership. Our family was settled in Moncton, and our options did not include relocating again.

Wendy had the presence of mind to get me to take the courses for my real-estate license, and, to the shock of my teachers, I passed on the first try! In the spring of 2003, I left Royal Oaks and joined Wendy at Re/Max Quality Real Estate in Moncton. We formed Team Howard—the real estate version.

We went to the Brier in 2004 in Saskatoon and it was my thirteenth trip, a record—one more than the legendary Bernie Sparkes. I'm especially proud of this mark considering all the great players who have competed in this event. We played well enough to make it as far as the tiebreakers. We had been playing well near the end of the round robin but lost in an extra end to Jay Peachey of BC. We faced him again in the tiebreaker, when he made everything and deserved to win.

I thought my curling career was over when I left my Ontario team in 1998 to focus on getting my career on track, but I managed a pretty good record in my years in New Brunswick. I've been part of teams that won five provincial championships and two mixed provincial titles. The latter two crowns came in 1999 and 2000, when Wendy elected to play. I had a wonderful time watching her in her first national championship. I could see the joy and excitement on her face. It was the excitement that kept me in this wonderful sport for such a long time. We finished 7–4 in both events, and once she was a two-time provincial champion, Wendy decided to retire.

Me and the Boys

11

BECAUSE I WAS A CURLER and a curling fan, I knew Toby McDonald. He had been third on Jack MacDuff's 1976 Brier-winning team from Newfoundland, the only rink from that province to win the national championship. Their story was one of the great ones in Brier history, and when I moved to New Brunswick—a province that has never won the big one—I heard more and more about MacDuff's big win, the story of the long shot coming in and defying the odds. The rink had come from nowhere to upset some of the top teams in the land, win the Brier and, in the process, capture the hearts of all in their home province. As I would come to learn, Newfoundlanders love to see their own do well; they get behind each other like no one else.

The MacDuff win was certainly a Newfoundland story, but it was also one for all of Atlantic Canada. MacDuff lived in Moncton, which added to the number of times the story was recounted.

My only face-to-face meeting with Toby McDonald had been in 1987, when my team flew to Newfoundland for a big cashspiel and he was our driver. From the time he dropped us off at the airport after that spiel until the spring of 2005, I didn't talk to him once. But when the phone rang in May, the voice on the other end of the phone sounded like a long-lost friend. "Russ," he boomed down the line from his St. John's office. "Toby McDonald. Do you have a minute?"

McDonald explained that he had taken over as coach of Brad Gushue's team. Gushue had qualified for the Canadian Olympic Curling Trials in Halifax, and they were looking for a fifth man. Each player on the team had been asked to draft a list of six players—three from the Rock and three from the rest of Canada. Most of the teams in the Trials had decided to use a fifth man to fill a void. For instance, Kevin Martin's team had selected Scott Bailey, the lead on Wayne Middaugh's squad. Martin knew his weakness was his lead, Don Bartlett, who had a bad back and might be felled at any point in the competition. Martin needed to know he could replace Bartlett.

Gushue's team realized its weakness was experience, or rather lack thereof. Brad had been to a number of Canadian junior champion-ships, winning one and topping it off with a world junior title. He'd also played in the Brier. But to win an event like the Olympic Trials was a large step. The team wanted to pull out all the stops, to give itself a chance. Part of their plan included me.

"You're number one on everyone's list," McDonald said. "Would you consider the position?"

I had been planning to watch the curling trials on television. My brother Glenn had made the field of ten teams, and I had entertained thoughts of driving to Halifax to watch him play. I hadn't given com-peting much thought.

The fifth man on a curling team is like the fifth wheel on a car. He doesn't serve much of a purpose, and the only benefit is a great seat to watch the games. Unless someone gets hurt or falls ill, chances of the fifth man throwing a stone in competition are pretty slim. It is almost like being an assistant coach.

I was considered as fifth man because of my knowledge and exper-tise, exactly what the team needed to take on and beat rinks like Martin,

Jeff Stoughton and my brother. I told Toby I needed to know how much time being fifth man would take. I had my curling team to consider. We now had Mark Dobson, an exciting young curler from Saint John; we still had my longtime teammate Grant Odishaw, and for the first time my son, Steven, was on the team: when we went to the Brier in 2004, we asked him to be our fifth player. It was a huge thrill for me.

At the start of every Brier, there is an event called the Hot Shots competition, an individual skills challenge for all the competitors. Top prize is a car. Players are scored on a number of different shots. I thought it would be a great opportunity for Steven to get out and play on Brier ice in front of the crowds, and my back was sore, so he took my spot. And he performed very well. At one point he ticked a guard, so he ended up with a score of zero. I heard what sounded like an elderly woman yell, "That's okay little fella!" Later he swept for Marc Lecocq, the team's second that year, and they nearly won the car.

When we were playing Randy Ferbey from Alberta, their fifth man and coach, Dan Holowaychuk, devised a prank and my son was to be the target. Steven was sitting with Holowaychuk watching our game in the special seating at ice level. Holowaychuk asked Steven if he could see the good-looking young woman in the upper deck in Section H. Steven, age twenty, was quite willing to check out the situation, and Holowaychuk kindly offered his binoculars. When Steven put the binoculars to his eyes, he had no idea the rims were coated with charcoal. I had been around this block a few times, and I could tell by the snickering from the Alberta team that something was up. In the third end, I talked Randy into telling me what they were up to. They were afraid Dad would blow the whistle. "Are you kidding me?" I said. "This is great."

We talked the on-ice cameraman into getting a good close-up of Steven as he took the binoculars away from his eyes. Someone told Steve to look at the large in-arena television, where eleven thousand people were laughing at Raccoon Boy. Welcome to the Brier, son.

Ashley was at the Brier too, during her spring break. And I was honoured with a plaque from the CCA for surpassing the legendary

Bernie Sparkes—it was my thirteenth Brier appearance. I was privileged to wear a Legends jacket with the likes of Ernie and Sam Richardson, Matt Baldwin, Fred Storey, Ron Northcott, Bernie Sparkes, and a few of the young guys like Rick Lang, Don Walchuk, Pat Ryan and Team Ferbey. It was exciting to have my family there to witness this gathering.

On the last Saturday of that Brier, Wendy and I went to the traditional closing banquet in the Brier Patch. Our team had been eliminated, but we felt it was important to be there. The room held five thousand people, and it was wall-to-wall when Wendy and I arrived. As I walked in, I was stopped and asked to sign a few autographs. Then someone said I should be up on the stage because they were doing Russ Howard impersonations. Wendy and I pushed through the crowd and saw a contestant screaming mock sweeping instructions. I peered at the stage. The impersonator was our son, Steven. He thought his mom and dad had gone to bed. With the help of a few beers, he started with a perfect "Hurry Hard" on Day 1, moved to a rough version midway through the week, then ended with a final-weekend, on-his-knees, veins-popping-out-of-his-neck, red-faced scream that only dogs could hear. The place went wild for two reasons. First, Steven was the best impressionist of the evening. The second was that I was now standing a foot and a half behind him, about to tap him on the shoulder. The look on Steve's face was priceless.

Going to the Brier with my son was my No. 1 goal for the season. It was unlikely I could help Brad's team and jump into the playdown schedule with my rink. There was also the matter of work. Our real-estate business was extremely busy, and it wasn't fair to leave Wendy to cover for me weekend after weekend, at work and at home.

I talked things over with Wendy and my team, and I talked to Toby about the time commitments. I had been to all the Olympic Trials, starting with the first in 1987; I could continue my streak and be among the best curlers in the world, an environment I loved. After plenty of thought, I called Toby back and told him I was in.

The Canadian Olympic Curling Trials were possibly the toughest event anywhere in curling. The qualifying process set up by the Canadian Curling Association for the 2005 event made it next to impossible to get in by luck. Teams qualified by winning the Brier or the Canada Cups (big cashspiels run by the CCA) or by finishing at the top of the Canadian Team Ranking System, a points system that tracked results in big events.

Ten of the best teams gathered in Halifax, all hoping for that trip to Torino, Italy. Randy Ferbey was probably the favourite going in, and with good reason. His team was a four-time Brier winner, and Ferbey had six titles. Kevin Martin, Ferbey's nemesis, represented Canada at the 2002 Olympics, losing the gold medal game to Pal Trulsen of Norway. He skipped one of the most profitable teams in curling history. Manitoba's Jeff Stoughton, a Brier and world champion, and Glenn and his Ontario team, were definite contenders. Two Nova Scotia teams were in the running: Mark Dacey from Halifax, who beat Ferbey in the Brier final in 2004, and Bridgewater's Shawn Adams, who lost to Ferbey in 2005. John Morris had a good young team based in Calgary. Pat Ryan, the wily veteran from BC, and Jay Peachey, also from BC, rounded out the field.

Brad's team comprised Brad as skip, Mark Nichols at third, Keith Ryan at second and Jamie Korab at lead. His rink earned its spot in the Trials by winning the Canada Cup East, a significant accomplishment against one of the best fields in Eastern Canada. They also captured the Newfoundland title and earned a spot in the 2005 Brier, where they finished with a 6–5 record. Toby knew the team had a long way to go to win the Trials. Over the summer Toby was blunt with Brad in his assessment: "You can't win the Trials with that team," he told the skip. "You have to make changes."

It was something Brad had trouble accepting, although he knew it was true. A curling team was not like a football or hockey team. Cutting players was done by other players, not by some management type who collected a big salary. A team was a small, tight-knit group. Brad's decision was complicated because the team that had earned the spot in the Trials should probably be the team that played in the Trials. But Toby and Brad agreed to leave no stone unturned in the attempt to win gold. Their decision was to drop Keith Ryan from the rink and bring Mike Adam in.

Those were the four—Gushue, Nichols, Adam and Korab—with whom I would work. I would try to shape their game so they could beat teams like Ferbey, Martin and Stoughton. We arranged a three-day practice session in Saint John in late August, coinciding with a junior curling camp where we were assisting.

The on-ice sessions were thorough. I showed them my drills and suggested that we throw the stopwatches away. Like most young teams, they used a stopwatch to determine the speed of a rock. I taught them how to judge a rock's progress accurately without a watch and they learned very quickly. The boys' deliveries were solid, so we worked on tendencies and idiosyncrasies. They had consistent deliveries, which made it easy to pick up their tendencies. I believed that if a player threw his out-turn three inches wide every time, the skip should accept that and adjust the ice rather than try to change the delivery.

At the first gathering, it was apparent that Brad had high expectations. He was intense and focused during the practice, the other three a little looser. All four could play, of that there was no doubt, but Brad was clearly the leader of the team. He was a driven individual, not only in curling but in his life. He had a tremendous work ethic and when he put his mind to something, there wasn't much that could stop him from getting it done. He was more serious than the others, but could share a laugh too. Mark was a soft-spoken but personable guy and a tremendous team player. On the ice he was pretty quiet, but when asked for his opinion, he was ready to offer it. He was also one of the best hitters I've ever played with. Mike had a great sense of humour and could turn the mood of the team around with one line. He was a great team player. Jamie was the live wire of the group, cracking lines that kept me laughing.

The weekend gave me a chance to see the boys on the ice, and it gave Toby a chance to fill me in on the overall personality of the team and what made each individual tick. It was a good start for the five of us, and we all left in a good frame of mind.

In early September, we met in Moncton. Toby wasn't able to come, and Brad had to pull out when his mom went in for surgery for recently diagnosed bowel cancer. Mark, who had won the Canadian Mixed Championship earlier that year, declined a spot at the World Mixed so he could attend the team practice. To me, this said volumes about this young man's dedication.

Moncton was alive—the Rolling Stones were playing at Magnetic Hill in front of eighty thousand fans. But the boys were there to practice and never considered going to the concert. After practice, I invited them to the house for a beer. Jamie quickly said, "How much beer do you have, boy?" I said we didn't have any but we'd stop at a beer store on the way. Jamie said, "I can do better than that," and he went to the side of the ice and grabbed four six-packs that were chilling for use in the club later. (Note to the Beausejour Club: I replaced the beer two days later.)

Mark, Mike and Jamie were prepared to bond with the old skipper that night. The casual beer I had suggested turned into Mike cooking ribs and steak on the barbecue. They made themselves right at home. At one point Jamie looked around and said: "I can't believe I'm in Russ Howard's house." Later, with a big grin, he said, "I can't believe I'm having a beer with Russ Howard."

I was taken aback by the comments. After all, these three had accomplished a lot in curling. I'd assumed they wouldn't be impressed by my accomplishments. I considered them fellow curlers. They had put me on a bit of a pedestal. Jamie's "can't believe" lines became a running joke throughout our journey. Later that night, the boys, accompanied by my son, Steven, decided to paint the town red. At 3:00 a.m. I opened the door and found Mike and Jamie in the two wicker rocking chairs on the front porch. They had obviously enjoyed their night. Jamie took one look at me and said: "I can't believe Russ Howard came to the door in his underwear."

We were full of optimism and energy when the team left me to start their season. They had an aggressive schedule with a budget of

$56,000 for travel and associated costs. Most of that would be done without me. The first few weeks didn't go so well. They started with two weeks in Norway, where they won a small spiel but didn't do well in the bigger spiel. In their next three spiels, in Canada, they failed to qualify. By the middle of October, the team had yet to earn a dollar in Canada. The alarm bells may not have been ringing but there was certainly some unease among the troops. I agreed to join them at the next event, a Grand Slam in Port Hawkesbury, Nova Scotia, where many of the teams they would face in the Trials would be competing. Toby called and suggested that I be ready to play. This was unexpected. I had assumed Toby and I would watch their games and critique their performance, offering up assistance on strategy and shot selection. But because the team had been struggling, he suggested I play one, maybe two games, thinking I could help out more by being on the ice. We went out for dinner before our opening game against Pal Trulsen, the defending Olympic gold medalist, and I was wondering how we were going to divide five curlers into four spots when Mike blurted, "I'll sit out the game tonight." Just like that, I was in. We agreed that I would throw second stones then call the game, maybe because the other three had seen me sweep. They were taking pity on the old man.

It wasn't a very positive start. In the first end of our first game together, Trulsen stole four. We fought back but lost in the last end. I was certain that would be it for me, so I offered some comments: the boys were missing the soft shots, the quiet-weight hits and the taps. As I gave examples, Brad listened intently. This was exactly what he wanted me for, and he was eating it up.

When I was finished, Gushue nodded, then said the lineup would stay the same for the second game. We won over Markku Uusipaavalniemi. (We faced him again in the gold medal contest.) We won the third contest over Peter Lindholm of Sweden, then lost to Winnipeg's Jeff Stoughton. Before every game, I thought I was going to get the hook, but Brad kept putting me in. When he did make a change, it was to take Jamie out and put Mike in at lead. We lost to Ferbey in the quarterfinals but the team earned $7,000, the first Canadian cheque of the year.

The next week, we played in New York and I was expecting to go back to my role as fifth man, but in the back of my mind, I was excited about how we played in Port Hawkesbury. Obviously Brad was too. He said he'd like me to continue playing. The performance with me on the ice had buoyed his attitude, especially after the poor start with the original lineup. He admitted that the front end had let the team down during the early part of the year and he was hunting for the perfect combination. Even if I didn't become part of the four-player team, he was no longer afraid of an injury or a slump; he knew he had a backup in me.

In New York, the hot hand continued. We won our first five games. I played all five; Mike played only one. We lost in the semifinals and picked up another $7,000.

Our mood improved considerably, and we bonded, thanks to some travel difficulties. We had flown to Toronto to make a connection to New York, but were grounded by bad weather. By seven, our two-o'clock flight hadn't left; we decided to rent a van and drive to New York. On the way back to Toronto, Brad and I had a long talk about the team. Had I seen any weaknesses? I offered what I thought they needed—and what every young team needs—finesse.

We parted ways at the Toronto airport. They were heading to Newfoundland for a few days before travelling to Calgary for a spiel that wasn't on my original itinerary. I left them with some kind parting words: "Hope you fall flat on your face out west," I joked. "Hope you don't qualify."

Actually, I was only half-joking. I could sense something special developing with this team when I was on the ice. But it was an awkward position in which to be. It was their team and I had only been asked to serve as the fifth man. I couldn't pursue anything other than what I'd been offered. They didn't qualify in Calgary, and the temperature got turned up considerably when they came home without a cheque. In the eight spiels before the Olympics, they were 1–5 when it came to cashing a cheque without me, and 2–0 with me. We weren't winning events but we were competitive.

While all this was going on, I was still trying to play with my own team. We had a spiel in Montreal before the Trials and were on our way when a snowstorm forced us off the road in Edmonston, New Brunswick. We went to a local restaurant for dinner, and my cell phone rang. It was Toby. "Russ," he said, "we're having a meeting in an hour to decide what the rotation's going to be for the Olympic Trials."

"Do you want my recommendation?" I asked.

"No," he replied. "Brad wants you to play. How do you feel about that?"

"I'd love to play," I answered. "But I'm not part of your team. You have a team that qualified for the Trials. I wasn't on that team. And if I'm in, who's going to sit out?"

That was why the meeting had been called, Toby said. Then he asked me where on the team I thought I would be most effective. I told him I'd always prefer to skip. I knew I was still a little rusty, and I hadn't been training for the Trials as the others had. I hadn't planned on playing much until the provincial playdowns in February. I thought I was playing at about eighty per cent.

Me throwing second rocks and skipping the team seemed to work fine, but I told Toby I would fit in wherever. I hung up the phone in a bit of shock. It was November 23; the Trials were set to start December 3, and they were talking about changing the team lineup? It was almost ludicrous.

The next day Toby called and said that Brad really liked the lineup from the two spiels. He loved having me call the game and felt it gave the team the edge it needed to win the Trials. Brad had confidence in having me in the lineup. I answered with three words: "Count me in."

When we got to the spiel in Montreal, I was on fire. We rolled through the field and won the spiel undefeated, beating future Brier champ Jean-Michel Ménard twice in the process. I couldn't believe that at forty-nine I was heading to the Olympic Trials to play. My mind was racing. How was the ice going to be? Could I get in enough practice before the first game? How was the team going to play? How was I going to play?

As we headed home from Montreal, Grant Odishaw, third on my New Brunswick team, asked if I knew who I was playing in the first game at the Trials. I said I didn't.

"Your brother," he said.

There was so much going on, so little time to prepare, but I was right where I wanted to be. When I came down from the initial high, I thought about what happened. I had not been at the meeting where the team decision had been made, but I heard the story. The team sat around the table and all the possible scenarios were laid out. Everyone spoke, and it became clear the best lineup was the one that included me. Then Mike stepped up and volunteered to be the fifth man. This would prove to be one of the most unselfish acts in Canadian history.

Toby had trained his team: when they sat down for a meeting, there were no egos. They said whatever was on their minds, and the good of the team was more important than hurt feelings. At the end of every meeting, the four walked out as friends. Mike's move still astounds me. He felt it was best for the team if he sat out. It was also tough because Mark was his best friend. One night at the spiel in New York, I was on the phone with Toby, who was checking in from Newfoundland. I told him that I thought Mark was awfully quiet.

"Do you think it's because I've replaced his best friend?" I asked.

Toby assured me it wasn't and he promised to look into it. As it turned out, there was nothing wrong. That was just Mark being Mark. I just didn't know these guys well enough yet to realize that. But it illustrated an unusual point. Most of the teams heading into the Trials had been together for years. We were about to play our third spiel together.

I gave Toby a lot of credit for creating a positive team atmosphere. He was even coaching me. He also served as go-between for me with the rest of the team, especially Brad. He knew them better and how to approach them. It was the same coming back. He could relate to an old dog like me. A lot of the media gave me the credit for turning the team around, but it certainly wouldn't have happened if Toby hadn't been there to facilitate it.

The Olympic Trials—officially the Tim Hortons Canadian Curling Trials—were in Halifax, and we convened there on the Wednesday before the opening draw on Saturday. The ice at the Metro Centre wasn't ready, so we had a team practice at a local club. A lot of the other teams were there too.

Just before I went on the ice, Toby pulled me aside and gave me some marching orders. "I want you to know that I'm the coach, but when you get onto that ice, you're in charge of this team," he said emphatically.

I said it was Brad's team and I was the Johnny-come-lately, but he'd have none of it.

"We got Russ Howard for a reason. Yes, maybe Brad will have the final say on his shot selection, but we got you because of who you are, so you be who you are." More coaching. But it was welcome and it made things clear for everyone. We all understood the rules and we all agreed with them. Toby had set the groundwork, which he did well, often times without us realizing it.

On the ice, there was a definite difference in our approach to the game. Brad's strategy was pretty solid, but it showed a distinction in generations. I might choose to guard a shot and force the opposing skip to draw the button to beat me; Brad would reply that he was going to play a hit and roll to the button off that rock way out in the wings. That was the type of shot the younger curlers used. To them, it was obvious. To me, not so much.

Toby recognized that we were two skips from two different age groups with two different philosophies, and he made sure we knew who was in charge and that everyone was in the proper space.

His philosophy was that it didn't matter if we won or lost a spiel in Gander or New York or Toronto. We had to be ready for the Olympic Trials.

The boys were also working with a sports psychologist, Bas Kavanaugh, who preached the same thing: all the stuff beforehand was preparation to get us to the final goal. I followed the Michael Jordan theory, which was to work as hard as possible and do as well as possible all the time.

I ran the practice and took special care to note their releases, trying to pick up any idiosyncrasies. At that point, I knew I could curl well enough, but my concern was whether I could I get the broom in the right spot for these guys. I learned quickly and felt confident heading into the Trials.

The Trials 12

BEFORE THE TRIALS, there was the usual assortment of banquets, photo ops and official meetings. We practiced on the arena ice several times, along with the other nine teams. I knew the rocks that were being used—they were the rocks used in the Brier—but they'd been sandpapered to improve their curl. That meant a little extra time matching them up.

I felt it was my job to ensure the rocks were matched as well as possible for the team. I won many games over the years because I had the advantage of two perfect rocks. We had to make sure that Brad, at the very least, had two good rocks with which he was confident. The other players went through the motions of rock-matching, but I wanted to be precise. If I gave Tiger Woods a Titleist and a range ball, he'd know instantly they were different. That's the way I was with curling rocks. I felt confident we were prepared heading into our first game.

A little extra momentum came from an unusual place. After our first practice, Brad and I were relaxing in our room. He was reading faxes that had come in from friends and fans all over the country. He suddenly popped up from the bed. "Have you seen this?" he asked. "Jeff Stoughton says that we have no chance."

I looked at the fax and saw a newspaper article that quoted Stoughton as saying the Gushue team had no chance to win due to the last-minute lineup change. I immediately knew I had to go into damage control mode.

I knew from past experience that this could be a big distraction to a team in a high-profile event. The media live for good quotes, and we didn't have to help them write the next ten articles by lobbing some back at Stoughton. Brad was upset, but he was handling it well. Could we, as a team, handle the negativity? Inevitably, the Stoughton quote would be the topic of the day, and we had to be prepared.

"You can't really blame him, Brad," I said. "You picked up a guy who's ancient, just minutes before the Trials and there are questions about our team chemistry. They're not saying you guys can't curl; they're questioning the eleventh-hour decision."

Brad was calm, but I knew we had to put this behind us before the first game. Toby and I addressed the situation at our next team meeting. We decided we would take the high road. Jamie said Steve Gould, Stoughton's lead, had called to apologize. Gould said the comment had not come out as Stoughton had intended and that it wasn't necessarily the sentiment of the entire team. He hoped there were no hard feelings. That was a classy move by Gould, and it was definitely appreciated by us. But all of Newfoundland and Labrador, most of Atlantic Canada and any Brad Gushue fans were pretty upset.

Our first match against my brother, Glenn, confirmed for the other teams that I was indeed going to play as a regular member of the Gushue team. Playing against Glenn was difficult, first, because we played together for such a long time, so he knew the way I'd think, and second, he's good!

Being brothers, Glenn and I can say a few things to each other that other skips probably wouldn't. If one of us threw a bad shot, the other might snicker and make a wise crack. We're also honest with each other so, if I wrecked on a guard, I asked him what happened, and he would tell me if I was narrow. For the most part, however, we were pretty professional out there. And I can assure you that we both dearly love to beat the other one. The victory is that much sweeter, in a fun, family way.

In that game, however, neither of us played to our potential. I missed a couple of key shots, and he did too. The difference was that his misses were skip's rocks and mine were second stones. We got lucky in the eighth end; it looked like we were going to give up four. Brad missed his last shot a little bit wide, and we managed to sweep it just in time to roll to a spot Glenn could not get at to remove it for a big end. He was forced to draw against two but came up a hair heavy. We went from giving up four to scoring two. That gave us a two-point lead, and we went on to win.

It was a great start for our team. Glenn's rink was one of the favourites. If we were going to make the playoffs, we had to beat the world-class teams, like Glenn's. I had told Wendy we needed a few wins early. Against this field, it would be tough to win five or six in a row to get out of an early hole and I knew the boys would lose confidence quickly if we lost a few early in the week.

After the game against Glenn, I noticed a difference in approach between the team and myself. I liked to break the game down and talk about what went right and what went wrong. Brad would discuss it a little bit, but Jamie and Mark wanted to put it behind them. In their minds it was over, and it was time to move on to the next game. It was almost as if they'd left work for the day. It took me a while to get used to that.

Our next game was against Shawn Adams from Nova Scotia; he had a lot of local support. We played well and benefited from a miss by Adams. He had a draw for two with his last rock in the seventh. All he needed was to hit the rings, and he missed. He got one but instead of leading we were tied. The miss seemed to play in his mind; and in the eighth, he took some chances to try to score, but we ended up getting three. That led us to a win, which pushed us to 2–0 and gave us a huge shot of confidence.

I followed my Brier system of breaking things down into three-game series. I tried to do no worse than 2–1 in each series. (My lifetime Brier winning percentage is about sixty-six per cent, which means I've accomplished my goal.) If we happened to win our third one, that was a bonus.

That third game was against Ferbey and a win would be icing on our first three-game cake. Before the match, Toby threw a little speed bump into our progress. He said that sometime during the week we had to play Mike. There was no rule about it, but Toby wanted to ensure he was game-ready. We all agreed. Then Toby said it would be better sooner rather than later, so he wouldn't have to start cold in an emergency. Being 2-0, Toby thought the game against Ferbey was the perfect opportunity to bring him in.

The competitor in me disagreed. Ferbey was 1–1 and struggling. I knew we could put them in a hole if we beat them. A win would put us two games up against the pre-event favourite. I told Toby over and over how big this game was and he decided to call a team meeting to talk it over. Brad agreed with me; even Mike agreed with me. If it ain't broke, don't fix it, was his attitude. It was a huge concession on his part and one I know a lot of other guys wouldn't have made.

In the game against Ferbey, neither team played all that well. At the fifth end break, they were one up, and we went into what we called our Pumpkin Patch meeting—a mid-game powwow so named for the bright orange jackets we wore. Toby tried to have us sit in a circle, which was fine for the young guys, but it took me ten minutes just to get my legs crossed!

As we sat at the meeting, I thought I needed to say something to pump these guys up, to get them thinking positive. But Jamie beat me to it, which was a little surprising because he was more a listener than a talker. "Guys," he said. "What are we worried about? We're playing like shit and we're one down to Randy Ferbey. That's not that bad."

Jamie's words put a spark in us, and when we went out for the second half, we were determined. We managed to get a point, stole another one and Dave Nedohin, who throws last rocks for Ferbey, had a free draw he threw through the rings.

I enjoyed playing Ferbey's team because they got so aggressive a steal was always a possibility. If they weren't firing on all cylinders, they were putting themselves in trouble. That doesn't happen that often, but the possibility is always there. We won the game and all of a sudden we were 3–0 without playing anywhere close to our potential. We'd been average at best. Our record meant we were getting plenty of attention from the media, and the guys were feeding off that positive vibe. It was also the first time Brad had beaten Ferbey, so he was thrilled. In our minds, we'd just beaten the best team in the world, even though none of us was playing very well.

At 3–0, we were on pace for my goal of 6–3. I figured that would be good enough for the playoffs. I wasn't sure we had the horses to finish at 7–2 or 8–1. All we wanted to do was make the playoffs, and our start gave us a great chance to do that. We'd won three and beaten two favourites. By my way of thinking, we could split our remaining six games and still make it.

Our next game was against Mark Dacey. We jumped to an early start, getting three in the first end, then stealing three more in the fourth. Sensing we had control of the game, we brought Mike in to get his feet wet, and I took a seat. We ended up shaking hands after the seventh end.

We were 4–0 and leading. I wanted to keep the guys focused on the goal so I reminded them we were a long way from done. "I was 4–0 in this the last time, boys," I told them. "You don't see me with any Olympic medals."

I had gone 5–4 the last time and failed to make the playoffs, so I knew we had a long way left to go. I kept drumming that into them and for the most part, they were aware of our position. They'd also had a lot of coaching from Toby, and they had been to Briers and Canadian Juniors. I wasn't telling them anything they didn't already know. I had a lot of pearls of wisdom, but I'm not sure they needed them.

The boys had also spent a great deal of time working with their sports psychologist, Bas Kavanaugh from Memorial University. They'd been with him since they were juniors. Before the Trials, they hired him to put together a full program, and in addition to sports psychology, he had them training all summer. They went to the gym, lifted weights and ran sprints; he pushed them really hard. At one point, Kavanaugh told Jamie and Mark they weren't working hard enough, and that if they didn't do it his way, he was leaving. That's what ended up happening. It wasn't that they guys weren't training hard—I saw enough evidence of their dedication—but Kavanaugh wanted them to train like triathletes. As far as he was concerned, they weren't committed.

Brad continued to talk to Kavanaugh regularly, relying on him to clear his mind and train his thinking. I was from the old school, long before sports psychology became popular, and I found it all quite fascinating. One exercise Brad and the others did was called scripting. Each invented a story about the perfect situation of winning the Olympic Trials. Their stories were extremely detailed, right down to the colour of socks they wore on the day. The stories were read into a tape player and set to music. They'd created the stories in August and continued to listen to them to reinforce the imagery of winning in their minds. They had to redo them when they won the Trials, because they needed new stories and images for the Olympics. They went something like this.

> I hear the alarm go off. It's December 11 and I'm in the Hyatt Hotel. I'm excited because this is the day I've been working for all my life. I can hear the cars outside. I roll over and there's Russ in the other bed. I'm feeling confident and ready. I walk to the bathroom to shower and the carpet is cold.

And on it went, right down to the smell of the rink and the sound of the slider on the pebble. Brad relied on such mental training to keep him sharp. At the end of his story, he made a draw to the four-foot to go to the Olympics, a shot he'd made lots of times in the past. This was way out there for an old guy like me. But as long as it worked, I let them do anything they wanted. I'm sure Eddie Werenich would die from hysterical laughter if he ever heard their tapes.

Our first loss came to Pat Ryan. It brought us back to reality and humbled us a little. After that we needed to win to keep our 2–1 scenario alive. The game was against Stoughton, and there was a lot of electricity in the air. Aside from Brier playoff games, I hadn't felt an atmosphere as electric as that one. The game was the feature on TSN, and we began to notice more and more people wearing orange, our colour. Some did it by slipping on orange garbage bags but it was clear the fans were coming over to our side.

The electric atmosphere, of course, stemmed from the comments Stoughton had made about our chances. We were really motivated to win that game, and it showed. It was a well curled contest by both teams, but Brad made one shot more than Stoughton. In the ninth, Stoughton came an inch too heavy, Brad made a difficult bigweight takeout, and we got four and won the game. We also won the crowd over; the cheers were so loud it felt as if they would bring down the roof. The win kept our 2–1 mark alive heading into our final three games.

Perhaps it was the thrill of beating Stoughton, but in our next game, we were flat against Jay Peachey. They played very well, and with his last rock, Brad had to draw to half of the button. It was one of the most difficult shots he had all week, as the line and weight had to be perfect. I called only for line and let the boys take it with the brushes. The guys swept it as hard and as well as any rock I've ever seen, and the stone came to rest perfectly, giving us the point and the win. The crowd exploded when Jamie and Mark raised their brooms to signal it was shot rock.

Don Bartlett, a Newfie who played lead for Kevin Martin, finished his game a couple of sheets over and stayed to watch the last rock. He came flying across the backboards to shake hands with Jamie and Mark. As a front-ender, he knew it was the sweepers who had made the shot.

With a mark of 6–1, we were in control of things. We were guaranteed a playoff spot. If we split our last two, we would be 7–2, and only a couple of other teams could finish that high. One of those was John Morris, whom we still had to play. We knew that game would likely be for first place.

Before that, however, we had to get past Kevin Martin. We went into the game more relaxed than the previous two contests, which I was happy to see. Martin was his usual self, constantly talking in my ear as the game was going on. He gave me the impression he believed he was out of it, but I'm not sure if that was gamesmanship or the truth. He was certainly on the bubble at 4–3, but he still had life.

We had motivation to win so we could wrap up first place, and we wanted to beat Martin so we could say we had done it. His team had really dominated Brad's over the years so a win would be extra sweet.

The game was pretty hairy. We went in with a different strategy: to keep our guards high so it would be tougher for Martin's team to use the run-backs, who played so well. There would be a lot more rocks in play, which meant more finesse shots, which had become our strength.

The game plan worked perfectly, and we got up four points playing nine. For his last shot in the ninth, Brad had an open hit to give up two or a more difficult double, where he needed to hit just a quarter rock. I wanted to play the open one, but he was adamant about the double. I kept talking about what could go wrong, but in his confident mind, missing wasn't a possibility—he was going to make it. In his way of thinking, if he made the double, the game was probably over. In my way of thinking, if he missed, we were going to give up three.

In situations like that, I always yield to the skip. But I gave him rather tight ice and he threw it up a bit, missing by a fraction, giving Martin a draw for three. We were only one up, so it was game on. Martin managed to get a couple buried; then, with his last rock, Brad calmly drew the button to beat him. It was another milestone for Brad, who held Martin in very high regard. He hadn't beaten him in a big game, and he couldn't have picked a better time to do it.

I was impressed with the way the team battled back after giving up the three-ender. Often, after a mistake like, that a team folded up like a cheap suitcase and lost everything, but these guys had the right attitude. They never got rattled. I can only assume that the work with the sports psychologist trained them to focus on what was ahead, not what had just happened. And they did it better than any team I've ever played for. All four of us remained calm and stayed in the moment.

Our last game was against John Morris, and the winner got first place. We got up early and controlled things throughout. I was surprised because they were a very good rink and Morris was a very talented skip, easily one of the best young ones in the world. I was worried about losing to them.

But on this day, Morris wasn't sharp. His team seemed flat, and we handled them easily. We won the game and the round robin. We were one game away from a trip to the Olympics. But we had to wait a while to get to that game—it was ridiculous how long we had to wait. Our win over Morris took place on Thursday night. The final was scheduled for late Sunday afternoon. We had two and a half days to sit around and kill time. If I was in charge of the curling world, I would change that in a heartbeat. It's not a good system and I've never understood it. I know television is involved, but it's unbearable for teams to sit around. For the next few days we had a steady diet of playing cards, visiting the casino, watching movies and throwing rocks. We tried to stay busy, but by Saturday night everything started to get a little hard on the head. Late Saturday afternoon, I was sitting in my room watching golf on television and Brad was resting quietly on his bed. We hadn't said a word to each other in an hour when all of a sudden he leaned over.

"Russ," he said. "Are you nervous?"

About nine different things rushed into my head but I finally owned up.

"Yup," I said. "A little bit. But I think that's a good thing. I find when I've got butterflies before a game, it's because I'm excited. I always felt I played better when I had those butterflies." I didn't want to call them nerves. I thought that might scare him. I asked how he was feeling.

"I'm going out of my mind," he said. "One minute I'm so excited that we're this close to going to the Olympics and the next minute I get really scared about what will happen if we don't win."

I told him I thought that was a pretty natural way to feel. I relayed a story about the '86 Brier, how we lost on the last shot and I was devastated for a month, but after that I realized that I'd played well, had a great week and finished second in Canada, which was pretty good. Coming in second at the Olympic Trials wasn't bad either.

I asked if he'd been nervous before and he had been, just prior to the 2001 Canadian Junior.

"Well Brad, how'd that work out for you?" I said, knowing he had won the title.

I wasn't a sports psychologist, but I decided the best way to deal with his nervousness was total honesty. All we could do was play our best and accept the outcome. My words seemed to calm him, and I was impressed that he'd opened up to me. It showed just how much we'd come to trust each other in a short time. There were no egos involved, just trust.

Normally, I like to watch the semifinal game if I'm in the final. I do it even though it usually ends up bothering me because I tend to cheer for the underdog who doesn't win as often. The match-up was Stoughton against Morris, and I was thinking Morris hadn't played very well at the end of the week and that our battles with Stoughton had been complicated by his comments, so for me it was, "Come on, John!"

This time, rather than watch, we decided to go out for dinner while the game was on. We heard in the restaurant that Stoughton won, and we knew we were in for a tough final. On Sunday morning, I was filled with a real sense of accomplishment. I knew I was going in to play a world-class team that was coming in hot, so I had to be realistic about our chances. It could all come down to one shot. Yes, we'd had a great week, but so, too, had Stoughton. He'd only lost two games, one more than us.

Part of me was nervous because it was such a huge game. I'd never been in a sudden-death game to go to the Olympics, but I did have more experience than anyone else on the ice. I'd been in big games, and I'd won some and lost some, and I'd lived through both. I think once I experienced losing a big game, I had a better chance of winning the next one.

The rest of the team was different. They were all a little tight, but Jamie was exceptionally nervous.

Brad and I continued our ritual of going for breakfast and sitting way off in the corner so we didn't have to talk to anyone. We came down the elevator and when the doors opened, who was standing there but Peter Smith. Peter was on the Scottish team we beat in the World Championship final in 1993, and I hadn't seen him since that game. We exchanged greetings, and he joked that I was giving all the old curlers hope. After he left, I said to Brad that had to be an omen. Brad hadn't even noticed. He was in another world. We went in and got our juice and a newspaper and sat at our table. I was about to attack the buffet when Brad said he wasn't hungry. I said I wasn't, either, even though I was; I figured it was better to keep Brad at ease, so we went to the room to kill a few more hours. Time seemed to drag. When we got to the rink, we were all trying to keep each other loose, and no one was better at it than Mike. He was always at ease and always ready with a joke or a wisecrack. He was invaluable to the team in those minutes before we went on the ice.

For the first time in my career, I tried to remain calm. I'm usually a bundle of controlled nerves before a big game, but I knew that it was important for me to appear calm. I realized that at my age and with my experience, if I showed nerves, the rest of the team would probably do the same. It was tough not to be a little anxious, especially when we were piped in and the arena was a wash of orange because of our supporters. The fans were loud, and there was a tingle throughout the building. Everyone was waiting for this one, especially us.

We had decided our best chance to get to the Stoughton rink was to put pressure on second Gary Van DenBerghe. There weren't many weak links on the team, but if I could outcurl their second, we might have a chance, especially in a big game with my experience.

We elected to go right after them in the first end, and it worked—we scored two after Brad drew the four-foot. If there was any doubt who the crowd was behind it was clear after that. Jamie and Mark had to sweep the last shot from one end to the other. It isn't often I was drowned out when I was yelling, but on that shot the fans were so loud, my molars were rattling.

As I held the broom and awaited that last rock, I thought there was an eighty-five per cent chance Brad would make the shot. I thought that if he missed it, we weren't going to win the game. It was only the first end, but I had a sense this was a very important rock. It would give us two points, and it would show Stoughton we weren't going to back down.

Stoughton didn't waver, however. They're a tough experienced team and they came right back with a deuce. We scored two the next end. The turning point was the fourth. We had a rock buried behind a long guard right on the top of the button. Brad and I talked about leaving it just short of the rings, which would probably guarantee a steal of one, but with the swing in the ice, we felt if we got it right in on top of our rock on the button, it would leave Jeff a difficult shot against two. The line looked a little tight halfway down, but Jamie and Mark swept it past the guard, and Brad's rock couldn't have been carried into a better spot, dead buried, frozen to our shot rock.

Stoughton had a very difficult cold draw to the side of the button. He barely missed—a rarity—and we scored two for a 6–2 lead.

We were elated for about three seconds and then fear kicked in. We were four up without the hammer and there were still six ends to go. If he took two, forced us to one, took two then forced us to one again, and so on, he could get back. That may sound crazy, having played so well up to that point, but that's the way I thought. The ice conditions were so swingy, we knew we weren't close to being finished. Especially playing Jeff Stoughton. I wished I'd never invented the free guard zone rule!

The call of "the Wounded Moose." Russ, at the 1987 Brier, in his characteristic pose, giving his full-on trademark yell to "Hurry Haaaaard!"

Michael Burns Photography

Even in an intense match, Russ finds time to share a laugh with Finnish skip Markku Uusipaavalniemi, during Canada's 10–4 gold-medal game win at the Winter Olympics in 2006.

Mike Ridewood / COC / CP Images

The famous Bear uniform. During the 1989 provincials, teams were forbidden from wearing their own sponsors' logos during the competition; only Ontario Curling Association sponsors' crests were allowed on team garb. In protest, Team Howard (from left to right), Russ, Glenn, Tim Belcourt and Kent Carstairs bought these cute bear sweaters made by their sponsor Goldline, and sported them all week.

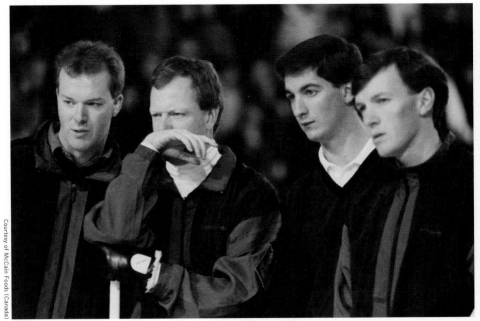

In a more serious moment, analyzing the play before the final game-winning shot in the 1991 Skins Game against John Bubbs. Russ loved the format of the made-for-TV Skins Games and—with the support of some great players like Glenn, Wayne Middaugh and Pete Corner, pictured with Russ above—appeared in eight Skins Games, winning three of them.

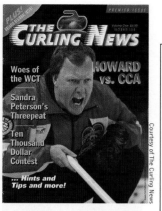

World Championships to use Howard rule in 1992

Stellar field shaping up for Owen Sound

Howard Wins Big in Skins Series

Kevin Martin and Russ Howard skip the two highest – profile teams in the land. Martin will lead Canada's Men at the 1992 Olympics. Howard is number one on the Gold Trail.

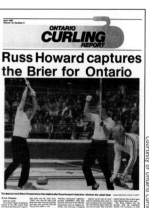

Russ Howard captures the Brier for Ontario

Howard Grabs Third Straight Skins Win

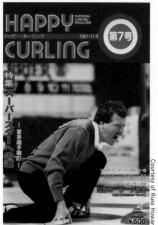

At the top of the game in Canada and around the world for over 30 years, Russ Howard has been the cover story on countless curling publications. Here, a selection of the headlines he has made in the *Canadian Curling News* (now *The Curling News*) over its fifty-year history, in the *Ontario Curling Report*, and even in faraway Japan.

The 1993 Canadian Champs with the coveted Tankard. From left to right: Russ, Glenn, Wayne Middaugh and Peter Corner.

On top of the world again. From left to right: Larry Merkley, Peter Corner, Wayne Middaugh, Glenn and Russ with the 1993 World Championship trophy in Geneva. Sandra Schmirler's rink also won for Canada that year on the women's side.

Curling has always been a family affair in the Howard household. Russ and Wendy on the ice with their two kids, Steven, 10, and Ashley, 5.

Passing down the Howard family tradition. A proud moment for Russ at the 2004 Brier in Regina, when he had his son Steven on the same team.

Russ and "the kids" in one of the proudest moments of his life. The gold-medal-winning Gushue rink show off their hardware, the first-ever Olympic men's gold medal in curling for Canada. From left to right: Brad Gushue, Mark Nichols, Russ, Jamie Korab and Mike Adam.

A winning moment. From left: alternate Mike Adam, lead Jamie Korab, skip Russ Howard, third Mark Nichols and fourth Brad Gushue.

Gathering of legends: At the 2004 Brier, 15 past Brier winners came together for this rare photo. From bottom left: Russ, Bernie Sparkes, Don Walchuck, Dave Nedohin, Rick Lang, Randy Ferbey, Marcel Rocque and Scott Pfeifer. Top, from left: Ron Northcott, Fred Storey, Bryan Wood, Ernie Richardson, Pat Ryan, Sam Richardson and Matt Baldwin.

Firefighters across Canada have supported and raised money for Muscular Dystrophy Canada for over 50 years. Russ, a National Ambassador for Muscular Dystrophy Canada, is pictured here with Moncton firefighters in his hometown.

The family celebrates Russ's gold. Ashley, Russ, Wendy and Steven. It doesn't get any better than this.

On the other hand, we still felt in control of the game and that we were oh-so-close to the goal. We hadn't expected to be four up. We knew we had to keep a lid on the optimism just as we had to keep control of the negative feelings. As we predicted, Stoughton fought back, and after seven ends, the score was 7–4, but they had last rock in the eighth and they made good use of it. With skips' rocks left, Stoughton was looking at the possibility of getting four if he made a perfect run-back double. We had shot rock, but he had one in front of it onto which he could run back one of his rocks from in front of the rings. There was also an open Stoughton rock out to the side. I suggested we hit the open one and make sure the worst we did was to give up three. That would mean a tie game with two ends to play, but we would have control of last rock. Brad wanted to guard the run-back and try to steal one.

If we didn't hit the open one, four was a definite possibility, and I wasn't going to be any part of that. Brad was equally adamant about playing the guard. I didn't object very often with Brad's calls, but this time was different. This time I knew we couldn't play the guard.

Finally, we called a timeout to talk to Toby. We pleaded our cases, and Toby agreed with me, saying it was time to play the scoreboard. As it turned out, Brad hit the open rock. This gave Stoughton the raise. He made the shot, but left us with a makeable double. Brad made it perfectly, spilling the two stones out, and Stoughton had to draw for two.

Before the ninth end, we were telling ourselves not to get too defensive, and we started to try to make freezes. With a couple of half shots on our part and some great shotmaking from Stoughton's team, Brad had to draw against three, albeit all in the twelve-foot, with his last one, which he did, to give us a two-point lead coming home.

Before that end we had a quick meeting, and I reminded the guys not to overthrow anything, to play as if it was the first end. Jamie took my words to heart with his first one. He didn't throw it heavy—he didn't throw it heavy enough. We asked for a rock on top of the four-foot but it ended up being a centre guard, exactly what we didn't want.

Stoughton, the veteran, immediately guarded Jamie's rock, knowing we would have peeled out our own rock if we had the chance. With two rocks out front, I elected to have Jamie come around them to the top of the eight-foot, choking off Stoughton's chance for a come-around. Jamie overcompensated and threw his second one through the rings. I felt sick for Jamie, who had played so well throughout the game and the week. His shot allowed Stoughton to throw a third guard off to the corner, setting up a potential three.

Somehow, I managed to work up enough weight to make a double peel and roll-out, killing off two of their guards and losing my own stone as well. I turned to the boys and gave them a wink, hoping to relieve a little of the pressure we were feeling. I also peeled away the next guard they put up. We felt we had dodged a bullet after that, but then we stumbled again. Remarkably, the best hitter on the team, Mark, nose-hit the next Stoughton guard, and it was game on again.

Stoughton got one in the rings around that guard and we ended up peeling off the guard. Then, after a long discussion, Mead made an almost perfect shot around a corner guard to sit two. We could see a small portion of it, and we thought about taking that one out, but decided to hit the open one and make him play a perfect hit and roll to get two behind cover. Brad made it dead on, and they tried the hit and roll. If they made it, we were in trouble. But they got a little too cute, and the rock hit and rolled—and rolled and rolled and came to rest right at the edge of the twelve-foot. (Mead was pilloried in the press after the game for missing the sweeping call, which was unfair. It had to be precise; to call that perfectly would have been more luck than skill.)

We peered over top to try to determine if it was in or out, and we were ninety-nine per cent certain it was out, although we had been around long enough to know that the rings were not always perfect.

Brad was certain it was out, I was not quite as certain and suggested hitting it, since it was three-quarters open. The other shot was a raise takeout on the shot rock. If we hit the back one, the worst outcome was an extra end. If we missed the raise and this little biter was in, we were finished. Brad wasn't worried about playing the raise takeout. He was pumped up and confident, and ready to throw his rock. I shut up, put the broom down and said, "Let's make it."

It was one of his favourite shots, and he made it perfectly. Brad was starting to celebrate, thinking the stone at the back of the house was out. He walked down the sheet with his hands in the air, and the cameramen, thinking the game was over and that Stoughton would concede, came in to capture the moment. I was sure Stoughton would throw his last one, and I wanted to be prepared if the measure showed that the stone was in. I told the guys to stay calm and wait for the measure. But Brad was unstoppable. He slid over to the next sheet, as excited as a kid at a carnival. Toby was desperately trying to get his attention to tell him to stay in the moment and remind him the game wasn't over.

Stoughton bravely went down and threw his last rock into the rings but seemed resigned to the fact his biter was out. The official came out with the measure and began to slide it around to the rock in question.

At the hog line, Jamie and Mark were holding on to each other, unable to look at the proceedings. Brad was peering in from the back of the sheet, pacing like a bull in a pen. I was standing next to the official and Mead in the rings, looking right down over the rock, as we awaited the results. A thousand thoughts were racing through my mind. What if it was in? Would we be able to win the game if it lost the measure? How would we regroup?

As the measure got within a couple of feet of the stone, I could tell it wasn't going to touch—it was going to miss by about an eighth of an inch. As the measure swung past the stone without hitting it, I pumped my fists into the air. Lord thunderin' Jesus, boys, we're going to the Olympics! The rest of the team followed, and the crowd went nuts. After celebrating with the team, I found Ashley, who had run the length of the arena to get to me, and gave her a big hug. Wendy and Steven were still trying to get close. Everyone was in tears.

It was an amazing feeling to win that game. It was the best, most thrilling game I had ever played. Both teams were at the top of their games, and with the measure, there was suspense and drama. A little metal bar swinging by that rock determined a week of play and our futures.

And now I was just a few weeks shy of my fiftieth birthday, and I was going to the Olympics.

During the ceremonies, I was still on cloud nine. We started to walk down the ice to the podium in front of that boisterous crowd, and Jamie said. "Slow down, boys. I don't ever want to forget this."

My kids were there, and I could feel their admiration and love pouring over me. Wendy was right there too, as always, with a big smile. I was close to letting the tears flow.

As we stood on the podium it hit me: no matter what happened in Torino, I was going to be an Olympian for the rest of my life. The very idea of the Olympics seemed strange. I had curled for so long and won a few titles, but the Olympics was so much bigger than that, and I was going. Me and the kids. What a crazy story this was. Six weeks ago I planned to watch this game on television at home. Now I was on my way to the Olympics.

My thoughts went to my parents. My mother was no doubt watching in Midland, and I knew my father was looking down from on high. I thought of all those days he taught me the game and all the times he reminded me to work on the fundamentals. Because of his lessons those many years before, I was standing on the podium at the Olympic trials.

At the ceremony, every speaker and every action seemed to reinforce the fact we were Olympians. One defining moment was when they gave us our team jackets, which were blue. As I put mine on, I thought that was strange. Twice before I'd received the red Maple Leaf as a Canadian champion, and here I was in a blue jacket. The CCA ordered the right jackets, but they didn't arrive in time. Elaine Dagg-Jackson, team leader for the women's side, used some ingenuity and scurried to The Bay that morning to buy five men's and five women's jackets, and all that was available was blue. She threw in a red scarf to try to jazz up the jackets.

When I got off the podium I rushed over to Wendy, Steven and Ashley to get a family hug. That was what it was all about to me. Wendy and I had been a team for thirty years, and I could see the joy in her eyes. To have our children there was also very special. They were both competitive curlers and understood the nature of the competition.

Then an ordinary-looking gentleman introduced himself and said he'd be escorting me. I had no idea what he was talking about. Then he offered me a bottle of water, which I took. I was called over to get some photos taken, and the man walked with me. Suddenly, I realized who he was—the drug-testing guy. He had to stay with me every step of the way. When we were having our pictures taken, he was right there. When I went to the media scrum, he was right beside me. I kept drinking water, and after my third bottle, he told me I could have no more until after the test.

When the media obligations were finished, the man took me into a back room where they had their paraphernalia all set up. Brad was in there; the other two guys, who didn't have to talk to the media, had already finished and were well into the celebration. After the three bottles of water, my fifty-year-old bladder was ready to provide a sample. Brad let me go ahead of him. I went into the stall, and my escort came along.

"Pull your shirt up and your pants down," he said.

I obliged and then tried to go as this gentleman looked on. It was a little unnerving, having this guy watch me, but if it would get me to the Olympics, I was ready to let everyone in.

The euphoria surrounding our win continued until Jim Waite called us into a meeting in the players' lounge. He said there were questions surrounding the next steps, especially from the families of players on our team and Shannon Kleibrink's rink, which had won the women's side. He wanted to provide as much information as possible. There wasn't much time to prepare for the Olympics, and family members who wanted to attend needed to make arrangements quickly.

Waite presented some pictures of Torino and Pinerolo, the small centre where the curling would be held. It looked idyllic, and none of us could wait to get there. We hadn't discussed it, but I assumed Wendy, Steven and Ashley wouldn't want to miss the Olympics. Then Gerry Peckham, the CCA's director of high performance, announced the cost of the adventure. "If any of your family is going, you'd better budget $8,000 per person," he said.

I quickly did the math—$24,000. I was shocked. No, I was in denial. I couldn't believe it could cost that much to go to the Olympics. Wasn't there some sort of financial assistance for families? The big expense would be accommodation, which would be at elevated prices. We all expected that flights and food would be costly. But it was a shock to find out that not even one family member would receive a free ticket to the curling games. When we represented our province at a national championship, our spouses received complimentary tickets to the games and free accommodations.

I tried not to get upset but had so much history with the CCA folks I was bothered. I approached Peckham, who was in charge of the Olympic program for curling, and questioned him about the costs. "Is there no funding here, Gerry?" I asked.

"We'll see what we can do," he answered. "I'll e-mail the CCA head office in the morning. They have some good contacts." Unfortunately, the response was that there wasn't any funding or sponsorship available. Maybe Jonathon Mead knew something I didn't when he called the sweeping on that fateful shot.

It was a sobering end to the night, although I was still on a high. I decided to continue with my tradition of a calm celebration with the family, minus Steve, who'd gone to the mass celebration in the Patch.

In Wendy's hotel room, we sat on the floor and watched highlights on TSN, reliving that remarkable afternoon. We ordered in room service. At one point, Wendy got up to get something from the dresser. As soon as she moved, the light fixture in the ceiling directly above her came crashing down. A moment earlier and she would have been seriously injured.

We took that as an omen of the good fortune that was to come. Maybe I shouldn't be so worried about the $24,000; maybe I should be thankful to have a happy, healthy family and a chance to celebrate my fiftieth birthday in Torino at the Olympics, with my family!

Wendy and I would be celebrating our twenty-fifth wedding anniversary in June 2006, and we had been thinking of taking a special trip. We couldn't think of a better way to celebrate such a milestone.

Off to Italy

THE MORNING AFTER winning the Trials, I woke up to the sound of Mike pounding on the door and yelling. "We got you on the flight," he bellowed.

I opened the door a little sleepily and he continued. "You're not going home. You're coming with us to Newfoundland."

I answered the only way I knew how. "When do we leave?"

I vaguely recalled that the team told me if we won, they were going to take me to St. John's for a big party. I didn't think much of it, but they had been serious, and I didn't see why not. Most of Newfoundland and Labrador had been on the edge of its collective seat watching our game. I was sure it was going to be an experience going there.

Most of Monday we stayed in Halifax, going through all the protocol and logistics necessary to make us Olympians. We were measured up for clothes, had pictures taken, met with national media, got the lowdown on what we could and couldn't put in our bodies and on and on. We flew out of Halifax in the early evening and on the plane I leaned over to Brad and expressed my doubts at what awaited us.

"This might be a big waste," I said. "Who in their right mind is going to be at the airport at ten o'clock on a Monday night?"

Brad shot me a quick grin, as if I was about to get the biggest surprise of my life. As I entered the terminal, there were people everywhere. They were covering every inch of floor space, hanging off railings, hanging over the escalator and standing on anything that would hold their weight.

Security had to stop people from entering the building, as it was over capacity, and the excess flowed into the parking lot. Television cameras were everywhere, and flashes popped like Canada Day fireworks. People came up and hugged us as if we were returning from the war. (I later learned they were aunts and uncles and cousins of the boys.) I met one of Brad's old coaches, and Mark's high school teacher, and there were politicians and policemen. Some had tears in their eyes as they embraced us. "Bless you boys," said one man, crying as if we were his own offspring.

We managed to get through the crowd and were taken in limousines to the St. John's Curling Club, where there was a party for us. Brad got up and spoke for the team. He gave a great speech, thanking everyone for all the help and support. After that was over and we'd had a chance to eat, they showed the tenth end of the final game on a big screen. It was the first time we'd seen the end in its entirety with the comments from the announcers. But what was more enjoyable were the comments from the people in the club. They booed Jamie's misses and then cheered when I made the double peel. I stood up and told the crowd that I was going to teach Mark how to make that shot before the Olympics, which brought a huge roar of laughter. Mark was quick on the comeback. "You mean make a double peel with hack weight?"

There was more laughter and frivolity, and it was apparent that the five of us, despite the difference in age, had bonded. We were able to joke with each other and knew what buttons we could push to have some fun. That was important for our team dynamic, which could have easily gone the other way. But those four guys were so good about having fun and getting to know me that it made it easy.

I don't remember much about the end of that evening except that about 4:00 a.m., Brad and his fiancée, Krista, and I were in a cab driving home to Brad's. The cab driver recognized us and sang the entire trip. I knew I was half in the bag, but I was a little worried that this guy was probably well ahead of me. At the end of the ride—somehow we made it—he refused to take a fare, saying he was honoured to "have you in my chariot."

After a night at the Gushue house, I flew to Halifax, where my car was, then drove to Moncton. Those hours alone on the ride back may have been the last quiet time I had for the next three months. On that ride I realized we may have climbed the mountain and won the Trials, but ahead of us was a much higher peak, and our preparations had to begin immediately.

I went on a strict diet, cutting out all the luxuries, and I hit the bike, trying to get into some kind of shape. (I lost about ten pounds before we left for Torino.) I wanted to take every action that would help me perform well at the Olympics. I even sent my shoes away to Balance Plus, the curling shoe company, for some repairs. The shoes went with specific instructions. I phoned the company owner, Scott Taylor, and said the sole had split and needed to be fixed, but he was in no way to alter the top of the shoe. If he couldn't fix the bottom without touching the top, then no repair. Taylor returned the renewed shoes the next day.

During this time, the media calls never stopped. I was used to such calls, from my previous Brier wins, but I had a full-time job. When I won the Canadian title, I was a golf pro, and my wins were pre-golf season. Wendy and I were trying to work hard to make up for the time we were away at the Trials and for when we'd be at the Olympics.

I continued to practice regularly putting in lengthy sessions. My main focus was to improve my peels. Unlike my team members, I wasn't able to throw big weight accurately with any consistency. I never learned because as a skip, I never needed to. But for a second stone, good peel weight was vital. The few peels a skip did play were usually outside in, to clear centre guards. But a second often played them inside out, usually on a corner guard, and then had to roll almost the entire width of the sheet to clear the shooter. It was an almost entirely new shot for me. The old down-weight Ed Werenich peel didn't cut it any more. So I worked on more leg drive and maintaining accuracy at the same time. By the time I was ready to leave for Torino, I wasn't throwing it with the same weight a Wayne Middaugh might, but I improved markedly.

Most of this practice was on my own. The team set up a schedule with regular conference calls. Toby, one of the most organized people I knew, arranged things so the other players were in his office when he called me. We burned up the phone lines talking over everything we could think of that needed to be covered.

I thought the pre-Olympics schedule would be fairly easy to set up. But we had a short time frame—about nine weeks from winning the Trials to our first game at the Olympics. As well, all our minds were telling us to take a break. We played in a huge competition, had some celebrations and we were all a bit worn out. On top of it all, Christmas was quickly approaching.

We did agree to two weeks of unstructured practice during which we would be on our own. But it wasn't exactly quiet time. I was constantly doing phone interviews, being called down to the local television or radio station, talking to newspaper reporters from around the world. Often they knew nothing about curling.

As the skip of record, Brad was taking a lot of the load. He wasn't working a day job, but even he was complaining about how much time the interviews were eating up. I was trying to sell houses to keep the wolves from the door. It was scary how many inquiries we had to answer and how much time it took out of a day.

Christmas was almost an afterthought, until the day actually arrived. The presents to the rest of the family were Team Canada Olympic clothing from The Bay and an Italian-English dictionary in preparation for the big trip. The kids, thank goodness, ate it up and were ready to get to Italy. It was a great day to relax and reflect, as well as enjoy some family time.

On Boxing Day, however, it was back to work. We had a golf course listed for sale, and I spent most of that day walking it with a prospective client. The course was covered in three feet of snow, and there was a steady drizzle, making it an extremely uncomfortable day. By 2:30, I was in the car for a four-hour drive through a wicked snowstorm to St. Stephen, New Brunswick, to watch Ashley play in the provincial junior. Showing that maybe curling is in the genes, Ashley (she was playing second) and her team managed to make it through the eight-team triple knock-out to face Andrea Kelly's rink. Kelly was the defending Canadian champion and had played the previous year's World Junior Championship in the building we would play in, in the small town of Pinerolo, Italy. People wondered, when they watched me screaming on television, how the elite teams handled the pressure. That was nothing compared to being a proud father, sitting behind the glass, not being able to read the ice, call the sweeping, discuss the strategy or even sweep. If I had known what I was putting Wendy through all those years, I would have recommended her for a gold medal. Ashley's team won a close game by stealing the extra end, and she won her first provincial title. As the girls hugged at the far end of the rink, Ashley turned to see her teary-eyed dad already at the far hog line.

Between her games, I was trying to throw some rocks—I had to drive an hour to find another club in St. Andrews—and hit the gym to keep my body in shape.

In between visits to curling rinks, Wendy and I were trying to co-ordinate the trip for the family. Steven and Ashley needed passports, we all needed vaccinations, and there were multitudinous arrangements to make. All the family arrangements had to be made within days after the Trials. At the top of the list was getting the tickets to the competition. For reasons I wasn't able to understand, tickets for curling were among the hottest in Italy, and there was a good chance they'd be sold out. We had to act quickly or risk the family not seeing the games. Each round-robin game was $70, the semifinal was $100 and it was $120 for the final. Those were the most expensive curling tickets I'd ever heard of, and I had to multiply each ticket price by three for Wendy, Steven and Ashley. To watch curling for a week was going to cost the Howard family more than $2,500. Of course, when we got to Italy, the curling tickets were selling in the village for $35 apiece!

Three days after Ashley won her title, I was on a plane heading to Winnipeg to meet the guys and play in a Grand Slam event. We desperately wanted some top-level competition. We hadn't played together since the Trials. And those ten Trials games were our only serious level match-ups.

It didn't matter if we won or lost in Winnipeg. We just wanted to play. But that was easier said than done. We all arrived exhausted and when we got off the plane, we were deluged with interviews.

Brad, for example left St. John's at 5:00 a.m., flew to Toronto, waited in the airport for a connection, landed in Winnipeg hungry in the late afternoon, and as soon as he stepped off the plane, he was cornered by a media liaison person from the World Curling Tour, who told him she was going to drive him to a local radio station to join Kevin Martin for a live interview. Brad begged the woman for a moment to eat, but was told there was no time. She put him in the car and refused to stop for food, taking him to the interview. When Brad got to the hotel, he was livid, a combination of being hungry and tired.

The next day, before our first game, we had to tape a television commercial on the sheet where we were to play. The shoot ran late, so our team and our opposition missed practice time, and the game started late. I was angry, but also felt bad for our opposition, Glen Despins and his team, because we had hampered them. We were run ragged. When we did play, we were rusty and had little motivation. It was tough to get up for another bonspiel when we knew we'd be in the biggest competition of our lives in a few short weeks.

After a few days in Winnipeg, Brad was just about at his wit's end dealing with the media. He told Toby it had to end. Toby was all about eliminating distractions, and shortly after that weekend, he had a press release sent out saying that the team would do interviews for one more week and then no more. No exceptions. That was a huge relief for all of us.

We were knocked out of the spiel in Winnipeg, and we had to stay two extra days to do some work with the CCA and the Canadian Olympic people. For most of the two days, we sat in a classroom and listened to a nutritionist, a physical trainer, a doctor and other experts. By the end of the two days, I was expecting the butcher, baker and candlestick maker to walk in, but it was all very well organized and informative.

One fellow came in and went through every type of pill or vitamin we were taking, then told us which were allowed. We'd been instructed to bring everything with us. The other guys had maybe a pack of Hall's and a bottle of Aspirin; I had a big bag of pills for all my aches and pains. Most of what I was taking was fine, although the expert suggested I switch a few brands because he was unsure where some of the pills were made. I had to drop a greens supplement, which bothered me, but he wanted to err on the side of caution.

Another session was with a media trainer. He'd videotape us as he asked tough questions to see how we'd react. I was pretty experienced so I had no trouble, but Jamie rarely had to deal with the press, and he froze. Mike, on the other hand, had even the trainer laughing. He was asked, "What other countries do you think will compete for the gold medal?"

"Well I think that we've trained hard and have really put in the time to give it our best shot," he said. "I know there will be a lot of really tough opposition over there but if I had to pick one country, I'd say it would be Timbuktu. They have a skip from Timbuktu who's amazing. In fact, we think he's probably on steroids, he's so good."

In his Newfoundland accent, the trainer had a tough time understanding him, but eventually he caught on, realizing Mike was mocking the session in a good-natured way. Jim Waite gave us a slide presentation dealing with the area where we would compete. We would spend the first few days in the Olympic Village, but the curling was in Pinerolo, about forty-five minutes from Torino. We'd be in different accommodation and without the benefit of the Village restaurant. Waite told us what restaurants were there, what our accommodation was like, and showed us pictures of the facility in which the curling would be held. He was trying to make sure there would be no surprises when we arrived.

I was interested in the facility and tried to get details about the building, the ice and the rocks to try to find out what the conditions would be like. If we could find that out, we could adjust our practice sessions to fit.

I already had some information about the rocks. The day I arrived home from the Trials, Shorty Jenkins called me from China where he was training some icemakers. He gave me the bad news that the rocks we'd be using at the Games were straight. He was adamant that they weren't going to curl. He'd used those rocks in a previous event and had a good read on them and wanted me to know the unfortunate news.

Waite told us his information was that the rocks were pretty good. He said the juniors hadn't had any trouble; the boys' team found a single bad stone and the girls had no difficulties. Although I respected the talents of our junior teams, I deferred to Shorty and told Brad and the boys to find the straightest ice they could to practice on.

One of the last sessions was with Marnie McBean, the Canadian gold medal rower, who gave us a superb motivational talk. We took a few phrases from her speech and used them throughout our trip. She told us of the time when she was in an important race and near the end she felt as if her arms would fall off and she would die of exhaustion. And she told herself, "Suck it up Princess." That immediately fell into our lexicon and came out any time we began to feel sorry for ourselves.

A big benefit to our stay in Winnipeg was bonding with the women's team, skipped by Shannon Kleibrink. Waite wanted the teams to join forces, to work as a unit, share information and root for each other.

He arranged for us to have an Italian night together. We had an Italian meal, tried several different types of Italian wine and there was a translator who helped us learn some of the basic phrases. It was a fun night that brought the two teams closer.

The women's team was a fun bunch, very bubbly personalities. I had met Kleibrink at the previous Trials. I had curled against their coach, Daryl Nixon, on the cash circuit years before. The other three—the team's third was Amy Nixon, Daryl's daughter— I'd never met, but we came together quickly.

I left Winnipeg feeling better about everything—except perhaps our curling. We had a better handle on what was coming. A lot of questions had been answered, and we had a plan for the weeks until we left.

And what a plan it was. There was no downtime. We were in Winnipeg from January 3 to January 10. I was home for three days then went to Newfoundland. In one weekend, we had two-a-day practices of two hours each, attended two parties in St. John's and drove two hours to Harbour Grace—Jamie's hometown—for a parade through the streets and two more parties. One was in the high school gym, which was absolutely jammed. We received several presentations, then the doors to the gym opened and in walked Don Bartlett, the lead from Kevin Martin's team and the most famous curler from Harbour Grace, carrying the Olympic torch. He'd flown from Edmonton, where he lived, to take part in the celebration. It was amazing for him to do that to honour us.

I flew home for four days after that, then packed my bags for the next month. I flew to Newfoundland for a practice session on January 20, then left for eight days in Thunder Bay, where I watched my daughter play in the Canadian Junior. They didn't finish as well as they would have liked, but I was impressed with the team. Al Hackner and Rick Lang, curling greats from Thunder Bay, were serving as co-chairmen of the event. They won two Briers together, in 1982 and 1985. They asked me to speak at the closing banquet and I accepted. They spoke first, then it was my turn. I told the story of how, after losing a game to Manitoba at the 2003 Brier, I was handed a fax. It read: "Congratulations Russ, on becoming the skip with the most losses in Brier history. Ha Ha Ha. Al Hackner." The record I'd broken had belonged to Al! Then I offered up the best description I'd ever heard of Rick Lang, the skinny third, who had also won a third Brier in 1975. In his prime, it was said, Rick weighed 140 pounds at the top of his backswing.

I believe the young audience got the message: we had all had wonderful memories throughout our long curling careers and we hoped they too would continue to curl competitively.

From Thunder Bay, I travelled to Kamloops to meet the rest of the team and play in the Canada Cup. We were besieged by the media, despite our edict of a few weeks earlier. We set ground rules again and told ourselves we wouldn't let the media interfere with our games or practice time.

I was worried about Brad. He had taken on the bulk of the interviews, and it was starting to wear him down. It was getting tougher and tougher to get out of the limelight.

We didn't qualify at the Canada Cup but we played better than in Winnipeg, and I felt better about our game. As long as we were improving, we were doing what we needed to do to prepare. Our play reassured us that we were on the right track.

Looking back, going to Kamloops was probably a bit of a mistake. We could have played in Europe then stayed until the Olympics. The American team had done that, and it made sense. We could have played in curling conditions similar to what we would have at the Olympics.

But the CCA pressed us to go to the Canada Cup because it was their event. The competition was good, and so were the conditions, but it was a long way to go, especially for the other players coming from Newfoundland. It also meant after the Cup we had a long flight to Toronto two days before we left for Italy and had to cope with a 9 hour time change. This was a concern.

We had no real plan as to what we were going to do when we landed in Toronto. Waite invited us to his house in St. Thomas, about two and a half hours from the airport, but I thought our best plan was to hide away somewhere no one—the press, family, friends—could find us. We needed a couple of days of doing nothing.

Then I had a brainstorm and told the guys about my mother's cottage near Midland, close to Georgian Bay. We could be alone there. It was Super Bowl Sunday, and I told the guys we could be at the cottage for the opening kickoff. We pulled out of the rental car garage in

Toronto as the snow started, and it didn't let up; our hour-and-a-half journey took three and a half hours. We got to Midland, picked up the key at my mom's house and even though I hadn't seen her in over a year, she kept the visit short, just long enough for Mike and Mark to shovel her driveway. We set off for the cottage, dodged a fallen tree in the road, and we were there. Snow blocked the driveway, but I trudged through waist-deep snow banks to the door. When I got close to the building, I could hear the alarm going off, indicating the power was out. The door had an electronic lock, which meant with the power out, I couldn't get into the place! I waded to the car to give the guys the bad news. We drove through the storm to Midland, got a few rooms at the Highland Hotel, and caught the last ten minutes of the game in the hotel bar.

The next morning I woke up about five o'clock, not sure what time zone I was in. Brad was still asleep, and I decided to take a spin to the cottage. The storm hadn't let up, and the cottage was still without power. I returned to the hotel, and Brad was up and I could see he was in discomfort.

"I think there's something wrong with my tooth," he said. "It's really hurting me. What if it gets bad in Italy? What would we do then?"

He had a point. The tooth had to be taken care of. Luckily my best friend in the area, Dave Scanlon, was a dentist. I called him, explained the situation, then took Brad over to get the tooth checked. Brad had a slight infection, and Dave prescribed antibiotics, which we checked thoroughly to ensure they didn't contravene the drug code. We picked up the boys at the hotel, then went to the curling club to practise. As we were finishing, some seniors and school kids came in for their regular sessions. We obliged them all with photos and autographs. But the word was out, and it travelled fast. We barely got to our hotel when the phone rang, and CBC Newfoundland was calling. They had a crew in Toronto and wanted to come up to interview us. It was hard to say no; we did a session with them at the curling club with us teaching the juniors.

Soon my cell phone started ringing with friends, relatives and locals. The newspaper wanted an interview, my nephew—Glenn's son—showed up at the curling club on a snowmobile asking if he could throw rocks with me. Our peace and quiet was gone. I sent the boys off on their own, and I visited my mother-in-law and my mother. I returned to the hotel late Monday, collapsing into bed.

We hadn't made it to Italy yet and I was already beat. The CCA and COA people had told us to get rest and then more rest. We were doing the opposite, and at 49, I was starting to feel it. My body started to ache and my head started to get foggy. Despite all I had done to try to stay healthy, I was run down. In Toronto, as I boarded the plane that would take us to Frankfurt and then on to Italy, there was no doubting it—I was getting sick. There couldn't be a worse time, and I was mad at myself for letting it happen.

We finally landed in Italy, and I had no idea what time zone my body was in. Between the jet lag and my cold, I felt like a bag of hammers. But there were more problems. We walked into the airport, to a special Olympic check-in area, and our credentials were all messed up. Each of us was supposed to have a dog tag with all the security information on it, but five or six of the tags were missing. We were ushered into a holding room where we sat for about two hours. While Waite had told us to expect problems like this, I was upset. The CCA had hired a special liaison person in Italy to ensure everything went smoothly, and the first step was messed up. Being as cranky as I was at this point, I was not impressed. All I wanted was to get into a bed somewhere and sleep.

Eventually they put us on a bus for the two-hour ride to Torino. When we got there, we had to wait for the missing dog tags. Then we went through two more security clearances; finally, we were allowed into the Athlete's Village, which was set up in a series of interconnecting pods.

I flopped onto the bed and tried to sleep, but my mind wouldn't let my body shut down. I wanted to drink in the experience. Not long after checking in, we went to our first official function. Near the village, there was a flag-raising ceremony, and we watched the

Canadian flag go up the pole. I cried when the Maple Leaf went up. Here I was at the Olympics, representing my country and there was the flag of the country I was representing. It was all so hard to believe. I was beat up, I was sore, I was sick…but I was here.

By then, sleep was calling me and my aching body. I went to the room and was out cold before my head hit the pillow. The next morning I got a taste of how big and thorough the Canadian contingent was. I felt horrible, so I found Toby and asked him if he could get me a doctor. He said the doctor was in the pod next to ours. The medical facility was amazing, with every piece of medical equipment I could think of and a full pharmacy.

The doctor checked me out and confirmed that I did indeed have something. He gave me a prescription and warned me that it was going to get worse before it got better. How right he was. In the next few days I rested as much as I could. But there were still jobs to do and events in which to participate. We had to get all fifty-three pieces of official clothing, which included two pairs of official long underwear, complete with the Canada logo on them.

The clothing was remarkable. There was a uniform for the opening ceremonies, a uniform for on the medal podium, one for wearing out and around, and more. If anything didn't fit, there was an alteration team ready to make adjustments. I had six pieces that needed adjusting, and they had it back to me in two days. Don't forget there were more than three hundred people in the Canadian contingent—that's a lot of needles pulling thread.

The food operation in the Village was even more impressive. It fed athletes from more than sixty-five countries, who came with different tastes and from different cultures. We could get just about anything we wanted twenty-four hours a day. If we wanted pork chops and sushi at 3:00 a.m., we could get it. There were huge coolers full of drinks. And there was a full McDonald's—it paid to be a sponsor, I guess.

A day away from the opening ceremonies, I was so sick I wasn't sure I would make it. This would have been a big problem if I had been the flag bearer—and apparently, I nearly was.

A few weeks before the Olympics, some of the high-profile athletes said they weren't interested in being the flag bearer. Some wanted to concentrate on their events; others weren't going to be in Torino in time. For example, the men's hockey team wasn't there for opening day.

Jan Carninci, a former CFL player who lived in Moncton, started a campaign to name me as flag bearer, and I was honoured to be considered. I was interviewed for a front-page story in *The Globe and Mail,* which seemed to ignite a fuse with the public.

Every sports association is allowed to nominate one person to be considered for flag bearer, and the CCA submitted my name. But the honour went to Danielle Goyette, a veteran of the women's hockey team and a deserving choice.

Some good came out of the process for me: the COA asked me to march into the stadium in the front row. I considered this a huge honour. When we lined up to march in, the Canadian group was fifty rows deep—the last row was in the parking lot when I was making my way into the stadium.

I didn't want to get more sick than I already was, so I put on both pairs of official long underwear, a turtleneck, a wool sweater and my big opening ceremonies jacket. I looked a little like the Pillsbury Doughboy, but I was warm.

Before we went in, the Canadian athletes were mingling and having their pictures taken with each other. One young skier paid me a compliment—sort of—when she said she wanted her picture taken with me so she could give it to her father, who was a fan. I was the oldest person on the Canadian team, and some of the athletes were younger than my kids.

We felt we were part of more than just a curling team—we were Team Canada. We were all in this together, for our country, 330 athletes doing our best for Canada.

Entering the stadium behind our flag was a moment I'll never forget. The facility was huge, and as Canada was announced, a huge cheer went up that sent chills down my spine. Flashes went off by the thousands, and I was speechless. The enormity of the spectacle was breathtaking. Suddenly the Brier seemed like a small event.

The ceremonies were marvelous, a great mix of just about everything: culture, history, sport and spectacle. The highlight for me was the F1 Ferrari, which came out and did five spins, drawing the Olympic logo in burned rubber on the platform in front of us. The cloud of smoke was so thick I couldn't see the car. The car drew the biggest cheer of the night. Ferrari in Italy is loved about as much as the Maple Leafs are in Toronto. When I was leaving the stadium later, I had my picture taken on the skid marks for Steven, who is a huge Ferrari fan.

The lighting of the Olympic flame was another great moment. It was almost like a fuse being lit: a couple of smaller torches ignited at one end of the stadium and triggered a domino effect onto other torches around the inside of the structure, then outside and finally to the main flame.

I will always remember the crowd, which was as loud as any I had ever heard. They were into it from the first moment and stayed into it throughout, rocking and cheering the entire night. It was an amazing spectacle, a ceremony these fans had waited years for, which wouldn't be repeated any time soon.

Let the Games Begin

14

THE DAY AFTER the opening ceremonies, we were scheduled to practise at a curling club in Pinerolo. But when I woke up, I knew there was no way I could get out of bed, let alone throw a curling rock. I couldn't remember another time I missed practice due to illness. I've been blessed with pretty good health, and I love curling so much I usually grit it out. This time, I wasn't about to suck it up, princess or not. I knew I needed rest more than rocks; if I tried to throw, I might get sicker and, in my weakened state, might get into some bad habits.

Toby agreed, so while the rest of the team practised, I stayed in the village. I grabbed a chair and sat outside in a little compound area. The temperature had soared to twelve or thirteen degrees, and I sat in the sun and tried to bake the bug out of me. The area had been freshly sodded, and the back legs of the chair sank down, providing me with a natural recliner. As athletes ran past in shorts and T-shirts, I sat in my two pairs of Olympic long underwear, a turtleneck sweater, gloves, toque and Olympic parka and sweated.

The next day I wasn't much better, but I went to the practice. It was a week since I'd been on the ice, and I worried about being ready for our first game. If I threw only twenty rocks, I'd get the blood flowing and the muscles working. Being on the ice made me feel a little better, but I was useless in terms of effective practice. I was weak, and my head was in a fog.

That was our last night in the Olympic Village for a while. The next morning we packed up our stuff and moved to Pinerolo, a town of about thirty thousand. The CCA arranged accommodation for us in an apartment building, the tallest building in the town, by about 14 stories. We were on the top floor, the nineteenth, which sounded wonderful until we got there and found three of the four elevators were out of service.

The fourth elevator was small, slow and unreliable. When the doors opened for the first time, Mike, Mark and Jamie got in with a couple of bags, and the elevator got stuck. We had to go up in shifts, and it was faster to walk up, although we didn't attempt that often.

By the time we moved in, it was the middle of the afternoon, and we decided to head out for something to eat and to check out the town that would be our home for most of the next two weeks. Pinerolo was a beautiful, quaint village full of small shops, and it was a pleasure to walk around. We came to a small restaurant that looked inviting, but the door was locked tight as a drum. We walked a little farther, found another restaurant, and it was closed too. The same at the next one.

We quickly learned that every day, seven days a week, all the stores and businesses had a siesta-type break. This had been in the information Waite had given us before we left, but it didn't register until we got into the town. Finally, at about five, one of the boys found a pizza place that was open.

The adjustments to Italy and the Olympics continued when we met our driver. He was a friendly man with a big smile, but he didn't understand a word of English, and we never got to know his name. He knew a handful of words in French, but only Mark knew any French and that was very limited. It became quickly apparent that we couldn't communicate with this fellow. I found it strange that after multiple visits by representatives from our association over the previous two years to check and re-check all the details, we got a driver who couldn't speak English. It was beyond comprehension, but we were stuck with him. Now we had to find a way to communicate. We resorted to pictographs: a picture of the apartment with the time told him when and where to pick us up. We drew a picture of the arena to get him to take us there. Venturing anywhere else in the van was a nightmare. During the competition, we walked down the line of vans for the teams, looking for a driver who spoke both English and Italian who could translate to this chap. One day I walked out of the arena with Markku Uusipaavalniemi, and when we got to his van, the driver asked him, in perfect English, how his practice went. And this driver was with the Finnish team!

I began to understand that at the Olympics, we had to expect the unexpected.

While we concentrated on preparing for the competition, the families were having their own struggles. Wendy, Steven and Ashley flew over with Toby's family. Wendy had made arrangements to get from Milan, where they landed, to San Secondo, a small village said to be a short walk from our venue in Pinerolo. Just before she left Canada, she reconfirmed the arrangements but was told the reservations did not exist. She booked a new minivan, but the price had gone from $600 to $1,800—for a two-and-a-half-hour return trip! The two families decided to split the cost and hope all the luggage would fit into the one minivan. After arriving, they found their driver, who didn't speak a word of English but convinced them to follow him to their vehicle. The luggage was going to fit without any difficulty—the "minibus" was a sixty-seater!

The group arrived at the small Hotel San Secondo, which turned out to be an hour's walk from Pinerolo. For some reason, the CCA liaison person had given up on accommodation in Pinerolo and opted for putting the families in a place that was marginally better but in a smaller village outside of town. When they arrived, there was more trouble; the reservations they had booked in December were gone—given to the Russian hockey team. The McDonalds and Howards had been moved to another hotel for two days, then they would stay at Hotel San Secondo. The rooms at the second hotel were extremely small, and the weary travellers had to sleep on cots with their luggage stacked beside them.

Two days later they returned to Hotel San Secondo and met with another snag. The reservations for the Howards and McDonalds had again disappeared, even though Wendy produced confirmation numbers and receipts of payment. It didn't seem to matter. The hotel had reserved rooms for the families of the Swiss and Canadian curlers, but the Howards and MacDonalds were not included on the reservation list. Wendy wasn't about to give up. Where else could she go?

Finally, the hotel found a room at yet another location that could hold one family. It had dripping taps, no heat, doors that didn't lock, a cot for Steven, appliances and a TV that didn't work and no hot water, all for $700 a night…priceless!

At two in the morning, Toby's family went into Pinerolo and moved into his small hotel room, and my family slept in the apartment with the dripping taps, etc.

The next day, they went back to the Hotel San Secondo to talk some more. Through a generous volunteer translator, Wendy spent the best part of the day trying to get a room, negotiating with the hotel manager, the booking agent, Mike Murray, who had made the arrangements on behalf of the CCA, and the translator.

Thankfully, Steven and Ashley were warned that there would be difficult times on this trip. They were troopers and rolled with the punches.

All around Torino, scores of people were desperately trying to find rooms. At one point, Mike Murray sat down with Wendy and started to talk, and broke down crying. It was all becoming too much even for him. Toby had arranged his family's accommodations through the CCA, who eventually secured an apartment in Pinerolo. Toby and Wendy stayed in touch as she battled for our family at the Hotel San

Secondo. Several alternatives were suggested, even putting Wendy and the kids on cots in the lobby with use of the main public washroom without a shower. There wasn't any way they could convince Wendy to agree to that. After a lot of talking, a suite mysteriously became available, and Wendy and the kids had a base.

I heard only tiny bits of the story; Toby and Wendy, seasoned veterans of curling events, knew the fewer distractions, the better the team would perform.

While Toby and Wendy could talk at the venue, there was no way to communicate with the families on a regular basis. All the athletes had free phones but families had nothing. Eventually I gave my cell phone to Wendy, and Brad and I shared his. Brad's fiancée, Krista, and his dad used my phone to keep in touch with Brad's mother, Maureen, who was in St. John's undergoing chemotherapy. Wendy and the family could reach me on Brad's phone.

Although the families settled in at the Hotel San Secondo, their challenges weren't over. Transportation became a huge problem at the Torino Olympics for all spectators, our families included. San Secondo was a quaint little Italian village, and the Hotel San Secondo was beautiful. It would have been a wonderful place for a holiday. However, the families needed to travel to and from Pinerolo for the curling events and to Torino for Canada House events, other sports events and the medal ceremonies. Leaving San Secondo was easy: a bus stopped around the corner from the hotel. The adventure was trying to get back. The families dubbed it "The Amazing Race" after the reality television show. Every day, the families scrambled to get food, water and some transportation home. There were only two taxicabs in Pinerolo, and both drivers stopped work at eight each evening. Buses also stopped in the early evening. Our games finished at 10:30. Some evenings they walked back through rain or snow. No matter what the conditions, they were there to support us, and they did everything they could not to distract us with their problems.

Trips into Torino were no less difficult. Torino was packed with people travelling in trains, buses and cars. The train schedules weren't altered to accommodate the larger volume of people traveling to and from. The trip between Pinerolo to Torino was made by train, and the families were constantly running to catch the last train, then debating how they would get from the station in Pinerolo to San Secondo. They became very creative. The manager at the Hotel Regina, where the CCA was staying, arranged a taxi for them through his friends. On other nights they walked the one hour-trip.

These problems experienced by our families could have been a major distraction to our team, and we were lucky to have someone as experienced as Wendy to ensure it was kept from us. Wendy has accompanied me to more than 20 national and international events over the years and the CCA always had vehicles to transport immediate family to and from games and special events. We were warned there might be problems like this, but I'm the type of person who tries to correct errors. I believe it is up to our association to be proactive. After all, this is the Olympics. It was also frustrating to see the CCA staff, who were there to provide support to us, with vehicles to get around. I can't believe it would have been that difficult to add a couple more vehicles to help the families.

Our first look at the curling facility impressed us. The building was great, with superb lighting and a nice, cozy atmosphere. Once we got onto the ice, however, opinions began to change. The sliding surface was nice, it felt fine under foot, but the conditions were as straight as I'd ever played on.

There were also all kinds of bad rocks. We identified them, but when play started, more bad stones popped up. Shannon Kleibrink, the skip of the women's team, used a stone that picked three times, which cost her the contest. We used the same stone because Brad had liked it in practice. It caught three times in our game and almost cost us the game against Switzerland.

A lot of stones were slightly faster or slower, and on my first day in the building, I threw until I couldn't throw anymore, trying to match them up. But the rocks were depressingly straight; clearly, it wasn't the ice that was the problem, it was the rocks. The more I threw, the more upset I got. During a break, I vented to Jimmy Waite who had been privy to this information since the Olympic Trials in Halifax.

"We've known about these straight rocks for at least two months," I said, recounting my conversation with Shorty Jenkins after the Trials. "This is only the Olympics. Why didn't someone look into this?"

We weren't the only ones complaining. During that practice session, Pal Trulsen, from Norway, said the same thing I was thinking: the ice was fine, but the rocks were brutal. A player from Norway—where conditions are usually straight—was complaining about how straight the rocks were.

After practice, some reporters asked Trulsen and I what we thought of the ice. We said the ice was good, but the rocks were a problem. The rocks had been refurbished with smooth inserts. (A small portion of the bottom of the stone, including the running surface, was carved out and replaced with new granite. The new granite needs to be roughed up so the stone can bite into the ice, especially on arena surfaces). The bigger problem with these particular inserts was they were travelling on the outside edge of the running cup. (Every rock runs on a small band that has an inside and an outside edge, as opposed to the inside edge.) Thus they were more susceptible to catching debris. These rocks did a lot of debris-catching.

All the teams were experiencing problems. The icemakers asked for our input and tried to create better conditions. First they tried softening the ice to create more curl, hoping the rocks would grab more. The combination of the softer ice and these particular inserts caused more rocks to pick. After three or four draws of that, the ice-makers turned down the temperature to harden the ice and make conditions more consistent. Their next move was to "dish" the ice by scraping the centre lower than the sides. This made the ice curl from the outside of the sheet into the middle. Rocks could not curl from the inside out, but it was certainly an improvement because most shots in a game are thrown from the outside in.

Halfway through the event, thanks to the icemakers' creativity, we had the best conditions we could hope for. I wondered why I couldn't at least have a constructive discussion with Jim Waite, our liaison with the international curling officials. We needed sandpapered rocks that would curl on arena conditions; such rocks would make our event a spectacle. We had the biggest audiences in the history of curling. We had the four-rock rule, ten national championship teams from around the world, and rocks that wouldn't curl. Without the curl, there is no strategy or excitement. Without excitement, curling wouldn't be an Olympic sport for long. Jim told us to expect at least three feet of curl to the ice. I knew, through Shorty, that there was no way these rocks were going to curl three feet. My frustration with Jim and the CCA went back a long way. Waite was our national coach at the World Championships in Geneva in 1993 where the ice was 12 inches thick at one end of the arena and less than an inch at the other. This caused the ice to be 12 to 15 feet faster in one direction. Thirteen years later our association, which has all the technology and know-how to create great conditions, kept its head in the sand, saying, "There's nothing we can do. Just take less ice." The game has passed these people by. It wasn't just a case of taking less ice; it was tough to out-skip a team when there was only one rock in play.

Jim was quoted in another book about this. "Russ is vocal, but he has to realize that the people are not making ice for Russ Howard. What we have to do is to train our teams better to play better on crappy or straight ice. We are not masters of straight ice. The other teams are catching up on our ice as they come over here all the time to play."

I never expected anyone to make ice for me. I thought Olympic curlers deserved the best conditions, the best rocks, the best opportunity to showcase the sport. It has always frustrated me that the CCA won't lobby harder for a higher standard of playing conditions at international events. For Jim to criticize one of his national team members and to suggest that our elite teams prepare for the biggest events of our lives on "crappy or straight ice" is shameful. We had the technology; we should have used it. Even the great Old Course at St. Andrews, Scotland, quit cutting the fairways with goats years ago.

I met with the president of the World Curling Federation, Roy Sinclair. "I hear you think there's something wrong with the rocks," he said. "I'll tell you that we had those rocks for a whole season at my club and they curl three feet. There's nothing wrong with them."

"Roy, we are not at your club. The surface has to be so much colder in an arena, and the pebble pattern is so different, the rocks that curl three feet in a curling club will only curl half as much in the arena. I'm trying to let you know that it's not the icemakers, it's the rocks. They won't curl. This is bad for curling." I spoke out whenever I was asked because that was the way I operated. I'd been around long enough to know that if the mistakes went unchecked, they continued. I was hoping something could be done. I suggested switching to the rocks we practised with at the Pinerolo curling club.

The rest of the team had been taught by the sports psychologists to accept what was presented to them and make the best of the situation. There was nothing they could do about the rocks, so they should learn how to play with them. Three times in the round robin, Mark Nichols, trying not to worry about the rocks, got caught with an unmatched pair and played three very poor games. Then he started to soften his release, which affected his laser-like accuracy, and by the end of the week his confidence was hurt.

The more I lobbied to rectify conditions, the more distracted the team became. At one of our nightly meetings Mark said they weren't sure how to make the old guy happy again and asked me for suggestions. I smiled at Mark (that was a tough thing for him to say) and said, "Don't worry about me; I'll do my talking on the ice." The next morning, I managed to curl ninety-six per cent against Great Britain. The press wanted to make it a Disney script, where the team struggled early (we were 4–1) and the team dynamic suffered, but we magically turned it around to be the heroes at the end of the week. Our team dynamic was the best I'd seen in forty years. Yes, we had

discussions on how to make the team better, but under the guidance
of Toby McDonald, ours was the best prepared team I'd ever seen.

In our first game, we played well against a German team that wasn't
sharp. Germany was a perfect opponent for us in Game One. They
were good, but we felt we could handle them. We weren't afraid of
them, as we might have been against Sweden or Great Britain, our
next two opponents. This was our first game of the Olympics, and we
were wearing the Maple Leaf on our backs—I'm surprised we weren't
more nervous.

We chose to play defensively for the first part of the game, to get
used to the ice and the atmosphere in the building. The Germans had
the same game plan, and the first five ends were pretty straightforward. The conditions were quite straight, with a tiny bit of curl. We
needed a good start and we got it, easing to a 10–5 victory.

Our second game was against Sweden and their talented skip,
Peter Lindholm. The Swedes had soft releases on their deliveries, almost as if they were dumping the rocks. They could get two or three
feet more curl from their rocks than we could. That meant they could
put a rock where we couldn't get to it. We were putting the broom
on the edge of the four-foot to draw the button. They were getting
to the button by taking ice at the edge of the eight-foot. Sweden
practised first, and we watched them throw. Jim Waite commented
on how swingy the ice was compared to our first game. I explained
that it wasn't the ice or the rocks; it was the Swedish releases. I've
played Peter Lindholm many times over the years and I was aware
of his team's ability to make the rock curl. I told Jim nothing had
changed. When we practiced, Brad threw his first two stones, turned
to me and said: "Uh-oh, Sweden can make those rocks curl." Brad and
Mark both throw from an inside position with a very positive rotation,
which results in less curl than normal. They could not possibly get in
behind the guards the way the Swedish team could. I tried to emulate

the European style by sliding slightly wide of the broom and feeding the rock in towards the target to create the desired curl.

Why I would try to alter my delivery in the biggest competition of my life was beyond me. The harder I tried, the worse it got, and I let the team down in that one. The stats had me shooting at sixty-seven per cent, one of the lowest marks I ever turned in, and even that was probably generous. I played a little better near the end of the game, and we took the Swedes to an extra end, but we lost when Brad's last two shots picked.

We were 1–1 and not playing the way we'd hoped. I was mad at myself for going away from my game. The mood in the dressing room was tough. Brad had thrown two really good rocks, with poor results. A heavy weight peel managed to hit a piece of debris and ended up nosing the Swedish guard, so his shooter stayed right on the centre line. His next one was a draw to the four-foot, which looked perfect only three feet from its intended target. As we were about to congratulate him on a great shot, the stone hit something and curled just enough to wreck on the Swedish rock. That cost us the game. Brad was pretty upset.

We needed to win our third game, which was against a very strong Scottish team representing Great Britain. The British (really the Scots) had gone a different route in picking their rink. The country's top curlers were put through various tests, and the organizers chose the best at each position. The team had played together for a year.

There were pros and cons to this system, but the bottom line was the British team was very, very good. I thought they would contend for the gold. We were coming off the loss to Sweden, and this game was vital. If we lost to the contenders—Sweden, Great Britain and Norway—we might not make the playoffs. It was a real confidence check.

But we came out on fire. We were spectacular. It was my best game of the week. A renewed attitude was key, and I was finally beginning to feel better physically. All of us seemed stronger, we were starting to recover from the travel schedule. As a team, we scored seventy-six per cent in the first two contests, a low number for us. That third game, we were at eighty-six per cent.

The Brits played well, but we played better, grabbing a big three-ender in the fourth and stealing one in seven for a 9–5 win.

Although we were on the same team, so to speak, we rarely saw the women's team. We were on different draws, and the only time we saw them was near the dressing rooms, where we exchanged pleasantries and asked about conditions. Kleibrink and her rink were concentrating on their work, and so were we. We kept up on their progress, but our days were pretty regimented—set meal times, set practice times, set travel times. Toby had organized our regimen. He learned some of it from his mentor, Sam Richardson, of the famed Richardson family that won four Briers. Sam Richardson was the driver for the Newfoundland team in 1976 when they won the Brier under Jack MacDuff. Richardson built a plan for his team and forced them to live to it, and it had worked. Toby borrowed it and used it for us.

Game Four was a great test for the team. We were into our next group of three games and up against Switzerland. The icemakers had scraped the ice so it was dished—there was finally some curl, although it was only from the outside in. When we saw the ice moving to the centre, it was like watching a beautiful sunrise—we were thrilled. But Brad had somehow not picked up on a bad rock in practice, and it nearly cost us. In the third end, he had a relatively simple draw that picked (one of three in the contest) and the Swiss stole three points. That put us down 4–1, but we got one in the fourth and stole singles in each of the next four ends to win 7–5. The victory felt great.

Our next opponents were Pal Trulsen and Norway. It was a significant contest against the defending gold medalists. Coincidentally,

I knew Pal and his team very well. In 2000 I had been invited to Norway to teach strategy to their elite men's teams, which included the jovial Pal Trulsen and his team. Pal's team had two losses, so we knew we could put a knife in their chances by beating them. We came out strong and played a great game. In the tenth end, the game was tied; with a series of good freezes, we forced Trulsen to make a very delicate come-around tap back, which he just missed. Brad didn't have to throw his last one.

At this point, I felt we were playing at about 90 per cent of our ability. We weren't playing poorly, but it wasn't the same as at the Trials; we were working a lot harder here. To some extent the conditions didn't allow us to play great, but we were winning and that's what mattered. But we suffered a setback in the next game, which was against Finland and Markku Uusipaavalniemi. It was close through the first two ends; in the third, they ended up with a couple of biters and we had a pair of rocks buried on the four-foot. They made a sensational shot that doubled our two counters out and left them sitting three.

A few ends later, they did the same thing. Uusipaavalniemi called and made an unbelievable shot for four, putting the game out of reach, although we did force him to make his last shot to win. I left that game with a very good impression of the Finnish skip. He had all the shots—the big weight hit, the soft touch shots—and he wasn't afraid to gamble in his strategy. The game really took me by surprise.

At 4–2, I still felt positive about our chances. If I'd known what was going to happen in the game against Italy, I might not have had such a rosy outlook. Weeks ago, when we were making arrangements for the families, I told Wendy that with the different events going on and the high ticket prices for curling, she and the kids might take a pass on our game against Italy, ranked near the bottom of the pack. But so was our team at the Olympic Trials. The family stayed but may have wished they didn't.

Before the Olympics, I thought we would easily beat Italy. But when I saw them play, I had a different opinion. They played well and were far from the free space on the curling bingo card I'd imagined.

They were coached by Roger Schmidt, originally from Saskatoon. I'd beaten him in the final of the World Championships in 1987, when he was curling for Germany. I knew he'd have his team prepared for us.

The Italians also had the hometown crowd behind them, and that crowd was huge. About ninety-nine per cent of their fans had likely never seen a curling rock thrown before. When the Italian skip, Joel Retornez, threw his final shot to blank the end and stuck to take a point, the crowd erupted in cheers.

In the game between Italy and Sweden, Lindholm had a tricky shot on his last one in the ninth to score two. He had to come through a narrow port and remove an Italian rock to secure the deuce. From the time Lindholm started his delivery, the Italian fans, with the true soccer mentality, booed him and the rock until it finally made it through the port and accomplished its job. Lindholm was livid and fired his broom against the backboards, setting off another chorus of boos.

In the first five ends of our game against Italy, we were flat. We'd get a chance for two set-ups, then not finish it off, or we'd get them in a great position for a steal and their skip would make a big shot to bail them out of trouble. After five ends, we were trailing 5–1. Later, Toby told us the second half of the game against Italy was when the Olympics started for us. We didn't come back to beat the Italians, but we started to play the way we had at the Trials.

It was tough to lose to Italy, but it was great to see the reactions of the Italian curlers as they celebrated beating us in front of a cheering crowd. As I left the ice, I saw Schmidt with tears of joy in his eyes and went over to congratulate him. He shook my hand and said, "I've been trying for twenty years to beat you."

We were 4–3 and not feeling too comfortable about our position. Toby did a great job of trying to rally our spirits and keep us thinking positive. Elaine Dagg-Jackson, the women's national coach, had organized a birthday party at Canada House to celebrate Jim's birthday (February seventeenth) and mine (February nineteenth). The celebrations included a slide show of the men's and women's teams competing at the Olympic Trials in Halifax, which was quite motivational for both teams. For much of the evening I talked to Mike Harris, the silver medalist from the 2002 Olympics, who was providing colour commentary on the curling for CBC. Mike was probably the only person in the room who knew what we were going through, and he was very supportive.

I hadn't seen Wendy and the kids much that week. As part of our preparation, Toby kept us in this bubble to eliminate any distractions, and that included family. In 30 years of curling around the world, Wendy was alongside me every step of the way, so this was foreign to me. Brad and the boys were single and used to competing on their own. We weren't out at night with our families, sightseeing or going for big dinners.

I couldn't even see Wendy at the rink. Security wouldn't allow any athletes to get too close to the fans until after the event. Waves were okay; hugs were not.

The party gave me a chance to reintroduce myself to my family. Steven and Ashley were competitive curlers and it was fun to talk about the first half of the Olympics, even though we were 4–3. I could feel their pride and excitement.

My life as a fifty-year-old began the next day with a game against New Zealand and we started to feel good about things. We were playing better, the ice was curling, and the jet lag was finally gone. (It took me the better part of a week to get over it.)

We went out and defeated the Kiwis 9–1. They were a fabulous bunch of guys—they presented me with a birthday gift that morning —but this late in the round robin, they weren't exactly grinding it. We grabbed three points in the sixth and three more in the seventh, after which they conceded.

The next day, our final round-robin game was against the Americans. Toby woke us up with some bad news: Jamie was so sick he couldn't play. There was a quick powwow with me, Toby, Jim, Mark and Brad. Should we bring Jamie in sick—something he was willing to do—or should we bring in Mike? I favoured bringing in Mike. Everyone agreed.

If we won the game against the U.S., we would wrap up the round robin. If we lost, we would be 5–4 and we would have to play a nightmarish series of tiebreakers. We would also let Sweden, Norway and Switzerland back into the competition.

Mike was nervous, something he admitted after the game. At the Trials, he played one end and made both his shots. That became the running joke before the game. I told him we wanted him to play only because his shooting percentage was one hundred for the year, and we wanted to knock that down. He was great throughout the game, made lots of shots and swept well. He finished the game at eighty-three per cent, the highest mark on the team.

The Americans were coached by Canadian Ed Lukowich, who beat me in the Brier final in 1986. He prepared the American team very well for the Olympics, and they gave us a great game. I was impressed with the skip, Pete Fenson, an excellent shotmaker. (We got another taste of that in the semifinals.) We were up one playing the ninth and Brad made a great hit and roll that led to a steal of one, which proved to be the key in the 6–3 victory.

We were two wins away from gold, but they were two of the most nerve-racking, anxiety-filled games of my career.

Medal Hunt

HEADING INTO THE PLAYOFFS, we got some good news. Jamie had recovered. As mysteriously as he'd become sick, he was well. He recovered so quickly and completely that he considered playing the second half of our last round-robin game against the Americans. What afflicted him remained a mystery.

After the last round-robin game, we decided to go to Torino to take in a Team Canada hockey game. We had a day off, and watching hockey would keep us busy, and we had not yet seen another event. While in Torino, we met up with some of the women hockey players, who had won the gold medal a day earlier. Mike and Mark were engaged in conversation with one of them and called me over.

"Russ, come and see the gold medal," Mike said.

I got to within a few feet and looked at it, but I didn't want to touch it. It was shiny and twinkling in the light. I wanted to hold it to feel what it was like. But I resisted. "I'm going to wait until I get one of my own," I told them.

The next day we went to the rink to practise and go through our normal set of drills. Near the end, Mark walked off the ice, clearly frustrated, which was completely out of character. He was always attentive and diligent at our practices. In the round robin, he had been struggling with his run backs. The shot took precision and weight, but was vital in the era of the free guard zone. It was also usually one of Mark's strengths.

Mark had a very pronounced arm push that added to the rock's speed. For the average player that move is almost always a kiss of death, but for a curler of Mark's skill, it was an asset. For some reason, during most of the round robin he let the rock go without the push, which affected the way he released the stone. Instead of being thrown out to the target line, the stone was starting off inside and weak.

I grabbed Toby and told him we needed ice time to work out Mark's problems. He said not to worry, that Mark would be fine and in any case, there was no ice available at the arena. But I persisted and he eventually got us a sheet at the curling club where we first practiced.

The boys had planned to watch another event in Torino, but I wanted to help Mark. At first it was just the two of us, then Toby showed up, followed a few minutes later by Brad. Next in the door was Jim.

Shot after shot, I made Mark throw his run back. Shot after shot he kept missing, especially with the inturn. As he threw, everyone chimed in with bits of advice, and finally I asked him if he was doing anything different than he had in the Trials. He'd been stellar in Halifax; I was trying to get him to revisit the Trials in his mind.

He said he had stopped pushing the rock on Jim's advice, following our victory at the Olympic Trials. I asked him why; he said he wasn't sure. "Let's try pushing it;" I said. The change was dramatic. He missed the first one by a hair; then he made seven in a row. They were perfect. Mark came off the ice beaming. I was smiling, Brad was aglow and Toby and Jimmy were happy.

The day off also allowed us to pursue one of the games we'd enjoyed throughout our stay in the apartment in the building we affectionately dubbed the Skyscraper. When we first stood on the balcony, surveying all of Pinerolo, I commented that a paper airplane would sure look good off this height.

Before the words were out of my mouth, the boys were inside folding up sheets of paper. The game was to see who could make the best plane, based on hang time and distance. There was a court about a block away from our apartment, and it was our mission to get a plane all the way there. Trying to build the perfect Avro Arrow helped us kill a lot of time during that week.

The semifinal against the United States was in my mind the most nerve-racking game of the Olympics. A win would give us a fifty-fifty chance of winning the gold medal with the luxury of a silver medal already in our back pockets. If we lost the semifinal, our dream of gold or silver was gone, and we would have a fifty-fifty chance of leaving Italy in fourth place. A great accomplishment, but without any hardware.

I felt a lot of butterflies before the semifinal, but they scattered as soon as the game started. We played exceptionally well, but so, too, did the Americans. It was a great game, and I told Wendy later that it may have been the most enjoyable game I'd ever played.

In the fifth end, Pete Fenson, the U.S. skip, made one of the all-time great shots I had witnessed. He got through a hole that looked like it wasn't even there. That gave them one and made the score 4–3. We kept coming at them every end. And, in almost every end, Fenson would pull off some tremendous shot and keep the game close.

In the ninth, we were one up with the hammer. I had a hunch they were going to pull out all the stops to try to force us to one, then score two in the tenth and take their chances in an extra end. Jamie and I set up the end well, and by the time Mark finished shooting, we were sitting five. With his last one, Fenson managed to get one half-hidden at the back of the eight-foot, and we had a choice: play soft weight and tap it out or blast it à la Brad. He chose the blast, removed the American stone, and we scored five.

We were guaranteed a silver medal. I was part overjoyed and part relieved, knowing I had a medal. I knew that for the rest of my life, I'd have that medal and I would know we had earned another tick in a column for Canada. One of the first calls I made when I got out of the rink was to my mother, who was in tears in Midland. She told me the semifinal win was the biggest of my career. The gold medal game was gravy, she said.

I agreed, but I still wanted to win gold. I had a lot of reasons, but one very special one: to honour a member of my family who had missed, despite the same opportunity nearly three-quarters of a century earlier. My great aunt, Jean Thompson, was a very good sprinter as a young woman. She was called the Penetanguishene Pansy and part of the Matchless Six, a group of women who dominated women's track and field in Canada in the late 1920s. Even competing was a small victory for women then, who were trying to get equality in a lot of areas of life. The first time Canada sent women to the Olympics was 1928, and my great aunt was on the team.

Thompson surprised many at the Olympic Trials, held coincidentally in Halifax, by winning the 880 meters in 2:21.5, thought to be a world record. (A German runner had bettered that mark the same day, but news travelled slowly back then.) It stunned many track experts who didn't know a lot about my great aunt, but soon after, predictions were that she was a shoo-in for a gold medal.

However, in training for the Games in Amsterdam, Aunt Jean was on the track running sprints when the men's 1,500 meter champion, Jack Walter, came past her. Not wanting to yield, she raced him, and the two set a blistering pace that ended when Thompson felt a twinge in her hamstring. She received lots of therapy, but wasn't quite herself. Still, she went to Amsterdam. Her determination and fortitude took over, and she entered the race. Spurred on by the great Bobby Rosenfeld, who paced her for much of the race, she was in position to win a medal when she was jostled by a Japanese runner. She lost her step and finished fourth. It was a story I had heard countless times growing up, and I was in a position to make amends for my great aunt's unfortunate finish. I wasn't about to let up.

I was happy with the way the competition unfolded. The teams I worried about at the start of the week—Sweden, Norway and Switzerland—hadn't made the playoffs. We advanced to the final four, and I would have placed the other teams in the following order: Great Britain, the U.S., Finland.

We'd beaten the U.S., and Finland had knocked off Great Britain. I thought we were playing the weakest of the three teams for the gold medal. Of course, Finland wouldn't roll over for us—we still had a tough match. And they'd beaten us in the round robin.

On our day off, we pored over the stats to see if there was a weakness in the Finnish lineup. Markku Uusipaavalniemi had enjoyed a brilliant week, finishing with the highest shooting percentage among the skips. His third, Wille Makela, was also playing well. We decided we had to jump on them at the front-end positions, forcing their lead and second to make big shots. If we got into any trouble, Mark, with his delivery back in synch, would be able to bail us out.

That plan didn't work that well in the first end: with his final shot, Uusipaavalniemi was looking at a hit for three. He scored only two after making a half shot on his last one, and the difference of a single point was huge. There were not a lot of three-enders at this level of competition, but there were all sorts of twos. We definitely had dodged a bullet.

In the next end I made a nice hit and roll followed by four great shots from Mark and Brad that set up a deuce to tie the game. In the third end we were all over the Finns, and Uusipaavalniemi had to make a great angle raise to cut us down to one.

In the fourth end we never missed and stole another point to go up 4–2.

The next end we slipped somewhat, and the Finns played well. On his last shot, Brad went with a higher risk shot by drawing through a hole for a tap. If he wrecked, we would probably give up three. He made it through the hole but rolled just a bit too far, giving the Finns a free draw for two—or so it appeared. Uusipaavalniemi came a bit heavy, and I jumped on it at the tee line and pounded it as hard as my 50-year-old body could. We ended up winning a measure, which meant one point instead of two.

Unforced mistakes had cost Uusipaavalniemi's team two important points. I could see how losing the measure knocked any wind they had right out of their sails. They were trailing by one without last rock, and they chose to go aggressive so they could get back in the game. Jamie made two good shots to start the end, and I followed with two delicate tap backs behind cover. With Mark's first rock, we had three in the rings, but two were little nibblers. Our third was shot rock on the button, but they had one dead in front of it, which scared us a great deal. Two long guards protected those two stones.

My thinking was if we only got one, we'd be two up. Of course we wanted to score two to go three up, but even a single would allow us to keep control. We couldn't get the rocks on the button because of the guards, so I called for Mark to peel the two guards and roll out, not a tough shot the way the rocks were sitting. I desperately wanted to get rid of the guards to keep things clean and ensure we had options with our last three stones. As well, removing the guards limited their chance to steal.

There were options with the double peel. If he hit too much of the target rock, Mark could drive one of the guards back onto the two stones in the rings. That wasn't all bad because it was our rock that would be running back into the pile, and the guards would be gone. But if we lost our own shot stone, Finland would be shot rock, and we would have two nibblers, with two guards out in front. Finland could either hit one of the outside rocks, which would probably give us a deuce, or guard the lone Finnish stone in the rings for their lives.

Mark was hesitant about throwing the double peel. I reassured him it was the right call and said I had every confidence in his ability to make the shot.

Mark threw peel weight, but was slightly narrow. As the rock came closer to the first guard, I realized we were not rolling out with the shooter as we wanted, so I called them off sweeping, hoping to run the first guard onto the second guard and back onto the Finnish rock in the rings. Instead, the stone came straight back, hitting a sliver of the Finnish rock, driving it at right angles past our shot rock.

Never in my wildest dreams did I imagine we could pick it clean. But that's what Mark did, removing the Finnish stone and leaving us sitting three. The crowd went absolutely nuts.

Once the dust settled, however, I could see it wasn't the perfect situation. Mark had thrown a tremendous shot, one that will be replayed thousands of times, but we weren't out of the woods yet. Up in the centre of the sheet was Mark's shooter, sitting there as a perfect guard. We were sitting three, but one perfectly placed come around by Uusipaavalniemi would force us to one point, two at the very best, and the game would still be on. With his last stone, the Finnish third did try to draw around the guard, but it stayed out in the open. Mark hit that stone and rolled perfectly. We were sitting four.

Uusipavalniemi tried the same shot and came around the guard perfectly with his first one, but was just heavy enough to rub off our shot rock and spill into the open. Brad hit that one and rolled partially covered. We were sitting five.

Uusipaavalniemi tried to come around and play a delicate one into the pile, but that rock bent a little sooner than he expected. As it was halfway down the sheet, I knew it was never getting past our guard that was just short of the rings. My mind started to race with excitement. I knew it was a big end, but I didn't stop to think there were five rocks already in the rings. I knew I had to run and sweep the one he was going to wreck on, because it could end up in the rings too. I swept the raised stone as hard as I could. As it stopped, I looked down. It appeared to be about a half-inch inside the rings.

Brad yelled, "Russ, Russ, this one, this one."

He was pointing to the Finnish shooter, which was about to cross the tee line and was precariously close to the edge of the twelve-foot. I haven't moved that fast in years. I jumped from the top of the twelve-foot and got to the Finnish rock just as it reached the tee line. I got four or five good swipes in before the rock stopped—no more than one inch outside the rings. "Is it out?" Brad asked. "Yup," I replied. There was a pause as both of us surveyed the house.

"We're sitting six," he said in a tone that indicated he was finding it hard to believe. It took a couple of seconds to comprehend. Then it sank in—this game was over.

Brad and I looked at each other with huge smiles. A moment later, Jamie and Mark came down the ice to survey the situation. "Is it out?" Jamie asked. This time Brad responded. "It sure is."

I could hardly hear them for the deafening noise of the Canadian fans. I don't think anyone in the crowd knew we were sitting six, but they knew it was enough. We knew it was enough. We knew we would be the gold medalists. But we still had another rock to throw.

"Maybe we should throw it through," Brad suggested.

I told him to play a draw, and I put the broom down in a spot that gave him a wide berth into the rings. He didn't want to play it that way, in case it picked. The Finns still had a rock in front of the rings; Brad worried his shot might pick and push their rock in. The odds were slim, but Brad had a point. Why take the chance?

I suggested taking the other turn and draw away from the guard, but Brad was worried about that shot too. Eventually he agreed with me and tore off down the sheet—sprinted actually—to throw the last rock. He asked me to move the broom at least three times, to get me to go closer to the boards and farther away from the only thing that could hurt us. As soon as he let it go, Jamie called, "We need backing." He knew it was far too heavy, so the guys kept it clean all the way down the sheet and watched as it slipped through the rings and into the hack.

Brad came down the sheet and apologized. "Sorry, guys, I was just pumped up. Where did that stop?"

I lied, "It just went through, Brad, just through the rings."

"I'm surprised it didn't hit the boards," Brad admitted. "I couldn't get my heart to slow down."

For the first time in my life, I had to use two hands to signal the score to the official holding up one full hand and the index finger from the other to give him confirmation of the six-ender. When the score was posted on the scoreboard, the Canadian fans erupted.

Before we started the next end, we got together, as we always did thanks to our training from Toby, to ensure we were all focused. Jamie told us to stay in the moment, to keep concentrating, to make sure we kept playing hard. He was talking a hundred miles an hour. I tried to calm them by just reminding them to stay consistent with the peel weight. All our mental preparation for the game had been directed towards a close contest, a nail biter, with the possibility of having to play an extra end. A huge lead wasn't something we had imagined, and so we weren't prepared for it. According to the rules, we had to complete eight ends before a team could concede, so we had to remain focused and sharp for at least two more ends. It was tougher than it might sound.

After I threw my two peels in the seventh end, I was hit by a wave of emotion. I was going to be a gold medal winner. I looked at the Finnish team and could tell they did not want to be out there anymore. But we were stuck for at least two more ends. It was crazy. When I came down to start the next end, I turned to Uusipaavalniemi and said I was sorry that we had to stay out there. I felt it was tough for him to be there with the scoreboard reading 10-3. But he said it was okay, he understood the rules. His team never quit trying to make shots, but they knew as well as we did that the game was over.

I tried to concentrate on the game, but my mind was awash with other thoughts. I knew I was going to doping control for another test. We had been warned that no family members could come over the boards to celebrate. All I wanted to do was hug Wendy and Ashley and Steven.

And then, as much as I wanted the game to end, as the rocks came down the sheet, I suddenly felt that I wanted the game to go on forever so I could continue to experience the euphoria. I knew I'd never be back on Olympic ice so I wanted to drink it all in. When it came time to shoot, I tried to focus. It was *almost* over, but it wasn't over, and I didn't want to be known as the guy who blew a seven-shot lead and lost the gold medal. It was the strangest set of emotions I'd ever gone through.

Uusipaavalniemi blanked the seventh, and when we got to the eighth, all the crazy emotions had gone. We were just curling, not worrying any more. Mark made a great double with one of his, and when Uusipaavalniemi was playing his first shot, Brad leaned over and whispered, "Do you think he'll quit?"

"If you make this next one he will," I answered.

Brad made his last one, a takeout, then slid down to stand beside me.

"Is he going to quit?"

"Yup, he's going to quit," I said. I had heard them talking while Brad was playing his shot.

As Uusipaavalniemi's rock came down the sheet, the crowd sensed it was over and began to rise. The Canadian flags were waving. When his rock came to a stop, Uusipaavalniemi lifted his hand to offer congratulations. I shook his hand and then immediately felt Brad hugging me.

"Thanks, Russ," he said into my ear.

It was the same thing he'd said to me after the Trials, and it was the greatest recognition he could have paid me. We met the other guys in front of the house and had a group hug. Mike came in, and there was another hug. Then Toby joined the group for another one. Then we started high-fiving each other and living the moment. Jamie looked at me and with a big smile said, "I can't believe I just won a gold medal with Russ Howard."

Brad, of course, raced to a phone and tried to call his mother who was watching back home, unable to travel because of her illness. It was a poignant moment for him.

I waved to Wendy and the kids. I could see there were some tears going on up there, and it was frustrating not be able to get to them. I looked at my family, then pointed towards the heavens. In that moment, I had won a gold medal for my country, but also for my dad. I knew he would have had tears of pride in his eyes. He was the ultimate curling father, a perfectionist, a teacher who was able to pass his passion for the sport on to me. In that moment, I could see that passion had been passed along to his grandchildren.

It was a strange celebration because of the way the game had played out. At the Trials, it had been tense until the measurement gave us the victory. Our game against Uusipaavalniemi had been more or less over from the moment we scored the six-ender, but we couldn't celebrate then. It was an amazing feeling to have won, but it was an unusual delayed and drawn-out feeling.

After we finished our celebrations we went through the routine— CBC live interview, the rest of the media interviews, then a small ceremony in the arena with all three medalists. After that it was off to doping control, which took forever because they could only do one person at a time. I thought of the prescription the doctor put me on when I was sick at the start of the Olympics as I filled up the bottle.

With that completed, we were trotted out once more for an interview with Brian Williams, which also took forever because of technical problems. At last, we were allowed to get changed and pack up our lockers.

The gold medal game started at 5:30 pm. When I finally stood with my family, it was 11:55. We met at the hotel in Pinerolo, where there was a big celebration going on. All of us were bawling our eyes out, and Ashley was so emotional she didn't know whether to laugh or cry. It was a great moment for the Howards. Wendy had given me so much support over the years, and for surviving this trip, she deserved her own gold medal. There was no way I could have made it without her or without the support of Steven and Ashley.

The next day, we packed up from the Skyscraper and moved back into the Olympic Village to prepare for the medal ceremony. There were special uniforms for the medal presentation, and we slipped those on, then headed off to get our gold. A police escort took us through a maze of streets to the plaza. We drove the wrong way on one-way streets and even on the sidewalk; we made the trip in minutes, a stark contrast to the many hours it took Wendy and the kids who had to leave San Secondo almost eight hours before to ensure they made the connections to get there on time. Their transportation nightmare continued but there was no way they were going to miss this.

The presentation area was tucked into a court and designed to look like a structure from medieval times. It was stunning, and a perfect place for such an honour. We were dropped off by the police, and as we started walking to a holding area, Brad's phone rang. He answered casually but his tone changed and we knew someone important was on the other end. Stephen Harper, the Prime Minister, had called to congratulate us. We passed the phone from player to player, and he spoke to each of us. I had met Mr. Harper at a couple of celebrity golf events, and he mentioned that as we chatted. He obviously had been briefed or was a big curling fan, because he talked about the game and our team as if he knew what was going on. By the time the phone was handed to Jamie, he knew who was on the other end and started his conversation with a question in a thick Newfie accent.

"How's your new job going, b'y?" he said to the recently elected prime minister. After the call, we walked into the holding area where the other two men's teams and all three women's teams were gathered. I made a couple of calls, one to my good friend and New Brunswick teammate Grant Odishaw, another to my mother. I was getting sentimental, and memories were flooding my mind.

Then it was time. We were called to the edge of the stage where a curtain hid us from the fans. As we stood there, the medals were carried past us, and we got our first look at the spoils. First the Americans went out, followed by the Finns, then us. The announcement came, "Gold medalists and Olympic champions...Canada." As I stepped past the curtain, my jaw dropped. There were nine thousand people jammed into the tiny plaza that had been empty a half-hour earlier. A lot of them were Canadian, and they waved flags. Cheers went up. I saw Wendy, Steven and Ashley dead centre in the second row.

And then came the moment I had never thought possible four months earlier. We received our medals, one by one. Each one of us had the opportunity to congratulate each other. My name was called, and I received my medal; it was an unbelievable feeling.

A few moments later, *O Canada!* started to play, and the Canadian flag was raised on the centre flagpole, with the Finnish and U.S. flags on each side.

At the Trials, they played the anthem before every game, and I sang it loud every time, at first drawing some strange looks from the boys, who never uttered a peep the entire week. At the Olympics, as the music played, all five of us were belting it out. And the crowd joined in. About halfway through the anthem, I took my eyes from the flag and looked at my family, and the tears started to well up. Wendy was in tears, Steven was grinning from ear to ear with tears in his eyes, and Ashley couldn't decide whether to smile or cry, so she was doing both. As the anthem continued, I held back the tears. Near the end of the anthem I looked over at Brad. He was a puddle. We were led to the front of the stage, where our families could take pictures and we could take in the grandeur of what was happening. To share these emotional moments with my friends Brad, Mark, Jamie and Mike, with my family so close by, is one of the most cherished memories of my life.

As people left the plaza, we were asked to go around the back to do more interviews. We walked to the interview centre and were fortunate to bump into our families as they were leaving the plaza. It was remarkable timing, and we were all laughing, talking, taking pictures of each other and enjoying the fireworks. How lucky we all were to be together.

Everything was hitting home, all the work, the sacrifices, the meetings, the travel, the sickness. And we were starting to learn how wild things had been back home. When we were playing the game in that arena in Pinerolo, which held twenty-five hundred people, we had no idea that all of Newfoundland & Labrador had come to a stop. We knew before the final that the schools had closed, but even then, we didn't grasp how big an event it was until we arrived home a few days later. I heard stories of the excitement in Moncton; the city had put up billboards to mark the occasion, and people were ecstatic after the games. Midland, my hometown in Ontario, was also alive with excitement. Wendy called my mom after the gold medal game, and there was a camera crew in Mom's house, capturing her as she watched us. She was a local celebrity.

Our flight from Italy landed in Toronto, and even though none of us lived there, when the doors opened to let us out, it was like something out of a Hollywood movie premiere with television cameras and flashes going off.

I headed to New Brunswick for the first time in a month, and the rest of the team returned to Newfoundland to one of the wildest scenes that province ever had. It was as if the entire province came out to meet them at the airport, and those who couldn't get in to see them lined the roads to get a glimpse of the new heroes.

No one knew when my flight was coming in that evening, but the Moncton airport was full of friends and well-wishers when I arrived.

In the next weeks and months, we received countless honours and tributes. We received honorary law degrees from Memorial University, had streets named after us in St. John's, Moncton and Midland, we were presented with their highest honour, The Order of Newfoundland and Labrador, got invited to hundreds of banquets and golf tournaments, were named the Canadian Team of the Year and more. It was humbling to know that our victory had touched so many people, and we were proud to know it had inspired people to take up the game or work towards a dream of their own, perhaps one that would come true in 2010 in Vancouver.

We came together under unusual circumstances and ended up on the top step of the podium. It was the pinnacle of my career, which took me from the ice in a club in a small town in central Canada to exotic places such as Italy, Japan, Germany, Switzerland, Norway and Scotland. I made countless friends along the way and shared my journeys with my wife and children. It's possible to find a curler almost anywhere in this country and, increasingly, around the world. And for the most part, they all share a special feeling about the game and a kinship with each other. Curlers are, quite simply, good people.

I hope to keep playing the game for as long as my tired body will allow, and at a competitive level at least until I stop making the shots. Even when that day comes, I know I'll always remain attached to the game, either providing commentary for the media, coaching or being a proud father, just as my father taught me to be. Because at the end of it all, it won't be the gold medal or the Brier or World Championship titles I remember. And it won't be the money or the trophies I'll think about. It will be the journey, the long and beautiful journey I've taken.

Index